Praise for *Creating Productive Cultures in Schools*

The culture of a school has a significant impact on the academic achievement of our students and on the community as a whole. Murphy and Torre have clearly defined the processes to implement an operational goal resulting in a productive school culture in which students are challenged and supported. This book enables leaders, specifically school principals, to facilitate reflective practices designed to engage students, teachers, and parents in achieving successful learning communities.

Gail Connelly, Executive Director
National Association of Elementary School Principals, Alexandria, Virginia

A comprehensive, detailed understanding of the challenges and constraints education leaders face when encouraging, guiding, and supporting positive learning environments. Recognizing the diversity of school cultures, the authors take bold steps to identify what can and should happen to make our nation's schools more successful. A must-read for those seeking realistic and specific strategies for change.

Barbara Schneider, John A. Hannah University Distinguished Professor
Michigan State University, East Lansing, Michigan

This text provides readers with arguably the most comprehensive, accessible, and carefully organized synthesis of evidence available about what school improvement leaders should focus their efforts on and how those efforts can be most productive.

Kenneth Leithwood, Professor Emeritus
OISE/University of Toronto, Canada

Murphy and Torre have constructed a masterful narrative from the daunting complexity of the literature on school improvement, leadership, and school culture. This book puts the learner at the center of the improvement effort and avoids the usual polarities between relationships and academic focus—a highly balanced and integrative review.

Viviane Robinson, Distinguished Professor
The University of Auckland, New Zealand

If the communities concept put forth in this body of work is fully embraced, every school can change and each student will learn and fulfill their potential.

JoAnn D. Bartoletti, Executive Director
National Association of Secondary School Principals, Reston, Virginia

D1003878

LC and canine friends
For Mami, Papi, Vale, and Lisandro

CREATING PRODUCTIVE CULTURES IN SCHOOLS

For Students, Teachers, and Parents

Joseph Murphy

Daniela Torre

CORWIN
A SAGE Company

CORWIN
A SAGE Company

FOR INFORMATION:

Corwin
A SAGE Company
2455 Teller Road
Thousand Oaks, California 91320
(800) 233-9936
www.corwin.com

SAGE Publications Ltd.
1 Oliver's Yard
55 City Road
London, EC1Y 1SP
United Kingdom

SAGE Publications India Pvt. Ltd.
B 1/I 1 Mohan Cooperative Industrial Area
Mathura Road, New Delhi
India 110 044

SAGE Publications Asia-Pacific Pte. Ltd.
3 Church Street
#10-04 Samsung Hub
Singapore 049483

Executive Editor: Arnis Burvikovs
Associate Editor: Desiree A. Bartlett
Editorial Assistant: Ariel Price
Production Editor: Stephanie Palermini
Copy Editor: Lana Todorovic-Arndt
Typesetter: Hurix Systems Pvt. Ltd.
Proofreader: Susan Schon
Indexer: Kathy Paparchontis
Cover Designer: Anupama Krishnan

Printed in the United States of America.

Library of Congress Cataloging-in-Publication Data

Murphy, Joseph, 1949-
Creating productive cultures in schools : for students, teachers, and parents/Joseph Murphy, Daniela S. Torre.

pages cm

Includes bibliographical references and index.

ISBN 978-1-4129-9569-6 (paperback: acid-free paper)

1. High schools—United States. 2. Public schools—United States. 3. School improvement programs—United States. I. Torre, Daniela S. II. Title.

LA222.M87 2014
373.22'4—dc23   2013048901

This book is printed on acid-free paper.

14 15 16 17 18 10 9 8 7 6 5 4 3 2

Contents

Preface

Schools that serve children and young people well are defined by two anchoring pillars, strong academic press and supportive culture, a mixture of nurture and intellectual challenge. We know that focusing primarily on the academic side of the equation is insufficient, especially for students placed in peril by poverty. That is, schools with strong press can still prove inadequate if they provide little attention to the social and relationship dimensions of education.

At the same time, we know that nearly exclusive attention to culture is problematic as well. A number of landmark studies have revealed how over emphasis on culture can lead to a lowering of academic expectations. More recent analysis confirms that featuring culture at the expense of academic press is not a wise pathway for school leaders to pursue, nor a destination to which principals should steer their schools. We must not lose sight of the fact that community is in the service of learning.

We also know that because there is an essential connection between learning and social interaction, that press and support work best when they are viewed as an amalgam or conceptualized as two strands of DNA that wrap around each other. They should be braided together to work best. Thus while in this book we focus on the cultural element of schooling improvement algorithm, academic emphasis is never far from the center stage. It is threaded throughout our analysis of culture.

According to Sweetland and Hoy (2000, p. 705), culture is a "concept used to capture the basic and enduring quality of organizational life." It encompasses the values and norms that define a school. It is those aspects of schooling organization that reflect underlying assumptions and beliefs. It can be thought of as the personality of the school. We describe school culture in terms of community, a construct that is defined in a variety of overlapping ways. It consists of ingredients such as membership, trust, and influence. As we illustrate throughout the book, community stands in juxtaposition to institutionalism and hierarchy as an organizational frame of reference and an approach to leading.

We begin our analysis by focusing on communities of pastoral care for students. We suggest that understanding of such communities is critical because at the heart of the educational narrative is this essential truth: Learning is voluntary for students and students do not volunteer effort when they are detached from school. Creating attachments is key to the work of educators and we need to learn all we can about accomplishing that goal. Analysis is also critical because supportive community for students exercises strong influence on school improvement defined in terms of student learning.

We provide a model of personalized community. We see there that supportive learning community is defined by essential norms (i.e., care, support, safety, and membership). These norms combine to produce intermediate outcomes such as student learning dispositions which, in turn, lead to academic engagement. All of this powers student learning.

The model employs a two-stroke engine, one working to overcome liabilities and the other to build up assets. To begin with then, communities of pastoral care suppress factors that undermine hopes for success, such as the formation of dysfunctional and oppositional peer cultures. Personalization damps down aspects of schooling that push students away from engaging the work of "doing school" well. Concomitantly, supportive learning environments create assets, social and human capital, to draw youngsters into the hard work that is required to be successful in school.

In the second part of the book, we address professional culture, culture reflected in collaborative communities of practice. We examine the "seedbed" from which professional culture grows as well as what some of the flowers look like when they have emerged. We provide definitions and list well-known frameworks of the components of professional learning communities. We present and unpack a model of community of professionalism for teachers.

On the "what" side of that model, we see that a professional learning culture is characterized by six core elements (e.g., shared work, shared accountability). It is these ingredients that define professional learning culture. On the "how" side, we see that a community of practice works by adding capital to the school. One dimension of this capital is knowledge. Thus professional community promotes learning (e.g., deeper content knowledge, enriched pedagogical skills). The other dimension is professional cultural capital. A community of practice deepens professional norms (e.g., efficacy) and accompanying attitudes (e.g., commitment). Increased capital, in turn, leads to changes in the ways teachers conduct their work with students, which in turn leads to better learning outcomes.

In the final part of the book, we focus on communities of engagement for parents and the larger group of stakeholders beyond the school building. We establish the framework to turn work with these critical players from public relations and simple involvement to meaningful engagement. The focus is on forging norms (e.g., trust) that support collaboration, collaboration that fosters student academic and social learning.

About the Authors

Joseph Murphy is the Frank W. Mayborn Chair and associate dean at Vanderbilt's Peabody College of Education. He has also been a faculty member at the University of Illinois and The Ohio State University, where he was the William Ray Flesher Professor of Education.

In the public schools, he has served as an administrator at the school, district, and state levels. His most recent appointment was as the founding president of the Ohio Principals Leadership Academy.

He is past vice president of the American Educational Research Association and was the founding chair of the Interstate School Leaders Licensure Consortium (ISLLC). He is coeditor of the AERA *Handbook on Educational Administration* (1999) and editor of the National Society for the Study of Education (NSSE) yearbook, *The Educational Leadership Challenge* (2002).

His work is in the area of school improvement, with special emphasis on leadership and policy. He has authored or coauthored 22 books in this area and edited another twelve. His most recent authored volumes include *Turning Around Failing Schools: Leadership Lessons From the Organizational Sciences* (2008), *The Educator's Handbook for Understanding and Closing Achievement Gaps* (2010), *Homelessness Comes to School* (2011), *Leadership Lessons for School Leaders* (2011), *Homeschooling in America* (2012), and *The Architecture of School Improvement* (2013).

Daniela Torre is currently pursuing her PhD in education policy at Vanderbilt University. Her research interests include school improvement, particularly for English learners and at-risk students. Previously, she taught for 5 years as an elementary school teacher in both traditional public and charter schools. She earned her BA from Washington University in St. Louis and her MA in Teaching English to Students of Other Languages from American University in Washington, DC.

Different school cultures can indeed be distinguished with different consequences for student outcomes. What is needed is more insight into the role of school leaders in developing and sustaining these cultures.

(Witziers, Bosker, & Krüger, 2003, p. 416).

1

Leadership for School Improvement

Getting Started

Leadership is an influential lever for change. (McDougall, Saunders, & Goldenberg, 2007, p. 83)

Schools that make a difference in students' learning are led by principals who make a significant and measurable contribution to the effectiveness of staff and in the learning of pupils in their charge. (Hallinger & Heck, 1998, p. 158)

Later chapters explore in considerable detail how principals lead schools where student success is the norm. In this introductory chapter, we take a larger view, setting the groundwork for the balance of the book. We underscore the importance of leadership in the school improvement equation. We also develop the scaffolding for how to view and practice school improvement leadership. We begin with a few notes about how we put this volume together.

BUILDING THE BOOK

This book can best be described as an integrative review or a narrative synthesis—an interpretation of the literature (Vescio, Ross, & Adams, 2008), a method that is especially useful when combing qualitative and quantitative research findings (Rodgers et al., 2009). We follow guidance from Hallinger (2013a, 2013b) in explaining the construction of the volume. The goal is to explore the broadest landscape possible to distill knowledge and understanding on the one hand and provide usable material on the other, all in the service of strengthening school culture to forge more successful schools. In the words of Battistich, Solomon, Watson, and Schaps (1997, p. 150), the aim is "to develop integrative explanatory concepts that provide people with a useful framework for considering action under particular circumstances." The topic at hand is explicit: leaders improving schools by strengthening school culture. Specifically, we explain how principal leadership makes a difference, exposing the pathways through which impacts materialize. This necessitates the development of the various models placed throughout the book, beginning with the overarching framework provided in this chapter. We are quite transparent in our commitment to build on the legacy of scholars who have worked these fields over the last three decades. We build not only from their empirical findings, but also on analyses of the strengths and weaknesses of the field of school improvement leadership.

In order to be as comprehensive as possible, we proceeded in our work as follows. To provide grounding, we examined some of the classic literature on leadership in general. We then moved into the education literature. We compiled hard copies of everything we could turn up on effective school leadership and school improvement through the various search engines from 1975 to 2011. Using Hallinger's (2013b, p. 14) language, we conducted an "exhaustive review." We separated the resulting bounty into four groups: empirical studies (quantitative, qualitative, and mixed methods), major reviews of empirical research, robust theoretical and conceptual work, and all others. We concentrated our efforts on the first two categories, although we did read a good number of pieces from the theoretical domain as well. As we read, we identified and secured studies that had eluded us in our initial search. We read extensively (see reference list) until we had almost complete redundancy of information and nuances of interpretation had largely vanished.

Based on 35 years of work on school improvement leadership, we developed an abbreviated outline of what is known in the area. We coded each piece of writing using our outline. We also developed a fairly hefty stack of "memo notes" to ourselves as we read, based on the outline codes. After recopying all the articles and books, we then cut codes and placed each code on a separate sheet of paper with the following information: the coded sentences, the code, names of author(s), date of publication, and page number. The process produced about 25,000 pieces of information. We then compiled like codes together.

Following the canons of qualitative data analysis, we then grouped and regrouped items within categories into coherent sets as patterns and themes emerged. In this way, we believe, we have been able to enrich the narrative on leaders building productive cultures in schools.

The audience for this work is fourfold. We believe that there are critical insights for policy makers at all levels of the educational enterprise. Developers will, we believe, find the conceptual designs and specific findings helpful as they create products and programs for colleagues in schools. In a similar manner, many of the ideas herein lend themselves to fairly direct application by practitioners, especially principals. Finally, it is our hope that researchers will find this integrative body of knowledge quite useful in shaping future explorations of school improvement leadership.

SCHOOL IMPROVEMENT LEADERSHIP MATTERS

Leadership is often regarded as the single most critical factor in the success or failure of institutions. (Bass, 1990, p. 8)

Leadership seems complicit in excellence. (Supovitz & Klein, 2003, p. 36)

The Core Ideas

We define school improvement leadership as an influence process through which leaders identify a direction for the school, motivate staff, and coordinate an evolving set of strategies toward improvements in teaching and learning. (Heck & Hallinger, 2009, p. 622)

School Improvement

School improvement describes a set of processes, managed from within the school, targeted both at pupil achievement and the school's ability to manage change—a simultaneous focus on process and outcomes. (Potter, Reynolds, & Chapman, 2002, p. 244)

As with most constructs, it is instructive to begin with a definition of school improvement leadership. We know that school improvement is often implicitly defined in the literature (Gray et al., 1999). Precise definitions are often missing. Borrowing from Bryk, Sebring, Allensworth, Luppescu, and Easton (2010) and Gray and colleagues (1999), we define school improvement as an increase in effectiveness over time, with effectiveness centered around organizational capacity and the impacts of the deployment of that capacity, especially on student learning. Thus we anchor school improvement in measures of growth or value added (Heck & Hallinger, n.d.; Jackson, 2000). Of course, this leaves the metrics yet to be established, that is, the growth measures and the amount of progress required to be called "improving." As we report throughout the book, there is considerable variation in the answers to these issues in the literature.

Leadership

We define school leadership as the identification, acquisition, allocation, coordination, and use of the human, social, and material resources necessary to establish the conditions for the possibility of innovation. (Spillane, Diamond, Walker, Halverson, & Jita, 2001, p. 919)

This book is devoted to educational leadership or, more specifically, what we have referred to over the years as instructional leadership, learning centered leadership, and school improvement leadership. Before we drill down on these ideas, however, it is helpful to start with an understanding of the broader concept at hand, i.e., leadership in general. The essence of leadership is (1) having a sense of where an organization needs to get to, or what it needs to achieve, and (2) creating the capacity and deploying that capacity to reach desired ends. It is about the process of influencing others, influence exercised through relationships (DuBrin, 2004; Howell & Costley, 2006; Yukl, 2010).

Educational leadership is simply the application of these core ideas to schooling: "actions intentionally geared to influence the school's primary processes and, therefore, ultimately students' achievement levels" (Witziers, Bosker, & Krüger, 2003, p. 403). It is this broad definition (Leithwood & Duke, 1999; Murphy, 1988) that is ribboned throughout this volume, one that takes an extensive view of the primary processes of schools.

We are abundantly clear throughout the book that leadership is not synonymous with roles (Heller & Firestone, 1995; Ogawa & Bossert, 1995; Pounder, Ogawa, & Adams, 1995). However, because school administrators are foundational for leadership, our focus herein is on how those in formal administrative roles in schools, especially principals, exercise leadership.

Importance

There is increasing evidence that leadership makes a difference in schools. (Louis, Dretzke, & Wahlstrom, 2010, p. 315)

Higher teacher perceptions of principal instructional leadership behaviors relate to higher student achievement. (O'Donnell & White, 2005, p. 61)

School leadership sits in the first position. It acts as a driver for improvement in other organizational subsystems. (Bryk et al., 2010, p. 197)

Across time, it has generally been assumed that good leadership is an important force in developing good schools, while poor leadership hinders improvement. It has only been in the last 40 years, however, that this assumption has been affirmed, beginning with the initial effective schools and instructional leadership studies (Bossert, Dwyer, Rowan, & Lee, 1982; Edmonds, 1979; Hallinger & Murphy, 1985; Murphy, Hallinger, & Mesa, 1985b) and continuing through the increasingly sophisticated studies of the last two decades by scholars such as Hallinger, Bickman, and Davis (1996), Louis et al. (2010), and Robinson (2008).

Analysts have also been active in documenting the magnitude of that importance, providing concreteness to the influence of leadership as a driver of school improvement (Gray et al., 1999; Southworth, 2002). Researchers provide this information from quantitative studies in a variety of ways, most of which are not intuitively clear to practitioners, developers, and policy makers. They employ correlations, effect sizes, months of growth, variance explained, and so forth.

An essential point to remember is that most children's "learning" is accounted for by nonschool factors such as family conditions and student aptitude (Berends, Lucas, Sullivan, & Briggs, 2005; Lee & Burkam, 2002; Rothstein, 2004). Schooling is responsible for something in the neighborhood of 20 percent of student achievement (Creemers & Reezigt, 1996; Leithwood & Jantzi, 2000a; Waters, Marzano, & McNulty, 2003). So one needs to see whether "effects" are of all student learning ("overall effects") or the part of learning attributable to schools ("school effects"). For example, if leadership explains 25 percent of "school effects," that is 5 percent of overall variance, a finding consistent with the best work to date (Leithwood, Day, Sammons, Harris, & Hopkins, 2006).

One also needs to be aware if researchers are measuring direct effects of leadership or all effects (i.e., direct effects and mediated or indirect effects). Since, as we will see, most of the impact of principals occurs through their influence on school culture and the instructional program, measures of direct effects are almost always quite low, while assessments that include indirect effects are more robust (Hallinger & Heck, 1998; Witziers et al., 2003).

On occasion, studies report influence in terms that are more familiar to practitioners. For example, Branch, Rivkin, and Hanushek (2003) use months of student learning as the metric, finding that effective leaders raise achievement levels for students between 2 and 7 months each year, while their ineffective counterparts lower achievement by those amounts. Bryk and colleagues (2010) reach a parallel conclusion using growth versus stagnation, as does the Center for Teaching Quality (2007) using growth expectations.

Collectively, through the use of different procedures and tools and employing different metrics, research affirms leadership as an essential variable in the overall equation of student success, i.e., one that includes environmental conditions outside of schooling. That influence is amplified when the "school effects" only algorithm is examined and both direct and indirect pathways of influence are included. The summative message is that leadership can and does have significant and meaningful effects on student learning.

We also know that leadership takes on added significance in certain places and in particular times. On the "times" front, we know that leadership becomes more essential when the environment surrounding an institution is roiling (Bass, 1990; Murphy & Meyers, 2008). In difficult times, the value and influence of leaders increases as well (Tichy & Cardwell, 2004; Zaccaro, Kemp, & Bader, 2004). So too in times of change, especially fundamental change (Valentine & Prater, 2011) and on the occasions when the pathway to the future is less than clear (Fullan & Ballew, 2002). On the "place" front, leadership is more critical in schools with high concentrations of students placed at risk (Cotton, 2003), in low performing schools (Ikemoto, Taliaferro, & Adams, 2012), in low-SES schools (Cotton, 2003), and in all challenged schools (Heck & Hallinger, n.d.).

Impact

> Leadership has very significant effects on the quality of the school organization and on pupil learning. (Leithwood, Day, et al., 2006, p. 10)

> Student achievement is consistently higher in schools where principals are perceived to have more competence than schools led by principals perceived as less competent. (Valentine & Prater, 2011, p. 13)

Studies over the last 35 years have connected leadership with the effectiveness of most of the major dimensions of education and every important outcome of schooling. On the conditions, variables, elements, or dimensions side of the ledger, there is empirical evidence that effective principals have positive impacts on

- use of technology in schools (Anderson & Dexter, 2005)
- use of data (Kerr, Marsh, Ikemoto, Darilek, & Barney, 2006; Lachat & Smith, 2005; Wayman & Stringfield, 2006)
- instructional practice (Camburn , Rowan, & Taylor, 2003; Correnti & Rowan, 2007; Wellisch, MacQueen, Carriere, & Duck, 1978)
- parental/community-school linkages (Bryk et al., 2010; Teddlie & Stringfield, 1985)
- staff collaboration (Rutter, Maughan, Mortimore, & Ouston, 1979; Wayman & Stringfield, 2006)

- professional development and organizational learning (Gall, Fielding, Schalock, Charters, & Wilczynski, 1985; Hallinger & Heck, 1998; Youngs & King, 2002)
- professional community (Scribner, Cockrell, Cockrell, & Valentine, 1999; Sebastian & Allensworth, 2012)
- staff commitment, trust, motivation, work orientation, job satisfaction, confidence, and accountability (Dannetta, 2002; Gurr, Drysdale, & Mulford, 2005; Leithwood & Jantzi, 2005)
- implementation of reform (Desimone, 2002; Murphy & Datnow, 2003b; Useem, Christman, Gold, & Simon,1997)
- program coherence (Murphy, 1992; Newmann, Smith, Allensworth, & Bryk, 2001; Sebastian & Allensworth, 2012)
- learning climate for students (Brookover et al., 1978; Crum & Sherman, 2008; Heck & Hallinger, 2009), including safety and order (Lasley & Wayson, 1982; Rutter et al., 1979; Sebastian & Allensworth, 2012)
- academic programs within schools, including special education (Sindelar, Shearer, Yendol-Hoppey, Liebert, 2006), vocational education (Woloszyk, 1996), and bilingual education (Carter & Maestas, 1982; Scanlan & Lopez, 2012)

On the outcome side of the ledger, effective principal leadership has been shown to influence

- student engagement (Leithwood & Jantzi, 2000a)
- sustainable change (Eilers & Camacho, 2007; Hamilton, Stecher, Russell, Marsh, & Miles, 2008; Murphy, Hallinger, & Mesa, 1985a; Robinson, Lloyd, & Rowe, 2008)
- effective schools (Clark, Lotto, & McCarthy, 1980; Hulpia, Devos, & Rosseel, 2009)
- school improvement (Heck & Hallinger, 2010; Leithwood, Jantzi, & McElheron-Hopkins, 2006; May & Supovitz, 2011; Murphy & Datnow, 2003b)
- implementation of large scale reform (Desimone, 2002; Shear et al., 2008; Useem et al., 1997)
- student learning (Bell, Bolam, & Cubillo, 2003; Leithwood, Louis, Anderson, & Wahlstrom, 2004; Robinson et al., 2008; Waters et al., 2003).

The obverse to these storylines is also true, however. Ineffective leadership can negatively impact school conditions and outcomes (Bryk et al., 2010; Robinson et al., 2008). Relatedly, leader stability has a role here as well. Leadership continuity is important (Desimone, 2002; Tichy & Cardwell, 2004) and churn in the principalship often has deleterious effects on the ingredients of quality schooling and the outcomes linked to those conditions (Heck & Hallinger, 2009; Stringfield & Reynolds, 2012).

Cautionary Notes

Before we move deeply into our exploration of school improvement leadership, a few introductory notes are in order. To begin with, we need to heed the reminder from Leithwood and Montgomery (1982, p. 336) that "effectiveness is a continuous rather than bipolar condition." While our attention is riveted on leadership, it is important to remember that it is an essential but insufficient element in fostering healthy cultures and explaining school improvement (Hallinger & Heck, 1996; McDougall et al., 2007; Sweetland & Hoy, 2000) and that the ability to attribute "cause" remains problematic (Crosnoe, 2011). Within the "people" domain specifically, there is abundant evidence that others play critical parts (Levin & Datnow, 2012). We need also remind ourselves that conclusions about the importance of leadership are not completely uniform (Brewer, 1993; Grissom & Loeb, 2011; May & Supovitz, 2011) and are consistently richer and more robust in qualitative than in quantitative studies (Robinson et al., 2008). As we will see momentarily, research that includes both direct and indirect impacts is always more sanguine about the effects of leadership than the one that includes only direct effects (Hallinger & Heck, 1996, 1998). In addition, the significance of context is ignored at peril (Hallinger & Murphy, 1986, 1987a, 1987b). We also must acknowledge that the job is larger than leadership for school improvement (Leithwood, Jantzi, & McElheron-Hopkins, 2006). We close with one last caution. The work of principals is difficult by nature (Ackerman & Maslin-Ostrowski, 2002). It is much easier to write about the leadership game than it is to practice leadership.

SCHOOL IMPROVEMENT LEADERSHIP

> Principal leadership effects [are] reciprocal rather than unidirectional. (Hallinger & Heck, 1996, p. 32)

The framework for our work is contained in Figure 1.1 (see page 16). In order to push toward "the elusive goal of clarifying the link between leadership and learning" (Wahlstrom & Louis, 2008, p. 459), we partition the narrative into segments. We open with a description of the antecedents that exercise purchase on leadership. We include here demographic conditions, knowledge and skills, values and beliefs, and traits and characteristics. Next, we explore school contextual variables that shape leadership practice. We then turn to leadership behaviors inside the domains of effective schools. Here we foreground material contained in the remaining chapters of the book. An analysis of the pathways of leader influence on the workings of the school closes our discussion of the framework.

To complete our assignment, it is necessary to compartmentalize findings. To some extent, this is artificial. School improvement is complex and messy. It is difficult at times to slice it into components. Ideas and findings crisscross the narrative and are interwoven across sections of the story (Southworth, 2002; Vescio et al., 2008). What is true for school improvement holds for leadership for school improvement as well. Additionally, the work we present represents the normal pathway to success. However, we must remember that there is no universal chronicle that is applicable at all times and in all situations (Heck & Marcoulides, 1996; Southworth, 2002). Also, for reasons detailed earlier, our attention in the model is devoted almost exclusively to variables linked to student learning. That is, ours is a constrained model. This focus is not intended to gainsay the importance of other elements of school leadership. Recall also that ours is a hinged or reciprocal model. That is, the principal both is directed by antecedents, environmental and school contexts, and school conditions and outcomes and influences these factors (Hallinger et al., 1996; Pitner, 1988). The model is multilevel and dynamic, not static (Hallinger & Heck, 1998; Heck & Hallinger, n.d.), a fact that can be forgotten when it is pulled apart for analysis.

Antecedents

Leadership is best predicted by an amalgamation of attributes reflecting cognitive capacities, personality orientation, motives and values, social appraisal skills, problem-solving competencies, and general and domain-specific expertise. (Zaccaro et al., 2004, p. 120)

Personal characteristics influence how principals enact their role. These antecedent variables include gender, prior teaching experience, and values and beliefs. (Hallinger & Heck, 1996, p. 21)

The most sophisticated and theoretically sound models of instructional leadership include a set of personal factors that shape the actions of principals (see Hallinger & Heck, 1996, 1998; Murphy, Elliott, Goldring, & Porter, 2007) and, in turn, are molded by those actions. While there is overlap within and across antecedent categories, they do provide a useful heuristic for understanding how personal conditions shape school improvement leadership (Boyan, 1988). Building on our earlier work in this area (see Hallinger & Murphy, 1986; Murphy et al., 2007), we propose four broad bundles of antecedents, or what Barnett and McCormick (2004, p. 410) refer to as "internal processes": demographic characteristics, knowledge and skills, values and beliefs, and traits.

The *demographic antecedents* of leadership behavior include gender, age, education, and experience. Research confirms connections for gender (Hallinger et al., 1996; Valentine & Prater, 2011), especially for instructionally centered actions (Cotton, 2003; Hallinger et al., 1996); education (Leithwood & Jantzi, 2005; Valentine & Prater, 2011); and prior teaching experience (Hallinger et al., 1996). Linkages between age, or stage of development, and administrative experience have yet to be established (Valentine & Prater, 2011).

In terms of *knowledge and skills,* there is research evidence that the intellectual or cognitive capacities of principals have sway on behavior, which in turn impacts school effectiveness (Dinham, 2005; Leithwood, Day, et al., 2006; Mangin, 2007). "General and domain specific expertise" (Zaccaro et al., 2004, p. 120) are influential as well (Friedkin & Slater, 1994; Leithwood, Day, et al., 2006). Relatedly, social-emotional capacities of principals shape actions and sequel to those behaviors (Ackerman & Maslin-Ostrowski, 2002; Fullan & Ballew, 2002). Important elements here include: tolerance for ambiguity (Valentine & Prater, 2011); self awareness, especially of one's emotions (Fullan & Ballew, 2002); self-efficacy (Leithwood, Jantzi, & McElheron-Hopkins, 2006; Wells, Widmer, & McCoy, 2004); interpersonal skills such as empathy and social appraisal skills (Fullan & Ballew, 2002; Leithwood, Jantzi, & McElheron-Hopkins, 2006); and coping skills (Louis & Miles, 1991). There is also some suggestion that intellectual acumen and social-emotional intelligence together exercise powerful effects on the behavior of leaders (Fullan & Ballew, 2002).

While there is more overlap here than was the case with the demographic and knowledge antecedents, linkages between *values* (and beliefs and dispositions) are also more robust. To begin, there is a sizable body of evidence that "values and beliefs inform the principal's decisions and actions" (Silins & Mulford, 2010, p. 74) and impact school success (Gurr, Drysdale, & Mulford, 2006; Riester, Pursch, & Skria, 2002). While it is foolhardy to attempt to compile a complete list of all the values that mold leader behavior, some dispositions rise to the level of high visibility and importance. That is, there are value-behavior linkages that influence school success (Dumay, 2009; Leithwood, Day, et al., 2006). One is a ferocious belief in the educability of children and the prime mission of ensuring their success (Leithwood, Day, et al., 2006; Riester et al., 2002). A second is a disposition toward equity and justice (Dinham, 2005; Roney, Coleman, & Schlichting, 2007). A third is the belief in the power of the community of stakeholders to arrive at decisions that are best for students (Leithwood, Day, et al., 2006), a disposition toward collaboration (Newmann, King, & Youngs, 2000).

Research on *traits* and their linkages to leader behavior and subsequent organizational performance has enjoyed a checkered history (Judge, Bono, Ilies, Gerhardt, 2002; Zaccaro et al., 2004). Originally, they held center stage in explanations of leader effects. They were then pushed off the stage altogether only to claw their way partially back into the spotlight in the last few years. Traits are best thought of "as relatively stable and coherent integrations of personal characteristics that foster a consistent pattern of leadership performance across a variety of group and organizational situations" (Zaccaro et al., 2004. p. 104). The most accurate conclusion we can draw is that traits do mold behavior (Blase & Blase, 1999; Gurr et al., 2006; Zaccaro et al., 2004). The fact that other antecedents and context variables also matter hardly diminishes the "personological" basis of leadership (Judge et al., 2002, p. 775). As was the case with beliefs, containers for characteristics can seem bottomless. They do cohere, however, into a handful of "common and consistent" elements (Gurr et al. 2005, p. 548): passion, optimism, persistence, authenticity, and a penchant for hard work (high energy).

Passion means that principals are proactive (Day, 2005; Leithwood, Jantzi, & McElheron-Hopkins, 2006). They have a bias toward action, risk taking, and innovation (Barnett & McCormick, 2004; Crum & Sherman, 2008; Dinham, 2005). A results orientation is also part of proactiveness (Sweeney, 1982) as is a personal dedication to obtaining those ends (Supovitz & Poglinco, 2001) and a penchant for inspiring others to do likewise (Gurr et al., 2005). Passion includes courage, especially to make difficult and unpopular decisions (Dinham, 2005). Passionate leaders are comfortable pushing back the boundaries that limit goal achievement (Day, 2005; Sather, 1999; Southworth, 2002).

Faith and optimism often move leaders to action (Leithwood, 2005; Southworth, 2002). This includes a predilection for positive thinking (Dinham, 2005), especially in times of uncertainty (Blase & Kirby, 2009; Goldenberg, 2004). Leader optimism produces behaviors that help others gain and maintain positive perspectives (Blase & Kirby, 2009). Optimistic leaders help people see the connections between their work and the success of students (Bryk et al., 2010; Southworth, 2002); they spread a "sense of possibility" (Dinham, 2005).

Successful school leaders are often quite persistent (Dinham, 2005; Gurr et al., 2005; Leithwood, Jantzi, & McElheron-Hopkins, 2006). They translate that sense of tenacity into actions that push, pull, and carry their colleagues to higher levels of effectiveness (Riester et al., 2002). They are "determined individuals" (Southworth, 2002, p. 82) in the pursuit of goals (Dinham, 2005).

Strong leaders are often defined as authentic, a characteristic that covers a good deal of ground. It includes what researchers describe as openness to others (Dumay, 2009; Judge et al., 2002; Zaccaro et al., 2004). Embedded here also are feelings of empathy and concern for others (Gurr et al., 2006) as well as a sense of conscientiousness, which includes dependability and consideration (Blase & Kirby, 2009; Judge et al., 2002). Authenticity suggests a stance of nonguardedness and trustworthiness (Dinham, 2005; Dumay, 2009; Judge et al., 2002). Gurr and associates (2006, p. 375) refer to it as "other centeredness," commitments to inclusiveness (Hayes, Christie, Mills, & Lingard, 2004), honesty (Blase & Kirby, 2009), and accessibility (Dinham, 2005; Southworth, 2002).

Many productive leaders are high-energy people, with powerful work ethics (Leithwood, Day, et al., 2006), what Southworth (2002, p. 82) describes as "an emblem that the leader is devoted to the school." This energy fuels actions that promote organizational health and student learning (Eilers & Camacho, 2007).

Context

The relation between principal and school effectiveness will be best understood through the use of models that account for effects of the school context on principal's leadership. (Hallinger et al., 1996, p. 544)

Instructional management appears to be influenced by environmental characteristics. (Leitner, 1994, p. 233)

Researchers over the last few decades have solidified an essential law of school improvement: Leadership for school improvement is shaped by the contexts in which schools and the leaders of those institutions find themselves (Hallinger & Murphy, 1987b, 2013; Murphy, Hallinger, Weil, & Mitman, 1984): "Leadership practice is situated in a multifaceted context, including particular students and families, teachers, and administrators; district, state, and federal policy; and local and national professional organizations. These multiple facets all come together and interact in complex ways to help define leadership practice" (Coldren & Spillane, 2007, p. 387).

Context includes conditions of the larger environment around a school (e.g., type of community, geographical location) as well as characteristics of the school itself (e.g., ages of students served, or grade levels included) (Moller & Eggen, 2005). We know that similar leadership behaviors can have different effects in different settings (Hallinger et al., 1996; Judge et al., 2002). We also learn that varied contexts often call for different leadership behaviors (Bryman, 2004; Hallinger & Murphy, 1986).

External factors that influence leadership include federal and state policies, laws, and regulations; district policies, procedures, and norms; and community conditions (Levin & Datnow, 2012; McLaughlin & Talbert, 2001; Morrissey, 2000), such as racial and ethnic composition and income and wealth (Hallinger & Heck, 1998). School conditions can also make leadership work either easier or more challenging. We know, for example, that school SES is linked to principal leadership (Hallinger & Murphy, 1987b; Leitner, 1994). So too is the robustness of parental involvement (Hallinger et al., 1996). Level of schooling, whether elementary or secondary, influences school leadership (Firestone & Herriott, 1982; Mazzarella, 1985; Murphy, Hallinger, Lotto, & Miller, 1987). Because of their complexity (Firestone & Herriott, 1982; Louis & Miles, 1991; Sebastian & Allensworth, 2012) and because they are notoriously difficult venues in which to introduce change (McLaughlin & Talbert, 2001), indirect leadership is more prevalent in secondary schools (Hallinger & Murphy, 1987b; Heck & Marcoulides, 1996; Witziers et al., 2003). Secondary schools also often require more attention to the administrative dimensions of schooling and less to instructional activities (Brewer, 1993; Robinson et al., 2008). School size is meaningful to leadership as well, with large size influencing behavior in ways similar to secondary schools (May & Supovitz, 2011). School status also pulls leaders in particular directions at times. That is, whether a school is failing, satisfactory, or highly successful is consequential for leadership (Murphy, 2008a, 2008b).

We leave our discussion of context with some key reminders. It is important to reinforce the point that while context is important in helping establish patterns of leadership, it is hardly determinate. Principals can shape environmental conditions as well as be influenced by them. External context can also be amplified or muted by conditions of schooling (Valentine & Prater, 2011; Wahlstrom & Louis, 2008). The elements of context are interactive (Eilers & Camacho, 2007), not independent and static.

The School Improvement Leadership Engine

There [are] marked differences in leadership in effective and ineffective schools. (Sweeney, 1982, p. 348)

The mechanisms through which principals influence students are complex and defy simple categorization. (Brewer, 1993, p. 281)

In the balance of the book, we explore the core of the model in Figure 1.1 (see page 16), what we think of as the engine of school improvement leadership. Our objective in this introductory chapter is simply to provide an overview of forthcoming analyses. As we will see, paradoxically our engine is surprisingly simple yet complex. Each element carries depth and nuance that belie simple labels. Most of the concepts are not mutually exclusive; there is a fair amount of overlap between and among them. Variables wrap around each other and mix together. At times, ingredients fall under the spotlight. At other times, they are backstage. Varied proportions and different weights hold at different times and places. Variables can be combined in various ways to fuel school improvement. The relationships among the pieces are complex. There is no single storyline. What we end up with looks a good deal like a stew. Our work is in many ways similar to disentangling thickets. While this labor is essential, it is messy and at times less satisfactory than we might wish.

Tasks

Activities

Our colleague Philip Hallinger and we have held for the past 30 years that leadership needs to be defined, eventually, in terms of observable and consequential practices. For us, then, school improvement leadership is the enactment of behaviorally anchored processes in the core dimensions of improving and effective schools (e.g., monitoring instruction, building linkages with parents, establishing growth targets for students). It is always a cocktail of functions and processes, of content and ways.

Since the inception of the effective schools movement in the late 1970s and early 1980s, analysts have provided a multitude of frameworks to capture school improvement leadership. In one of the earliest, based on their California study of effective schools, Hallinger and Murphy (1985) featured the following domains (framing school goals and objectives, developing and promoting expectations, developing and promoting standards, assessing and monitoring student performance, protecting instructional time, knowledge of curriculum and instruction, promoting curricular coordination, promoting and supporting instructional improvement, supervision and evaluation of instruction, and creating productive work environment) and processes (communication, conflict resolution, group processes, decision making, and change processes). Around the same time, Sweeney (1982) culled out six core bundles of actions that define school improvement leadership: highlight student achievement, establish common instructional strategies, foster a safe and orderly environment, monitor student progress, coordinate the instructional program, and nurture and support teachers. In 1985, we consolidated all available work at that time into the framework in Table 1.1.

Table 1.1   Dimensions of Instructional Management

Defines the Mission	Manages Instructional Program	Promotes School Culture
Framing school goals Communicating school goals	Supervising instruction	Supportive learning communities for students
	Coordinating curriculum	Communities of professional practice for teachers
	Monitoring student progress	Communities of engagement for parents

Leithwood, alone and with a variety of colleagues, has been extremely influential in crafting broad frameworks of leadership for school improvement. Perhaps his best known model features setting direction, developing people, redesigning the organization, and managing the instructional program (Leithwood, Patten, & Jantzi, 2010). Another framework includes goals, culture, participatory decision making, and connections to parents and communities, along with the practices to bring these ingredients to life in schools (Leithwood et al., 2004).

Other scholars highlight the role of the principal as developer of capital in their portraits of leadership (Fullan & Ballew, 2002). Spillane, Diamond, Walker, Halverson, & Jita (2001) focus on human, social, and physical capital. Smerdon and Borman (2009) underscore human, material, and social capital. From our analyses of capital perspectives, we suggest that leadership for school improvement is best understood in terms of six types of capital: human, production, resource, cultural, social, and integrative.

Other designs have been employed as well. For example, May and Supovitz (2011) partition school improvement leadership into practices, styles, and processes. In her review, Cotton (2003) outlines overarching domains of principal work (with embedded practices): a clear focus on student learning interactions and relationships, culture, instruction, and accountability. Bryk and colleagues (2010) define leadership anchored to school improvement as the ability to positively impact instructional guidance, professional capacity, school community connections, and a student-focused environment.

In one model, Hallinger and Heck (1998) unpack leadership behaviors into four essential domains: purpose and goals, organizational structure and social networks, people, and organizational culture. In another, they describe five roles: being a catalyst for change, maintaining an improvement focus, fostering the leadership of others, supporting instructional effectiveness, and providing tangible support for youngsters and teachers (1996). Supovitz, Sirinides, and May (2010) wrestle behaviors into three pens: focusing mission and goals, encouraging a climate of collaboration and trust, and supporting instructional improvement. Fullan (2002, p. 2) outlines five "action-and-mind-sets": moral purpose, dynamics of change, emotional intelligence, coherence making, and knowledge.

In our model (see Figure 1.1), we build from these and other empirically anchored frameworks about school improvement leadership over the last 35 years. We employ two domains to capture behaviors: managing the instructional program and creating the culture. Chapters 4 through 8 will carry us deeply into the cultural part of the model. The domains or "dimensions" provide the foreground for those chapters. The "processes" are threaded into those dimensions, visible but not always in the spotlight. For this reason, it is useful to say a few words about the processes before we proceed. One can identify a great assortment of processes (e.g., communicating) that give meaning to content (e.g., curriculum) from the research on leadership for school improvement. Many of these come from studies of leadership and the various lines of analysis on school improvement (e.g., school restructuring, turnaround schools, comprehensive school reform, achievement-gap closing schools). Others are found buried in studies addressing a plethora of other areas of interest (e.g., professional development, programs for English Language Learners, homeless children). We group many of these processes into three bundles: organizational functioning processes, human relations processes, and inspirational processes. Organizational functioning processes include planning, organizing, implementing, coordinating, resourcing, monitoring, boundary spanning and buffering, and assessing. Human relations processes feature problem framing and problem solving, decision making, communication, and conflict resolution. Inspirational processes include modeling, teaching, maintaining visibility, and sensemaking.

Characteristic elements of practices

Before leaving our overview of tasks (the cocktail of content and processes), it is important to introduce what we refer to as the characteristic elements of leadership practices. To begin with, there is the issue of the *quality* of practices, which can be arrayed on a continuum from effective to poor. Practices also vary in *frequency*, from routinely performed to rarely undertaken. *Scope,* a characteristic first empirically surfaced by May and Supovitz (2011), addresses the number (or percent) of people touched by a leader's practice, from one to all. *Intensity* is an important element of practice as well, ranging from high or deep to light. *Range* addresses the coverage of behaviors from few to many. *Integration* refers to the extent to which practices are discrete or tightly bundled.

Figure 1.1   School Improvement Leadership Model

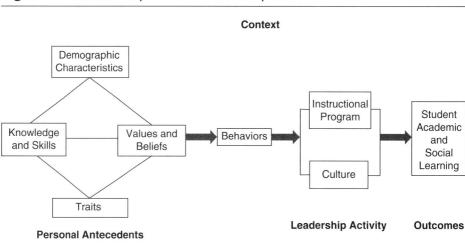

Style

Over the last half century, a good deal of ink has been devoted to the topic of leadership style, "the modes by which principals express themselves" (May & Supovitz, 2011, p. 335). Early analyses focused on whether principals were task oriented or people oriented. Derivations of this work often define style in terms of directiveness, supportiveness, and formality.

Another line of work considers style in terms of power and control. One strand here focuses on whether the principal displays an authoritarian or democratic style of leadership. A second addresses style in terms of whether the principal holds power centrally or distributes it to staff. A third genre of work presents style in terms of the leader's penchant for professional or hierarchical control.

Bolman and Deal (2008) help us see the ways principals express themselves somewhat differently, defining style by the frames that leaders employ—political, structural, symbolic, and human. Still others define style in terms of leader activeness, from highly active to laissez faire. Building on the work of Burns (1978) and other seminal scholars in the area of organizational leadership, Leithwood (Leithwood & Jantzi, 2000b, 2005, 2006) introduced the topic of transactional and transformational leadership styles to education. Closely related here are the discussions of charismatic versus noncharismatic styles (Yukl, 2010).

Styles anchored in the nature of work privileged by the leader has been common, at least since the pioneering efforts of Cuban (1988), who highlights political, managerial, and instructional orientations. Style has also been presented in terms of whether the leader features authority-based, morally-based, or personality-based practices. We see a good deal of writing featuring "change" in analyses of style as well, with principals being characterized as either status-quo leaders or change-oriented leaders (proactive, innovative, risk-taking individuals). Finally, the idea of integrative styles has arisen over time (see Marks & Printy, 2003, for an especially good empirical example).

The collective body of scholarship on leadership "style" has been helpful in mapping important dimensions of leadership work, deepening the leadership narrative. On the other hand, evidence on the effectiveness of styles has been both elusive and largely noncumulative. Looking at the full array of work, here is what we can report with some degree of confidence. There is no one-best style for all places and times. Leaders with varying orientations have been identified as effective. Alignment between leader style and context seems worthy of further investigation. There is some sense that leaders of improving schools are often "authoritative" (not authoritarian) and that a laissez faire or passive leadership style is rarely productive and often proves to be quite problematic. Styles that highlight distributed or shared leadership have yet to be linked tightly with improvement (Miller & Rowan, 2006), while those that feature commitment to learning and teaching often are found to characterize principals in improving schools (Murphy, 1990).

Leadership Pathways

> Successful leadership influences teaching and learning both through face-to-face relationships and by structuring the way that teachers work. (Robinson et al., 2008, pp. 659–660)

Earlier we reported that principals' effects on students are largely indirect. Their actions are mediated by the instructional program and the school culture (see Figure 1.1). Here we add that principal effects on these mediating variables can be direct or indirect as well (Ogawa & Bossert, 1995). For example, a principal can visit a classroom and provide feedback to an individual teacher. Or she can meet with a grade-level team to think through some curricular issues. These are direct effects on teachers. Alternatively, principals can do things, which in turn touch teachers or shape school climate. For example, a principal can create time to permit and protocols to guide collaborative work. Or she can require the use of curricular pacing guides. These actions have indirect effects on teachers. Something is situated between the principal and the teacher.

Researchers have also uncovered the mechanisms by which principals operationalize indirect effects on teachers and culture. School structures (e.g., how the day is organized, where teachers are located in the building) provide one influence strategy. Policies provide a second (e.g., all teachers cover both high and low track classes, all special education students must be mainstreamed). Standard operating procedures and norms (ingrained routines, systems, and expectations) offer principals a third indirect avenue of influence (e.g., staff members personally greet each child at the classroom door every class period). Additionally, as Spillane Diamond, Walker, Halverson, and Jita (2001) and Ross, Sterbinsky, and McDonald (2003) remind us, tools and artifacts provide another avenue of impacting teachers and culture indirectly (e.g., meeting protocols, lesson plan formats). Finally, principals exercise indirect leadership by the way they allocate resource. Leadership activity across all five of these pathways shapes the ways teachers conduct their work.

We underscore both direct and indirect pathways in our analyses in Chapters 4 through 8. Both appear to be influential in the process of school improvement, although the use of direct approaches is often constrained by factors such as school size and level (i.e., elementary vs. secondary).

CONCLUSION

In this introductory chapter, we overviewed the full landscape that we will be exploring in the balance of the book. We explained the methods used to gather, compile, and analyze the research. We summarized the literature documenting the cardinal position of leadership in the chronicle of school improvement. In the second half of the chapter, we presented the model undergirding our work. We unpacked the essential personal factors (antecedents) that help shape leader practice. We also described factors in the schools environment (context) that push and pull leaders to act in certain ways. We closed with a preliminary look at the school improvement leadership engine, the tasks (the processes linked to domains) defining effective leadership, and the pathways (direct and indirect) that practices follow.

2

Schooling in the Postindustrial World

The North Star for Leadership

A central tenet of our scholarship over the years is that leadership must be viewed in terms of how schooling is evolving and the forces that are driving those changes. For us, therefore, a decontextualized understanding of leadership is insufficient. Our models inform us that both the understanding of leadership and the practice of leadership need to backward map from knowledge about the type of schooling needed in a postindustrial world. This, in turn, necessitates, among other things, an understanding of the economic, cultural, and sociopolitical environment in which schooling is nested.

This chapter explores the evolution of schooling from the industrial world (1880–1990) to the current technological era. As we will see, the scaffolding on which schooling in the twentieth century was built is crumbling. New pillars required to meet new values and goals are being framed up. Whether this reconstruction work is productive will depend in large part on leadership.

We begin by providing an overview of the model that guides our analysis of change in schools over the last 125 years. We then show how one major revolution produced an understanding of schooling that defined the practice of education throughout the industrial era. We close by exposing the tenets of a second revolution underway currently, one that is forming our understanding of schooling in the postindustrial world of the twenty-first century. And to make the point one more time, this emerging understanding of schooling exerts considerable influence over our conception of school leadership.

A MODEL OF ORGANIZATIONAL EVOLUTION

Over the last half century, scholars have invested considerable energy in the quest to uncover answers to the question of how industries and organizations evolve, devoting special attention to the influence of environmental movements on the shape and functioning of institutions. In the mid-1980s, in an effort to bring coherence to this work, Tushman and Romanelli (1985) crafted their seminal theory of organizational evolution, the punctuated equilibrium model of organizational change. At the core of their model, Tushman and Romanelli hypothesize that "organizations progress through *convergent* periods punctuated by *reorientations* which demark and set the bearings for the next convergent period" (p. 173). According to the theory, convergent periods cover long time spans during which incremental and marginal shifts that refine and elaborate organizational elements (e.g., goals) toward increased alignment dominate. Reorientations, on the other hand, encompass "periods of discontinuous change where strategies, power, structure, and systems are fundamentally transformed toward a new basis of alignment" (p. 173).

In short, industries and organizations within them tend to go along for extensive periods of time with only marginal changes. Then, for reasons explored below, they get pushed out of their orbits. At these times, fundamental changes are needed to ensure success.

According to the model, it is external shocks to the system that necessitate radical change (transformation), shocks that "punctuate" change. Researchers in this field maintain that these disturbances arise from social, legal, cultural, political, economic, and technological shifts in the environment. For example, technological shifts are forcing newspapers and magazines to leave well-established routines and seek out new foundations on which to build, in much the same way that afternoon newspapers found it necessary to adapt (unsuccessfully) to significant cultural shifts in the environment in the 1960s and 1970s. Researchers also conclude that a sustained period of poor performance can induce disturbances that demand transformation.

THE INDUSTRIAL ERA OF SCHOOLING: WHERE WE WERE

Change Forces (1890–1920)

Sense of Failure

As just noted, prolonged poor performance is one of the two forces that provide the fuel to cause institutional disequilibrium, to push organizations out of well-established operational orbits. Moving into the twentieth century, there was a widespread and growing feeling that the system of schooling of the nineteenth century was in trouble. On the one hand, because the center of gravity for the institution was preparation for college, enrollments were quite low and schooling was failing to address the needs of the majority of students who were not planning on attending college (Odell, 1939). In short, schooling at the turn of the nineteenth century was not educating the great bulk of America's youngsters and was preparing almost no one "for life."

Equally important, schools were seen as failing society, in particular the rapidly emerging industrialized society. By and large, because the socialization and skill sets needed to function in the new economy were not being provided, schools were seen as out of step with needs of a post-agrarian society. Nor were they providing much help in dealing with the problems accompanying the mass immigration of the time (Murphy, 2006).

Changing Environment

According to Tushman and Romanelli (1985), environmental shifts provide the second axis on which major institutional changes are scaffolded, especially significant alterations in the ambient economic, political, and social contexts impacting an industry. On the *political front*, the change with the greatest impact on education as we moved into the industrial era was the rise of progressivism and the development of the liberal democratic state. Rooted in discontent with political corruption and an expanded recognition of government as too limited for the new industrial era, the political landscape was noticeably recontoured in the late nineteenth and early twentieth centuries. Direct citizen control and machine politics began to give way to bureaucratized institutions led by a cadre of educational experts (Callahan, 1962; Tyack, 1974).

The *social tapestry* was also being rewoven during the period from 1890 to 1920. The central dynamic was "the transformation of American society from one characterized by relatively isolated self-contained communities into an urban, industrial nation" (Kliebard, 1995, p. 2): Industrialization and demographic changes were reshaping the nation (Tyack, 1974). Most important from our perspective here is the fact that these shifts in social conditions resulted in significant changes in schools. As Cremin (1961), Kliebard (1995), Tyack (1974), and Wraga (1994) have all demonstrated, "With the recognition of social change came a radically altered vision of the role of schooling" (Kliebard, 1995, p. 1).

Turning to the economy, we see the emergence of new *economic realities* brought on by the industrial revolution (Wraga, 1994). At the core of the matter was the transformation from an agricultural to an industrial economy, or perhaps more accurately, given the social changes outlined above, to an industrial society (Cremin, 1955). The nation was witnessing the "advent of machine production and its accompanying specialization of occupation" (Koos, 1927, p. 310). Stated in language that eerily would be reintroduced nearly a century later in reshaping the school to the realities of a postindustrial world, it could be said that by 1890 "national concerns about international economic competition" (Spring, 1990, p. 220) and the demands of "advancing technology" (Krug, 1964, p. 209) began to influence the design of the blueprints being used to shape the foundations of the newly emerging model of education.

Convergence (1920–1990)

The period between 1890 and 1920 began with the publication of one of the two most important reports on education ever produced in the United States and ended with the publication of another—the 1893 *Report of the Committee on Secondary School Studies*, commonly referred to as the *Report of the Committee of Ten*, and the 1918 report from the National Education Association titled *Cardinal Principles of Secondary Education*. It was the time when the learning and teaching foundations that defined comprehensive schooling for nearly a century were poured. It was here that the educational response to the new industrial world that would define the twentieth century was forged. More specifically, it was during this era that the ideology that would define schooling was developed and implanted in education. We pull the strands of this shifting ideology into three clusters: core values and purpose, technical core, and organizational architecture and governance.

Core Values/Purpose

Although public education started out as a practical endeavor, by the end of the nineteenth century, it was dominated by college interests. Preparation for college largely determined what was taught. Agreement on the central aim of public education was short-lived, however. By 1920, the purpose of schooling would be radically redefined.

In their famous 1893 report, the Committee of Ten attempted to resolve the question of purpose by "merging the high school's two functions into one" (Herbst, 1996, p. 109). The eerily current perspective of the committee was that there was no difference in these two aims and that preparation for life should lead naturally to preparation for college. As Cremin (1955) and others have highlighted, it was the Committee's belief in the primacy of "improving intellectual ability by disciplining the mind" (p. 297) that allowed them to arrive at this resolution: "The best preparation for life was to strengthen the intellect. . . . The discipline-centered college preparatory curriculum was viewed as the program best suited for all youth" (Wraga, 1994, p. 2). Practical knowledge, they held, would come later, from work and everyday life (Sizer, 1964).

Analysts have concluded that "the report of the Committee reflected the crossroad between an educational system designed to provide everyone with a common education and an educational system organized to provide everyone with a specific education based on a future social destination" (Spring, 1990, p. 200). The signals provided by the committee—that the purpose of education was to develop the mind—pointed schooling in a direction that urban, industrialized America of the twentieth century was unwilling to follow: "The Committee had in fact written an epitaph instead of a blueprint for the future" (Herbst, 1996, p. 108). "The Committee did not see the vast scope of the issues facing American schools and thus did not prescribe for them in any way. As a result, the suggestions in the *Report* became obsolete within two decades" (Sizer, 1964, p. 170).

Those who believed that the aim of education was intellectual development were not able to hold the high ground. Between 1890 and 1920, a new agenda, education for social control, buttressed by a new science of learning known as social efficiency, gradually came to dominate education. This newly forming purpose rested on a rejection of what critics believed to be an outdated view of schooling (Sizer, 1964; Spring, 1990). According to many analysts of education during the early years of the twentieth century, "Intellectual development was of course vital, but it had to be reconciled with the school as a social institution and its place in the larger social order" (Kliebard, 1995, p. 54).

Subject to the pull of the environmental conditions described earlier, a focus on individualism began to give way to the social purposes of schooling. The dominant leitmotif was that of schooling as a mechanism of social control (Kliebard, 1995). Social efficiency, in turn, became the central concept in influencing the reconfiguration of schooling (Spring, 1990) or, as the great historian of the American high school Edward Krug (1972) concluded, schooling became "the cathedral of social efficiency" (p. 150).

Education for social control included the introduction of new ideas, such as specialization, and a reformulation of older ones, such as equality of opportunity (Spring, 1990). It represented a rejection of the prevailing position on the academic function of education and provided an affirmation of the practical aims of schooling (Powell, Farrar, & Cohen, 1985; Spears, 1941). It acknowledged the role of the school in addressing new socially anchored responsibilities. Analysts argued that "educational functions traditionally carried on by family, neighborhood, or shop [were] no longer being performed; somehow they must get done; like it or not, the school must take them on" (Cremin, 1961, p. 117). Social efficiency meant fundamentally that the function of schools would be to prepare students for the new industrial world that was redefining American society—for what Spears (1941) called "the great and real business of living" (p. 56). Advocates of the new goal of social control "wanted education to produce individuals who were trained for a specific role in society and who were willing to work cooperatively in that role" (Spring, 1990, p. 201).

The Technical Core

The period from 1890 to 1920 was marked by "a vigorous drive to replace what was commonly regarded as a curriculum unsuited for the new industrial age and for the new population of students entering . . . secondary school in larger numbers" (Kliebard, 1995, p. 156). One change was that academics would be illuminated much less brightly than they had been before the turn of the century (Ravitch, 1983). As the belief that schooling was too academic became ingrained in the American culture, the curricular spotlight was redirected elsewhere (Latimer, 1958; Reese, 1995).

As the academic scaffolding supporting schooling in the nineteenth century was dismantled, a new infrastructure rose up to take its place—one constructed more from the raw materials of personal and practical experiences than from the frameworks of the academic disciplines: Practical education was required and the opportunity for employment took on added significance (Kliebard, 1995). Schooling for life was no longer education for college but rather preparation for a job. When social control as the foundation for schooling, and social efficiency as the theory of learning, became dominant threads in the tapestry known as education, a diminished—and continually decreasing—role for academics would also be woven into the fabric.

The pieces that complete the pedagogical aspect of industrial-era schooling focus on the organization of the curriculum and on student access to subject matter. Students would no longer be educated alike, with similar, or at least equivalent, curricular experiences. Instead, a number of new ideas would emerge to help reground the curriculum and to shape the variety of learning experiences available to students. One of these perspectives grew directly from the incipient body of knowledge being codified by child development psychologists (Tyack, 1974). Indeed, although not quite pushed into ascendancy, the belief in the student as the axis of the school curriculum was advanced during this era (Krug, 1964). This viewpoint maintained "that children, not books and teachers, ought to be the schools' starting place" (Powell et al., 1985, p. 261) and "that the child's own natural impulses could be used as a way of addressing the question of what to teach" (Kliebard, 1995, p. 37).

A second perspective, social efficiency, would hold even greater influence over the organization of the curriculum during the development of schooling for the industrial era. Like their colleagues who saw adolescent needs as the appropriate ground for curriculum development, social efficiency advocates clamored for greater variety in the learning menu. Unlike their colleagues, however, they saw the landmarks on the new curricular frontier defined not by individual interests of students but by societal needs and goals. Students were viewed not as individuals but as members of groups. Subject matter would be organized in different bundles to be parceled out to students in these varied groups (Krug, 1964). As Kliebard (1995) documents, "Predicting future destination as the basis for adapting the curriculum to different segments of the school population became a major feature of curriculum planning" (p. 13) during the period from 1890 to 1920. What was called for was education that matched young people to appropriate work roles (Wraga, 1994).

Organizational Architecture and Governance

The revolutionary changes that took root in education from 1890 to 1920 were not confined to vision and learning and teaching. The methods used to govern education and the designs employed to structure schools also underwent significant alterations, which were in directions heavily shaped by the powerful political, social, and economic currents outlined above. The defining element of the organizational revolution was the shift from lay control, which dominated the governance landscape before 1890, to a "corporate bureaucratic model" of governance (Tyack, 1974, p. 6). As was the case in the construction of the learning infrastructure, the new scientific models of school organization and governance provided some of the defining components of education for a postagrarian world.

The organizational transformation that marked the evolution of education was laced with two central ideologies, a "corporate form of external school governance and internal control by experts" (Tyack, 1974, p. 146). Both elements drew freely from models supporting the development of the postagricultural business sector (Callahan, 1962; Newlon, 1934). "Working under the banner of the depoliticalization of schooling and eliminating political corruption, reformers sought to remove the control of schools as far as possible from the people" (Tyack, 1974, p. 167), to eliminate community control. As was the case with the development of the differentiated curriculum, the struggle to separate education from politics was powered in part by both antidemocratic ideology and class prejudice. In terms of influence, we know that this movement accomplished much of its goal. By 1920, throughout the nation, a closed system of governance that would dominate education for the next 75 years had replaced much of the more open system that had prevailed at the end of the nineteenth century.

Shifts in the basic governance equation during the early decades of the twentieth century were accompanied by a reconfiguration in the way schools were managed and structured (Callahan, 1962). One distinctive development was the appearance of a class of administrative experts to whom government agents delegated control for the management of schools (Tyack, 1974). Borrowing from the new models of organization and management being forged in the corporate sector, reformers began to develop analogs between the leadership of business enterprises and the management of schools (Callahan, 1962; Newlon, 1934; Tyack, 1974). They argued that to reform education power needed to be concentrated at the top.

In order to facilitate the use of this centralized power and to maximize its potential to effect change, reformers drew up blueprints for a new structure for their institution (bureaucracy) and cobbled together a new philosophy of leadership (scientific management), borrowing freely from materials originally crafted in the corporate sector. In so doing, they brought forth the array of operating principles that would form the organizational backbone for schooling throughout the twentieth century, principles such as authority vested in office, differentiation and specialization of roles, professionalism, separation of management from labor, chain of command, and so forth (Murphy, Beck, Crawford, Hodges, & McGaughy, 2001).

POSTINDUSTRIAL SCHOOLING: WHERE WE ARE HEADED

Change Forces

Sense of Failure

As we entered the 1990s, the foundation of schooling that had stood for nearly three quarters of a century had begun to show significant deterioration. As was the case at the dawn of the twentieth century, there was a widespread feeling that schools were performing poorly. Crosnoe (2011, p. 3) hit the mark directly when she reported that "these are definitely not the glory days of the American educational system." What analysts saw as frustration over the continuing inadequacies of education in the United States was a multifaceted phenomenon. Or, stated in an alternate form, the perception that the level and quality of education in schools is less than many desire was buttressed by data on a wide variety of outcomes. Specifically, critics argued that data assembled in each of the following performance dimensions provided a not-very-flattering snapshot of the current performance of the American educational system: (1) academic achievement in basic subject areas—compared to student performance in other countries; (2) functional literacy; (3) preparation for employment; (4) the holding power of schools (drop-out rates); (5) knowledge of specific subject areas such as geography and economics; (6) mastery of higher-order skills; and (7) initiative, responsibility, and citizenship (Murnane & Levy, 1996; Murphy, 2006).

Two issues in particular ribboned analyses of educational outcomes at the turn of the twentieth century: (1) the inability of the educational enterprise to enhance levels of productivity to meet the needs of the changing workforce and (2) the failure of schools to successfully educate all of the nation's children, especially the poor. While analysts acknowledge that student achievement has remained fairly stable over the last quarter century, they fault education for its inability to keep pace with the increasing expectations from a changing economy (Committee for Economic Development, 1994; Consortium on Productivity in the Schools, 1995; Marshall & Tucker, 1992).

One side of the problem critics discuss is the belief that systems that hold steady in today's world are actually in decline (Murphy & Meyers, 2008). While others see stability, they see damaging obsolescence (Murnane & Levy, 1996). The other side of the productivity issue raised by these reviewers is the claim that because of the changing nature of the economy outlined below, the level of outcomes needed by students must be significantly increased. They find that the schools are not meeting this new standard for productivity. Complicating all of this is the knowledge that high levels of performance must be attained by nearly all of society's children (Murphy, 2010a).

What appears to be especially damaging to public education at the current time is the perceived inability of schooling to reform itself. Questions raised by analysts who take the long-term view on this issue are particularly demoralizing. What has resulted from reform efforts, critics argue, has not been an increase in educational quality but rather a proliferation of professional and bureaucratic standards (Hill, Pierce, & Guthrie, 1997), the creation of subsidies for bureaucracy (Beers & Ellig, 1994), a widening gap between professional educators and the general public (Marshall & Tucker, 1992), and the strengthening of a centralized educational system that disadvantages taxpayers and parents (Murphy, 2012; Payne, 1995). Beers and Ellig (1994) make this point in dramatic fashion when they claim that "in a very real sense we have tried to run the public schools the same way the Soviets tried to run factories, and now we're paying the price" (p. 20). The effect, critics maintain, is that reform has reinforced the very dynamics that are promoting self-destruction in education. The natural consequence, they hold, must be the emergence of new forms of educational institutions.

Changing Environment

Economy

At the same time, and consistent with the Tushman and Romanelli (1985) model, American education finds itself in a roiling environment of economic, political, and social changes. To begin with, it is almost a fundamental law that the economy is undergoing a significant metamorphosis. There is widespread agreement that we have been and continue to be moving from an industrial to a postindustrial or information economy. Key aspects of the new economy include: the globalization of economic activity, the demise of the mass-production economy, a privileging of information technology, an increase in the skills required to be successful, and an emphasis on the service dimensions of the marketplace. The ascent of the global economy has brought an emphasis on new markets and cracks in the model of public monopoly (Murphy, 2006).

Along with these changes, as we discuss below, have come increasing deinstitutionalization, deregulation, and privatization of the American system of education. There is a growing belief that markets offer more hope than the public sector—a belief in "the assumption that left to itself economic interaction between rationally self-interested individuals in the market will spontaneously yield broad prosperity, social harmony, and all other manner of public and private good" (Himmelstein, 1983, p. 16). Supported by market theory and theories of the firm and by the public choice literature, there is a new spirit of market-based entrepreneurship in play (Murphy, 1999, 2012).

Sociopolitical changes

The political and social environments also are undergoing important changes. There has been a loosening of the bonds of democracy (Barber, 1984; Elshtain, 1995). The infrastructure of civil society also has been impaired (Dahrendorf, 1995).

As a consequence of these basic shifts—the weakening of democracy and the deterioration of civil society, especially in conjunction with the ideological space that they share with economic fundamentalism—important sociopolitical trends have emerged. One strand of this evolving sociopolitical mosaic is plummeting public support for government (Cibulka, 1999; Murphy, 1999). In many ways, Americans "have disengaged psychologically from politics and governance" (Putnam, 1995, p. 68). As Hawley (1995) chronicles, "Citizens are becoming increasingly alienated from government and politics. They do not trust public officials" (p. 741) and they are skeptical of the bureaucratic quagmire of professional control that defined education for almost all of the twentieth century (Murphy & Shiffman, 2002).

A second pattern in the mosaic is defined by issues of poverty (Cibulka, 1999; Murphy, 2010a; Reyes, Wagstaff, & Fusarelli, 1999). Many analysts have explored the accelerating movement toward a society marked by great wealth and great poverty. According to Dahrendorf (1995), this economically grounded trend represents a new type of social exclusion. He and others are quick to point out that this condition seriously undermines the health of society: "Poverty and unemployment threaten the very fabric of civil society. . . . Once these [work and a decent standard of living] are lost by a growing number of people, civil society goes with them" (pp. 25–26).

Consistent with this description of diverging life chances is a body of findings on the declining social welfare of children and their families (Reyes et al., 1999). These data reveal a society populated increasingly by groups of citizens that historically have not fared well in this nation, especially ethnic minorities and citizens for whom English is a second language. Concomitantly, the percentage of youngsters affected by the ills of the world in which they live, for example, poverty, unemployment, illiteracy, crime, drug addiction, malnutrition, poor physical health, and homelessness is increasing (Murphy & Tobin, 2011).

Convergence

Across the last quarter century, we have argued that a new convergence has emerged in the American schools, one that parallels in scope the changes seen in that institution from 1890 to 1920. Three central alterations are visible: (a) at the technical level, a change from teaching to learning and a change from transmission to social-constructivist views of learning; (b) at the organizational level, a change from bureaucratic and hierarchical systems to more communal views of schooling; and (c) at the institutional level, a rebalancing of the governance equation, one that adds more weight to market and citizen control while subtracting influence from government and professional elites (Murphy, 2006). Below we examine these changes.

The Core Technology

As we discussed above, from the onset of the industrial revolution, education in the United States has been largely defined by a behavioral psychology-based model of learning—a model that fits nicely with the bureaucratic system of school organization in play during the last century. This viewpoint in turn nurtured the development of the factory and medical practice models of instruction that dominated schooling throughout the twentieth century. Under these two models, the belief that the role of schooling is to sort students into the able and less able—those who would work with their heads and those who would work with their hands—became deeply embedded into the fabric of schooling (Goodlad, 1984; Powell et al., 1985; Murphy et al., 2001).

What is important here is that the current period of upheaval just reviewed has placed us "in the midst of redefining, even recreating conceptions of learning and teaching in schools" (Prestine, 1995, p. 140), that is, a shift in the operant model of learning is a fundamental dynamic of the current struggle to redefine education. The behavioral psychology-based model that highlights the innate capacity of the learner has been challenged by notions of constructivism and situated learning (Prawat & Peterson, 1999; Rowan, 1995) and by the components of authentic pedagogy (Newmann & Wehlage, 1995). As Prawat and Peterson (1999) inform us, "Social constructivism represents more than an addition to the traditional, individualistic perspective that has dominated research on learning for most of [the twentieth] century. It . . . represents a dramatically different approach to learning, requiring fundamental changes in how . . . educators think about the process" (p. 203). Under this approach to learning, schools that historically have been in the business of promoting student adaptation to the existing social order (Krug, 1964, 1972; McLaughlin & Talbert, 2001) are being transformed to ensure that all youngsters reach ambitious targets of performance (Murphy, 2010a).

The Organizational Architecture

For some time now, "critics have argued that the reforms of the Progressive Era produced bureaucratic arteriosclerosis—and the low productivity of a declining industry" (Tyack, 1993, p. 3). There is an expanding feeling that the structure of schooling that was hardwired into the system between 1890 and 1920 and that has dominated education ever since has outlived its usefulness. In particular, it is held that the management tools of the bureaucratic paradigm pull energy and commitment away from learning. Reformers maintain that the structure cemented in place during the first recreation of schooling between 1890 and 1920 is not capable of supporting excellence in education and that, even worse, bureaucratic management has actually been damaging learning (Elmore, 1993; Murphy et al., 2001).

It is also argued that bureaucracy has led to siloed schools (Elmore, Peterson, & McCarthy, 1996; Lynch & Strodl, 1991; Pellicer & Anderson, 1995), that the structure that defined twentieth-century schooling is counterproductive to the needs and interests of educators in postindustrial schools. In particular, these reviewers find that the existing structure is incompatible with a professional orientation (Curry, 2008; Little, 1987). They maintain that the hierarchical foundations laid during the reform era (1990–1920) of the industrial period have neutered teachers and undermined "the drawing power and holding power of strong collegial ties" (Little, 1987, p. 502). These reviewers contend that "it has become increasingly clear that if we want to improve schools for student learning, we must also improve schools for the adults who work in them" (Smylie & Hart, 1999, p. 421).

As might be expected, given this tremendous attack on the basic organizational structure of schools, stakeholders at all levels are clamoring for significant reform, arguing that the bureaucratic framework of school organization needs to be rebuilt using different blueprints and materials (MacBeath, 2009; Martin & Crossland, 2000; Olivier & Hipp, 2006; Sackney & Dibski, 1992). There is widespread agreement that the top-down, authoritarian approach to leadership has taken us about as far as it can (Frost & Durant, 2003; Gronn, 2009). There is a significant demand for new ways of organizing schools, especially changes in the way they are led (Donaldson, 2001).

New perspectives of education feature these new methods of organizing and managing schools (Beachum & Dentith, 2004). In the image of schools for the twenty-first century, the hierarchical bureaucratic organizational structures that have defined schooling since the early 1900s are giving way to systems that are more focused on capacity building (Crowther, Kaagan, Ferguson, & Hann, 2002) and that are more organic (Murphy, 2005).

In these redesigned, postindustrial school organizations, to which Louis and Miles (1990) have given the label "adaptive model" (p. 26), there are basic shifts in roles, relationships, and responsibilities: Traditional patterns of relationships are altered; authority flows are less hierarchical, for example, traditional distinctions between administrators and teachers begin to blur; role definitions are both more general and more flexible—specialization is no longer held in such high regard; because influence is based on expertise, leadership is dispersed and is connected to competence for needed tasks as well as formal positions; and independence and isolation are replaced by cooperative work (Katzenmeyer & Moller, 2001; Murphy, 2005). Furthermore, the traditional structural orientation of schools is overshadowed by a focus on the human element (Crow, Hausman, & Scribner, 2002; Sergiovanni, 1991a, 1991b). The operant goal is no longer maintenance of the organizational structure but rather the development of human resources (Mojkowski & Fleming, 1988; Schlechty, 1990; Tichy & Cardwell, 2004). Building learning climates and promoting organizational adaptivity replaces the more traditional emphasis on uncovering and applying the one best model of performance (Gray et al., 1999). A premium is placed on organizational flexibility and purpose and values (Ancess, 2003; Louis et al., 2010; Sergiovanni, 1990, 1992).

A new model for school leadership acknowledges that shared influence strengthens the organization (MacBeath, 2005). Institutional perspectives no longer dominate the organizational landscape. Rather, schools are reconceptualized as communities, professional workplaces, and learning organizations (Ancess, 2003; Visscher & Witziers, 2004). Professional community-oriented conceptions that challenge historical bureaucratic understandings of schools as organizations move to center stage (Bulkley & Hicks, 2005; Hayes et al., 2004; Smylie & Hart, 1999). Ideas such as community of leadership, the norms of collaboration, inquiry communities, and the principle of care are woven into the fabric of the school organization (Ancess, 2003; Lieberman & Miller, 1999; Robinson, 2007). The metaphor of the school as community is brightly illuminated (Beck & Foster, 1999; Murphy, 2013b, Sergiovanni, 1994).

Institutional Dynamics

Some analysts of the institutional level of schools—the interface of the school with its larger (generally immediate) environment—argue that the industrial approach to education led to a privileging of government and a "cult of professionalism" (Sarason, 1994, p. 84) and to the "almost complete separation of schools from the community and, in turn, discouragement of local community involvement in decision making related to the administration of schools" (Burke, 1992, p. 33). Critiques of extant governance systems center on two topics discussed extensively above: (1) frustration with the government-professional monopoly and (2) critical analyses of the basic governance infrastructure—bureaucracy.

Many chroniclers of the changing governance structures in schools envision the demise of education as a sheltered government monopoly dominated by professionals. As noted above, in its stead they forecast the emergence of a system of schooling driven by economic and political forces that substantially increase the saliency of market and democratic forces (Murphy, 1996; Tichy & Cardwell, 2004). Embedded in this conception are a number of interesting dynamics. One of the key elements involves a recalibration of the locus of control among levels of government. Originally called "democratic localism" (p. 305) by Katz (1971), it has more recently come to be known simply as localization or, more commonly, decentralization. However it is labeled, it represents a backlash against "the thorough triumph of a centralized and bureaucratic form of educational organization" (p. 305) and governance of the industrial era of education.

A second ideological foundation can best be thought of as a recasting of democracy, a replacement of representative governance with more populist conceptions, especially what Cronin (1989) describes as direct democracy. While we use the term more broadly than does Cronin, our conception of the solidifying convergence here shares with his a grounding in (1) the falling fortunes of representative democracy, a "growing distrust of legislative bodies . . . [and] a growing suspicion that privileged interests exert far greater influence on the typical politician than does the common voter" (Cronin, 1989, p. 4) and (2) recognition of the claims of its advocates that greater direct voice will produce important benefits for society (Murphy & Shiffman, 2002).

A third foundation encompasses a rebalancing of the control equation in favor of lay citizens while diminishing the power of the state and (in some ways) educational professionals. This line of ideas emphasizes parental empowerment. It is, at times, buttressed by a strong strand of antiprofessionalism that underscores citizen control, and local involvement (Murphy, 2012).

The ideology of choice is a fourth pillar that is also rebuilding linkages between the school and parents and community stakeholders. Sharing a good deal of space with the concepts of localism, direct democracy, and lay control, choice is designed to open up both the demand and supply side of markets (Murphy, 1996).

CONCLUSION

We find that schools are generally resistant to and able to deflect and accommodate reform efforts during the long stretches of time when previously turbulent economic, political, and social environments have cooled and activity domains have hardened. No matter how hard reformers hammer education during these periods of convergence, change occurs on the margins, if at all.

On the other hand, there is also considerable evidence that the hard equilibrium that defines American education is indeed subject to destabilization and reforming. It does seem to require considerable energy to punctuate the status quo, however. In particular, change depends on major and overlapping strands of environmental pressures. In the last two centuries, we have seen these conditions appear twice. One occurred as the nineteenth century turned into the twentieth and schools changed to respond to the perceived needs of an industrial economy and a postagrarian web of politics and culture. The second arose as the twentieth century melded into the twenty-first and education began its struggle to recast itself consistent with the political, social, and economic DNA of an information society. The essential elements in the domains of activity that came to define the periods of convergence that preceded and followed the first era of turmoil were documented above. In addition, our understanding of the cardinal dimensions and elements that will define postindustrial education were described. It is the latter set of changes that define schooling and establish the frames for school leaders today.

3

The Threads of School Improvement

School improvement is about the "stuff" that needs to be addressed. Over the years, the "goods" have been called correlates, factors, elements, ingredients, and so on. This book is about cultural dimension of the school improvement narrative. But it is also about conditions and supports that both link elements and provide some of the fuel for them to work well, for example, cohesiveness. Appropriately, we illustrate these threads of the school improvement story throughout the chapters on the elements. In this chapter, because leadership for school improvement requires a clear understanding of and ability to work with this knowledge, we pull these conditions and supports from the background and put them on center stage. We start with some guidelines about the road to school improvement and move on to analyses of core supporting concepts such as context and coherence. It is important to begin with an acknowledgment that there is considerable overlap among these supports and conditions.

GETTING STARTED: NAVIGATING THE TRIP

> I never underestimate teachers' skill in continuing to do what they consider works for them and resisting that with which they do not wish to engage. (Hattie, 2009, p. 215)

Things get in the way, people object, established routines assert themselves, competing demands intrude, there are conflicting opinions, there are conflicting personalities, there are conflicting interests, and insecurities and uncertainties emerge. (Goldenberg, 2004, p. 2)

Major figures in the study of organizational change such as Fullan (1982) and school improvement such as Bryk, Sebring, Allensworth, Luppescu, and Easton (2010) and Smylie (2010) have described the school improvement pathway as uneven and full of unexpected twists and turns (McDougall et al., 2007; Wilson & Berne, 1999). Or as Newmann (1992, p. 192) so nicely notes, "productive school change does not proceed on a tight linear path from a detailed plan to . . . success in terms of original intention." Scholars in these domains portray change as evolutionary as well as planful. The voyage according to Ancess (2003, p. 32) is marked by "a pattern of fits, starts, retreats, and starts again rather than as a smooth linear path."

In particular, analysts have discovered that school improvement work is often characterized by increased tensions, the unsettling of comfortable routines, cultural resistance, new enactments of micropolitical behavior, and the surfacing of legitimate concerns (Datnow & Castellano, 2001; Goldenberg, 2004; Sweetland & Hoy, 2000). Thus, they document that change is often accompanied by an implementation dip (Curry, 2008; Fullan, 1993; Louis, 2007). Things are likely to trend downward, both in human terms such as confidence and morale (Fullan & Ballew, 2002; Louis, 2007) and performance (Bryk et al., 2010; Fullan, 1993) before they turn upward.

Relatedly, we learn that success is fragile (Galletta & Ayala, 2008; Goldenberg, 2004). Victory is hardly inevitable and, once garnered, requires some vigilance to maintain (Betts, Zau, & Koedel, 2010; Bryk et al., 2010). Turnover of personnel is often accompanied by regression (Dede & Honana, 2005; Firestone & Martinez, 2007; Goldstein, 2004). Energy naturally leaks out of the system (Dinham, 2005; Spillane, Halverson, & Diamond, 2001), and the loss is often unnoticed or, if detected, not replenished (Goldenberg, 2004; Sindelar et al., 2006). The environments in which schools find themselves are always evolving, pushing one reform forward only to be replaced by another a short time later (Brunner et al., n.d.; Dede & Honana, 2005; Malen & Rice, 2004). Mandates proliferate, overload sets in, fragmentation increases, meaning dissipates, and people withdraw (Finnigan & Gross, 2007; Malen & Rice, 2004; Murphy & Meyers, 2009) to the safety of the past and the comforts of old routines (Ackerman & Maslin-Ostrowski, 2002; Blumenfeld, Fishman, Krajcik, Marx, & Soloway 2000; Olsen & Kirtman, 2002). Change becomes a ritual that washes over the school (Cuban, 1984a, 1984b; Galletta & Ayala, 2008; Malen & Rice, 2004). Sustainability is undermined (Fullan & Ballew, 2002; Stoll, Bolam, McMahon, Wallace, & Thomas, 2006).

COLLECTIVE, MULTIFACTOR WORK

School reform initiatives are "impoverished" when they ignore the factors outside of schools that contribute to failure. (Galletta & Ayala, 2008, pp. 1981–1982)

Only comprehensive designs offer hope of success. (Murphy, 2010a, p. 234)

One of the most important understandings that has emerged from the broad field of school improvement, especially improvement for students placed at risk, is that troubles and problems are traceable to the broader society in which schools are nested (Downey, von Hippel, & Broh, 2004; Rothstein, 2004; Shannon & Bylsma, 2002). Therefore, school improvement efforts must extend beyond the school (Berends et al., 2005; Lee & Burkam, 2002; Spradlin et al., 2005). This means collective work (Murphy, 2010a; Murphy & Tobin, 2011; Smerdon, Borman, & Hannaway, 2009). To start, it means a larger role for nonschool agencies in reshaping the political, economic, and cultural forces that disadvantage many children (Kober, 2001; Miller, 1995; Newmann, 1992). Second, it suggests that schools and other institutions and systems of support need to work in tandem (Reynolds, 2002; Shannon & Bylsma, 2002; Singham, 2003). None alone are likely to be successful, especially when improvement means turning around troubled situations (Murphy, 2010b). Third, it necessitates greater efforts on the part of schools to extend their work beyond the traditional boundaries of schooling, to take ownership for a wider array of services (Entwisle, Alexander, & Olson, 2000; Hughes, 2003; Jordan & Cooper, 2003).

We have also learned over the years that there is no single factor, element, or component that will lead to dramatic school improvement (Baenen, Dulaney, Yamen, & Banks, 2002; Balfanz & Byrnes, 2006; Stiefel, Schwartz, & Ellen, 2006). What is required is a collective attack (Chatterji, 2005; Halverson, Grigg, Prichett, & Thomas, 2007; Thompson & O'Quinn, 2001), "a mix of strategies" (Thompson, 2002, p. 5). A productive school improvement design would be comprehensive, providing a combination of elements (Ancess, 2000; McGee, 2003; Sweeney, 1982). It would provide significant initiatives on a number of fronts (Felner, Seitsinger, Brand, Burns, & Bolton, 2007; North Carolina State Department of Public Instruction, 2000; U.S. Commission on Civil Rights, 2004), that is, be multilayered and multitiered (Bryk et al., 2010; Roscigno, 1998). As we discuss in detail below, the design would be interconnected, aligned, integrated, and coordinated (Murphy & Hallinger, 1993; Reynolds, 2002; Silins & Mulford, 2010). It would feature what Miller (1995, p. 376) calls the principle of "complementarity" at both the strategy and institutional levels. It would attend to both the short and long term (Kober, 2001). It would offer redundancy (Miller, 1995).

The chronicle on multistrand school improvement work contains a number of key subthemes. We know, for example, that there are some components that are necessary not because they push the needle forward but because their absence can derail the rest of the bundle of work. A safe and orderly learning environment falls into this category (Bryk et al., 2010; Wynne, 1980).

We also know that weaknesses in any of the key pieces of the overall design make improvement problematic (Stringfield & Reynolds, 2012); each element needs to reach at least the moderate level of effectiveness (Bryk et al., 2010). Additionally, there is some evidence of a multiplier effect in play (Brewer, 1993). "A" may be weak by itself, as might "B." Together, however, they might produce a moderate to strong effect, what Hattie (2009) refers to as an "interaction effect." It is a combination of small effects working together that make a difference (Felner et al., 2007; Murphy, 2010a; Quint, 2006).

Studies of school improvement with nearly every group of students at risk inform us that the more disadvantaged the population, the more effort is needed to reach success (Elbaum, Vaughn, Tejero Hughes, & Watson Moody, 2000; Murphy, 2010a, 2010b; Newmann, 1992), and the more constant that work must be (Rumberger & Palardy, 2005). For example, while middle-class school communities benefit from school improvement ingredients measuring at mid-level strengths, only high strength leads to improvement in at-risk communities (Bryk et al., 2010).

Researchers have also uncovered another dimension of the multiple factor law. For students placed at risk, both academic and cultural levers need to be engaged (Croninger & Lee, 2001; Fredricks, Blumenfeld, & Paris, 2004; Rothstein, 2004). As Becker and Luthar (2002, pp. 204–205) remind us,

Methods that demand higher educational standards without a similar emphasis on the social-emotional needs of early adolescents will not result in much success, efforts to improve the social-emotional needs of disadvantaged students without a comparable application of instructional and curricular methods to attain academic excellence will be similarly ineffective.

Clearly then "instruction matters and it matters a lot; but so does the social context in which it is embedded" (Bryk et al., 2010, p. 209; Battistich, Solomon, Kim, Watson, & Schaps, 1995). Indeed, "the greatest achievement effects follow from strong combinations of communality and academic press" (Shouse, 1996, p. 47; Stoll et al., 2006; Rumberger, 2011).

There is emerging evidence that the multifactor package of school improvement components must not pivot solely on remediation. Successful work requires simultaneous movement on both helping youngsters catch up and keeping them in sync with their classmates. An effective design needs to include both remediation and acceleration (Murphy, 2010a). The corollaries are that (1) early intervention efforts almost always trump later work and (2) prevention of problems trumps remediation of problems (Betts et al., 2010; Balfanz, Herzog, & MacIver, 2007; Ensminger & Slusarcick, 1992).

Some of the most important sublessons threaded into the role of collectivism in school improvement research address issues of time. We learn, for example, that sufficient time to get reforms germinated is quite important (Goldenberg, 2004; Murphy & Hallinger, 1993). We also learn from studies (Betts et al., 2010; Bryk et al., 2010; Goldenberg, 2004; Henry, Fortner, & Thompson, 2012; Huberman, Parrish, Hannan, Arellanes, & Shambaugh, 2011; Louis & Miles, 1991; Rumberger, 2011) and integrative reviews (Borman, Hewes, Overman, & Brown, 2003; Desimone, 2002; Hattie, 2009) that it takes considerable time for improvement initiatives to flower (McKenna & Walpole, 2010).

An analog in this story is that, in general, improvement is developmental, and it appears gradually and incrementally (Leithwood, 2008; Quint, 2006; Smerdon et al., 2009): Schools by and large do "not make dramatic improvements, but rather incremental improvement over time" (Huberman et al., 2011, p. 9).

Success is by no means ensured in the school improvement game, especially when situations and environments are turbulent and when schools are in troubled condition (Balfanz et al., 2007; Huberman et al., 2011; Murphy, 2009). Because of this, and for substantive and symbolic reasons, small wins over time are heralded in the school improvement literature (Bryk et al., 2010; Huberman et al., 2011). These small impacts are often quite meaningful (Quint, 2006).

An important but less developed time theme is that some interventions play out differently across the career of students (Murphy, 2010a; Rumberger, 2011). For example, teacher expectations carry more weight with younger students. Other time, themes were noted previously; early is better than later and prevention trumps remediation (Davison, Young, Davenport, Butterbaugh, & Davison, 2004; Heckman, 1995; Hill, Rowan, & Ball, 2005).

CLIMATE AND SEEDBEDS

Structural changes in and of themselves never have and never will predict organizational success. (Murphy, 1991, p. 76)

It is not obvious that changes in teaching practice follow from changes in structure. (Elmore, 1995, p. 24)

Of course structural changes are important, but they do not define differences in student achievement. (Hattie, 2009, p. 33)

Perhaps the most essential threaded law that leaders and policy makers need to burn into their minds is that structural changes do not predict organizational outcomes, "structural change changes structure, not substance" (Ancess, 2003, p. 140; Fullan & Ballew, 2002; Newmann, 1992). Numerous studies have affirmed this fact over the last quarter century in nearly every domain of schooling (Antrop-Gonzalez, 2006; Cooper, 1999; Murphy & Beck, 1995) and nearly every school leader has been frustrated by this truth (Adams, 2010; Rodriguez, 2008; York-Barr & Duke, 2004). Additionally, what holds for structures holds for resources (Creemers & Reezigt, 1996; Spillane, Diamond et al., 2001) and policies (Louis & Miles, 1990; Newmann, 1981; Smerdon & Borman, 2009) as well. This is particularly unsettling knowledge because leaders have been inculcated to rely on structural change to power reform (Elmore, 1995; Murphy, 1991). Additionally, for reasons that Elmore (1995) explains in his classic essay (i.e., ease of use and high symbolic value), policy makers and other reformers routinely perpetuate the logic and practice of structural change.

Four lines of explanation shed light on the disconnect between structure and school improvement. One focuses on the fact that structures are a long way from outcomes: "the path between macro-level reconfigurations and micro-level processes and activities is long, many-jointed, and loosely linked in a number of places" (Murphy, 1991, p. 76). Structures need to produce changes in the conditions of learning if they are to be successful (Hattie, 2009; Murphy, 1991; Newmann, 1992). However, it is a problematic bet that they can do so (Elmore, 1995; Rodriguez, 2008; Smerdon & Borman, 2009). For example, moving from a regular schedule to a blocked one does nothing to change the quality of instruction or the robustness of the curriculum in classrooms. Advisory periods are as likely to be sterile as they are to foster personalization (Murphy, 2013b; Newmann, 1992).

A second line of analysis concludes that schools are characterized by deep patterns of who they are and how they do the business of education. Structural patterns that are inconsistent with the existing grammar of schooling routinely fail to produce desired change (Betts & Shkolnik, 1999; Felner et al., 2007). The existing conditions, if you will, almost always cause new ideas to conform to the prevailing ideology rather than to shape it (Murphy, 2013b). This is the hallmark contribution of Fullan (1982, 1993) to education: The culture needs to change to make structures viable.

Third, there is considerable evidence that structural changes are often introduced with little sensitivity to the local context or situation in the school, regardless of whether or not there is congruence with the prevailing climate. We examine this problem in more detail in the following section.

Finally, schools are generally subject to the mistaken belief that the "goods" they want to import are an integral part of the structure they are inviting in (e.g., "community" always accompanies structural changes in the size of a school). The problem is that the assumption is false. The result is that the structure is imported, but the DNA that made it work elsewhere is not. Schools end up with structural shells—empty forms—that do not power school improvement (Murphy, 1991, 2013a).

The great paradox here is that while reworking the climate, or the seedbed, of the school, is the main work, structural changes are required to hold new patterns and understandings in place (Murphy, 2013a). That is, while structures have only limited influence on conditions that enhance learning without them new perspectives will dissipate (Datnow & Castellano, 2001).

CONTEXT

> The situation or context is crucially important. (Phillips, 2003, p. 257)

> School reform plans cannot be forged in a vacuum; local context has a huge impact. (Gold, Cucchiara, Simon, & Riffer, 2005, p. 4)

> The complexities of these varied contexts introduce a complicated web of factors that influence whether or not a particular characteristic or practice will produce the desired results. (Guskey, 2003, p. 16; Bryman, Stephens, & Campo, 1996)

School improvement sleuths examining every aspect of change, arriving at the conclusion that regardless of the "reform agenda" context is a cardinal, but not determinate, variable in the change growth process (Jimerson, Anderson, & Whipple, 2002; Murphy & Hallinger, 1993; Penuel et al., 2010), not simply a "container" for the work (Spillane, Halverson, & Diamond, 2001). Context helps set the rules and norms as well as the constraints that shape improvement work (Adams, 2010; Hallinger & Murphy, 1985, 1986; Mitchell & Castle, 2005). Because situations are idiosyncratic, reforms must be molded to fit the context at hand (Bruggencate, Luyten, Scheerens, & Sleegers, 2012; Dede & Honana, 2005; Scheerens, 1997).

To begin with, it is important to remember that district context can heavily influence school-based improvement work—for better or worse (Mangin, 2007; Rumberger, 2011; Shear et al., 2008). Relatedly, a massive amount of evidence has accumulated that community contexts create powerful forces that can bolster or hinder improvement initiatives (Bryk et al., 2010; Crosnoe, 2011; Heck, 2000). Socioeconomic status, ethnicity, language, housing conditions, urbanicity, history, and so forth all matter (Adams, 2010; Leithwood, Louis, Anderson, & Wahlstrom, 2004; Marks, 2000).

Hattie (2009) in his hallmark meta-analysis documented that classroom contexts exert considerable pull over improvement efforts as well (see also Birch & Ladd, 1997; Louis et al., 2010; Supovitz et al., 2010). Teachers bring their own cultural understandings, skills, and backgrounds to the job (Grossman, Wineburg, & Woolworth, 2001; Palincsar, Magnusson, Marano, Ford, & Brown, 1998). Each develops a grammar of instruction that impacts how he or she views and engages with change (Hattie, 2009; Scheerens, 1997). The importance of teacher as "person-in-context" (Ford, cited in Geijsel, Sleegers, Leithwood, & Jantzi, 2003, p. 232) is an important theme that is often overlooked in conducting school improvement work. For example, investigators often report that younger teachers with fewer years of experience are more apt to actively engage in reform efforts (Desimone, 2002; Walker & Slear, 2011). Subject matter taught and department affiliation also have a role in this narrative (Goddard, Hoy, & Hoy, 2000; Palincsar et al., 1998; Supovitz et al., 2010).

School context also influences the viability and meaningfulness of improvement efforts, both directly and through the way it shapes activities in classrooms and the sensemaking of individuals (Chrispeels & Martin, 2002; Clark, Dyson, Millward, & Robson, 1999; Penuel, Fishman, Yamaguchi, & Gallagher, 2007). We know, for example, that "level" often produces different interpretations of change efforts (Marks & Printy, 2003; Silins & Mulford, 2010). Geographical location has been found to be influential (Gonzalez & Padilla, 1997; Leithwood et al., 2004). So too has the health of the school and the extent of the challenges they confront, that is where they fall on the continuum from troubled to highly effective (Heck, 2000; Robinson et al., 2008; Stoll et al., 2006). Lack of enrollment stability, or high student mobility, also shapes school improvement efforts (Bryk et al., 2010). Because youngsters from different environments view education and schooling in different ways (Crosnoe, 2011; Farrell, 1990; Newmann, 1992), demographics of the student body is regularly uncovered as a school-level contextual variable that influences school improvement work (Conchas, 2001; Munoz, Ross, & McDonald, 2007; Murphy, 2010a). The nature of the community of adults in the schools is also consequential, especially the nature of relationships in place (Connolly & James, 2006; Guskey, 2003; Mitchell & Sackney, 2006).

The fact that context matters, and that it matters a good deal, has implications for school leaders. We begin with some caveats. To maintain that context is important is not the same thing as arguing that it is determinate, and understanding acknowledgment does not require principals to be held hostage to context (Borman et al., 2003). Also, to underscore the importance of the situation does not mean that generalized reform ideas are dead on arrival. Indeed, as Leithwood (2005, pp. 620–621) reminds us, "leadership practices are common across contexts in the general form but highly adaptable and contingent in the specific enactment." Or turning to Bryk and associates (2010, p. 67), "the most effective managerial form for an organization is contingent on the technical and environmental circumstances affecting the core work of the organization." Thus the notion that all school reforms need to be completely homegrown is scientifically unjustified (Goldenberg, 2004). The objective is flexibility to meet or adapt to local conditions.

At the same time, leaders need to acknowledge the place of situation in school improvement work, to understand that reform does not "occur in a vacuum, devoid of its surrounding context" (Coldren & Spillane, 2007, p. 18). They need to learn that context is not simply a "container" for reform (Spillane et al., 2001) but an essential aspect of the work itself. Included here is the understanding that what works easily or smoothly in one school may require the investment of considerable capital and energy in another school (Cuijpers, 2002; Newmann, 1992). It also means acting in ways that honor the limitations of telling and mandating as engines of school improvement (Newmann, 1992; Smerdon & Borman, 2009). Improvements have to play out at the street level (Goldenberg, 2004). While the prize is never abandoned, localization and customization are needed (and appropriate) to gain it (Bossert et al., 1982; Leithwood et al., 2004; Penuel et al., 2007). Strategies must be formed to fit the situation (Cosner, 2009; Phillips, 2003) while working simultaneously to influence context in directions that support improvement. To be sure, the process cannot be permitted to produce "lethal mutations" (Penuel et al., 2007, p. 931) of reforms, but adaptation will be the norm (Borko, 2004). Leaders also need to be cognizant of the fact that this adaptive school improvement work is likely to produce unintended consequences (Hamilton et al., 2003; Murphy, 2010a).

COHERENCE

> The main point [is] that implementing effective practices in an integrated, schoolwide fashion holds much greater potential than a piecemeal approach. (Cotton, 2000, p. 8)

> Coherence is vital for successful change; coherence is the result of consistency and integration from one setting to the next. (Goldenberg, 2004)

Building on the findings from the pioneers in the effective schools movement, we distilled consistency, coordination, integration, and alignment (i.e., coherence) as one of the three essential beams supporting successful improvement (Murphy, 1992; 2013a, 2013b). This conclusion has been affirmed on a regular basis over the last 20 years (Barnes, Camburn, Sanders, & Sebastian, 2010; Bryk et al., 2010; Desimone, 2002). More important, analysts peering in on successful practice have unearthed the dimensions or essential aspects of coherence:

- Integration within each component of school improvement work
- Alignment across subject areas (e.g., a single point of view about writing across all academic domains)
- Integration between and among components of the work (e.g., between mission/goals and professional development) or what Goldenberg (2004, p. 35) calls "several factors working in concert"
- Coordinating the four pieces of the instructional program—standards, instruction, curriculum, and assessment
- Working as a collective rather than as a discrete set of individual actors, what Bryk and associates (2010, p. 217) refer to as engaging "collective social capacity"
- Abandoning practices and policies that get in the way of improvement, that foster fragmentation and overload
- Keeping the core issues at the center, maintaining a ferocious focus on what counts
- Shaping influences from beyond the organization (e.g., the state, the community) to fit the school context and goals
- Cascading improvement efforts and values across organizational levels (e.g., district-school-classroom), not isolating them to a single area
- Employing resources in an integrated manner, especially personnel
- Getting organizational policies, structures, operating systems to operate in tandem and in mutually reinforcing ways (e.g., around time usage)
- Building redundancy into improvement work
- Aligning the formal and informal aspects of the organization
- Filtering discordant messages and demands
- Shaping the sensemaking frames that hold the high ground in the school
- Linking short and long-term perspectives
- Thoroughly compressing variability in the academic program and the school culture
- Integration between school and work

We close our discussion of alignment and coordination with a few important reminders. It is the principal who is the prime actor in the coherence narrative, the one who wields the tools to forge integration (Bryk et al., 2010; Murphy, 1992). For a variety of reasons, coherence is not a natural state in schools. Things are more likely to pull apart than cohere. Alignment, integration, and cohesion require a strong hand (Csikszentmihalyi & Larson, 1984; Goldenberg, 2004).

CAUTIONS: COSTS AND CONSEQUENCES

> For policy makers and practitioners to decide what interventions to support and implement, they must consider costs. (Rumberger, 2011, p. 232)

> Leaders would be wise to anticipate unintended as well as hoped-for-actions. The operant caution is to assume that there will be some. (Murphy, 2010a, p. 20)

Some important guidance in the area of school improvement attends to "costs." One guideline reminds us that the reforms that have the greatest power to drive improvement tend to be the most costly too (Hattie, 2009). At the same time, because these costs often do not require new outlays of funds (e.g., people already on the payroll are shifted to new responsibilities), these costs often go uncounted (Hattie, 2009). Third, reliance on additional external resources generally does not work well for long-term improvements (Curry, 2008; Stoll et al., 2006). Finally, it is necessary that benefits not be the sole criterion of helpfulness or impact (Levin, Belfield, Muenning, & Rouse, 2007). School leaders need to remember that interventions have both benefits and costs. And while it is often difficult to isolate the impact of particular interventions (Thompson, 2002), "Considerably more effort than is now the norm needs to be devoted to assessing both of these dimensions of reform efforts and trying to determine the ratio between the two, to determine where efforts are most cost effective" (Barton, 2003, p. 37).

We also have discovered that it is difficult to predict the exact consequences of improvement efforts (Newmann, 1992; Murphy, 2010a). As reported earlier, the fact that the school improvement road is bumpy, reciprocal, nonlinear, and jumbled makes this nearly inevitable. We also know now that unintended consequences, both good and bad, find their way into school improvement endeavors (Blumenfeld et al., 2000; Fullan & Ballew, 2002; Scanlan & Lopez, 2012), what Leithwood (2008, p. 18) describes as "collateral outcomes." One message for leaders is that they need to spend some time working on these consequences. The unplanned for can often be foreshadowed with some effort and insight. Another message is that leaders need to be prepared to deal with these consequences, both in advance and after they arrive on the scene (Murphy, 2013a).

CONCLUSION

The balance of the book highlights the elements or components of leadership for building a productive school culture. While the "laws" of school improvement will be visible, they do not occupy center stage in the remaining chapters. For that reason, we made many of them explicit in this chapter. Leaders who fail to honor these principles and guidelines in the work of school improvement will find more struggle than joy in those endeavors.

4

Supportive Communities of Learning for Students

COMMUNITY AND ACADEMIC PRESS

> This powerful combination of high academic expectations and meaningful student-teacher interpersonal relationships form the basis of authentic caring as an alternative to traditional schooling. (Antrop-Gonzalez & De Jesus, 2006, p. 419)

> A press toward higher academic standards must be coupled with ample personal support. (Bryk et al., 2010, p. 60)

> Technical improvements in teaching and curriculum are necessary, but they are unlikely to be put to work for the benefit of students unless they are supported by a positive organizational climate, culture, or ethos. (Newmann, Rutter, & Smith, 1989, p. 221)

As we established in Chapter 1, schools that serve children and young people well are defined by two anchoring pillars, strong academic press and supportive culture. Ancess (2000, p. 595) refers to this as "a combination of nurture and rigor or affiliation and intellectual development," and Bryk and team (2010, p. 74) characterize it as "a press toward academic achievement . . . coupled with personal support from teachers." We reviewed the evidence on this mixture, and reported that focusing primarily on the academic side of the equation is insufficient (Shannon & Bylsma, 2002; Thompson & O'Quinn, 2001), especially for students placed in peril by poverty (Becker & Luthar, 2002; Rumberger, 2011). Academic press alone "does not attend sufficiently to the quality of social relations required for effective teaching and learning" (Goddard, Hoy, & Hoy, 2000, p. 293). That is, schools with strong press can still prove inadequate if they provide little attention to the social and relationship dimensions of education (Crosnoe, 2011; Felner et al., 2007; Quint, 2006).

At the same time, we know that nearly exclusive attention to culture is problematic as well, that it is a "necessary but not sufficient factor in promoting worthwhile forms of student achievement" (Newmann et al., 1989, p. 225). A number of landmark studies have revealed how overemphasis on culture can lead to a lowering of academic expectations (Cusick, 1983; Powell et al., 1985; Sedlak, Wheeler, Pullin, & Cusick, 1986). More recent analysis confirms that featuring culture at the expense of academic press is not a wise pathway for school leaders to pursue, nor a destination to which principals should steer their schools (Murphy, Beck, Crawford, Hodges, & McGaughy, 2001; Shouse, 1996). Too great an emphasis on providing nurture and support can constrain educators from promoting serious academic engagement (Farrell, 1990). The concern is that students may "be exposed to socially therapeutic rather than intellectually demanding values and activities, and that their schools' efforts to build supportive and cohesive communities may actually help divert attention from academic goals" (Shouse, 1996, p. 52). Communal support for students, separate from focus on achievement, creates distinct complications for students (Newmann & Wehlage, 1995; Page, 1991). When teachers want "more than anything . . . [for] students to know [they] care about them" (Nystrand, 1997, p. 53), they can "kill with kindness" (Sadker & Sadker, 1994, p. 124). When this occurs, "there [does] not seem to be any subject matter other than . . . cordial relations" (Cusick, 1983, p. 53), and caring separated from challenge contributes to student disengagement (Page, 1991). We must not lose sight of the fact that community is in the service of learning (Ancess, 2003; Antrop-Gonzalez & De Jesus, 2006; Shouse, 1996).

We also know that because there is a "fundamental relation between learning and social interaction" (Eckert, 1989, p. 183) that press and support work best when they are viewed as an amalgam (Murphy, 2013b), or conceptualized as two strands of DNA that wrap around each other (Dinham, 2005; Kruse, Seashore Louis, & Bryk, 1995; Strahan, 2003). "Rigor and care must be braided together" (Fine, cited in Antrop-Gonzalez, 2006, p. 274) to work best. There are some differences in the literature, however, about the relative importance of each strand and the order in which they load into the success equation. What is not in question is the fact that both need to be present and that the specific context will help determine issues of importance and timing (Murphy, 2013b).

THE POWER OF COMMUNITY FOR STUDENTS, TEACHERS, AND PARENTS

> Stronger bonds among the members of the school community build the school's social capital, broadening the space for teachers to expand students' learning beyond their self-imposed limits. (Ancess, 2003, p. 112)

In this volume, the focus is on the cultural element in the school improvement algorithm. However, given what we just reported, academic emphasis is never far from the center stage. Yet, the spotlight is consciously centered on culture. According to Sweetland and Hoy (2000, p. 705), culture is a "concept used to capture the basic and enduring quality of organizational life." It encompasses the values and norms that define a school (Dumay, 2009; Franklin & Streeter, 1995; Rossmiller, 1992). It is "those facets of organization that reflect underlying assumptions guiding decisions, behavior, and beliefs within organizations" (Scribner et al., 1999, p. 155). It can be thought of as the personality of the school (Hoy, Hannum, & Tschannen-Moran, 1998). In this volume, we use culture, climate, and environment synonymously.

We describe school culture in terms of community, a construct that is defined in a variety of overlapping ways (Beck & Foster, 1999). Battistich, Solomon, Kim, Watson, and Schaps (1995, p. 628) use community to capture "the psychological aspects of social settings that satisfy group members' needs for belonging and meaning." It consists of ingredients such as membership, integration, and influence (Baker, Terry, Bridger, & Winsor, 1997; Osterman, 2000). As we have illustrated throughout earlier chapters, community stands in juxtaposition to institutionalism and hierarchy as an organizational frame of reference (Beck & Foster, 1999; McLaughlin & Talbert, 2001; Murphy, 1991; Scribner et al., 1999; Sergiovanni, 1994).

> Communally organized schools are marked by three *core components:* (1) a set of shared and commonly understood organizational values and beliefs about institutional purpose, what students should learn, how adults and students should behave, and students' potential as learners and citizens; (2) a common agenda of activities that defines school membership, fosters meaningful social interaction among members, and links them to school traditions; and (3) the distinctive pattern of social relations embodying an ethic of caring visible in both collegial and student-teacher relationships. (Shouse, 1996, p. 51)

In later chapters, we attend to "communities of professionalism" for teachers and "communities of engagement for parents." Here the focus is on "communities of pastoral care for students." We suggest that understanding of such communities is critical because at the heart of the educational narrative is this essential truth: "It is students themselves, in the end, not teachers, who decide what students will learn" (Hattie, 2009, p. 241), and students do not volunteer effort when they are detached from school (Crosnoe, 2011; Newmann, 1981; Weis, 1990). Creating attachments is key to the work of educators, and we need to learn all we can about accomplishing that goal (Murphy et al., 2001). Analysis is also critical because, as we document below, supportive community for students exercises strong influence on school improvement defined in terms of student learning (Carbonaro & Gamoran, 2002; Rodriguez, 2008; Rumberger, 2011), "it explains a large amount of the variation in school effects" (Leithwood, Jantzi, & Steinbach, 1999, p. 83). Indeed, "failure to examine school culture can easily lead to ineffective reform" (Rodriguez, 2008, p. 760).

SUPPORTIVE LEARNING COMMUNITY FOR STUDENTS: A FRAMEWORK

> Students' engagement and achievement are affected profoundly by experiences that cannot be identified simply by listing what is prescribed in the formal curriculum, what students do in their classes, and what is tested. Instead, the effects of any specific school activity are best understood as cultural phenomena. (Newmann, 1992, p. 182)

Backdrop

> There is startling evidence that many children do not have nurturing relationships to support their academic work or their personal development. (Baker et al., 1997, p. 587)

> Young people . . . are in schools every day struggling to find their way in institutions that often do not recognize or meet their needs as learners or individuals. (Joselowsky, 2007, p. 270)

We begin by reintroducing the essential point raised above: Schooling for students is profoundly voluntary. Children have to "go to school." They need to debark from the bus and go into the building. Beyond that, especially as they mature, the decision to "do schooling" is substantially their own. This means, of course, that they are key decision makers in the learning production. The major purpose of supportive learning community is to positively influence students' willingness to learn what the school believes they require to be successful in life, to cause students to embrace academic challenges, and to help them reach those ends. Two corollaries arise here. First, to a much greater extent than has been the case, schooling needs to be understood through the eyes of students, not as a goal in itself but rather because it provides the framework for a school to achieve its mission: ensuring that all children reach ambitious targets of academic success. Second, adult actions need to be shaped based on those insights from students.

Educators here have three choices: ignore this reality, fight to change it, or use it as a platform for action. The first and second options have been the tools of choice for education historically. This is hardly surprising given the institutional nature of schooling and the managerial logic of school leadership (Callahan, 1962; Cuban, 1988). The problem is, however, that these choices have not been especially effective (Boyer, 1983; Crosnoe, 2011; Cuban, 1988; Eckert, 1989; Farrell, 1990; Goodlad, 1984; Newmann, 1981; Patterson, Beltyukova, Berman, & Francis, 2007; Sizer, 1984; Weis, 1990), especially for students placed at risk by society and schooling (Alexander, Entwisle, & Horsey, 1997; Chavis, Ward, Elwell, & Barret,1997; Murphy & Tobin, 2011). Supportive learning community for students moves us to option three, weaving the wisdom, needs, concerns, interests, and worries of students deeply into the "doing of schooling" without sacrificing academic press. Or more globally, it requires educators to acknowledge that achieving valued outcomes for students "involves, as a first step, recognizing that school culture is the setting in which [students] are being educated" (Crosnoe, 2011, p. 40). For example, we know that social concerns form the caldron of interest for students in schools (Crosnoe, 2011; Newmann, Wehlage, & Lamburn, 1992). We also understand that to reach working-class youngsters, we need to address social connections beyond the schoolhouse (Eckert, 1989; Farrell, 1990). The charge for school people is to learn how to work these and related realities productively in the service of helping students master essential academic goals.

In terms of background knowledge, it is also important to underscore a deep line of empirical findings in the research. Specifically, the school communities in which many young persons find themselves, especially older students and youngsters in peril (Adams, 2010; Baker et al., 1997; Quint, 2006) do not exert the positive influence and support necessary for them to commit to "do schooling" (Balfanz et al., 2007; Croninger & Lee, 2001; Newmann et al., 1992). While this is not the place to examine this line of analysis in detail, we need to point out that student disengagement, often passive, sometimes active, is common in schools (Conchas, 2001; Patterson et al., 2007; Quint, 2006). This is hardly surprising given that one of the pillars of institutions and bureaucracy is impersonality (Murphy, 1991). As Ancess (2003, p. 83) reminds us, because of this, "schools are conventionally organized as though relationships are not only unimportant and irrelevant, but an obstacle to efficient operation."

Model

> Pupils who experience acceptance, or a sense of belonging, are more highly motivated and engaged in learning and more committed to school. Engagement and commitment are closely linked to the quality of student learning. (Mulford & Silins, 2003, p. 180)

Analysts have uncovered a good deal of knowledge about what supportive communities of pastoral care for students look like and how they function. Building from that work, we provide our model of personalized community in Figure 4.1. We see there that supportive learning community is defined by essential norms (e.g., care). These norms combine to produce intermediate outcomes such as student learning dispositions, which, in turn, lead to academic engagement. All of this powers student learning.

The model employs a two-stroke engine, one working to overcome liabilities and the other to build up assets. To begin with then, communities of pastoral care "foster productive learning by removing developmentally hazardous conditions" (Felner et al., 2007, p. 210). They suppress factors that undermine hopes for success, such as the formation of dysfunctional and oppositional peer cultures. Personalization damps down aspects of schooling that push students away from engaging the work of "doing school" well. A supportive learning community provides a "protective power" (Garmezy, 1991, p. 427) while attacking social problems that place students in peril (Christle, Jolivette, & Nelson, 2005; Crosnoe, 2011). It helps create a "social environment that neutralizes or buffers home stresses" (Alexander & Entwisle, 1996, p. 77) and community problems and individual characteristics that foster social marginalization and academic disengagement (Demaray & Malecki, 2002b; Garmezy, 1991).

Figure 4.1   Communities of Pastoral Care for Students

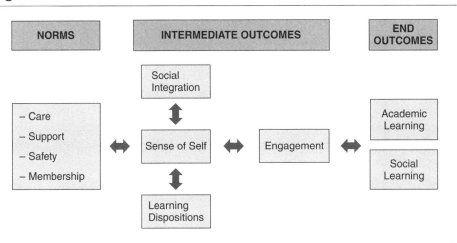

Concomitantly, supportive learning environments create assets, social and human capital, to draw youngsters into the hard work that is required to be successful in school (Ancess, 2003; Goddard, 2003; Supovitz, 2002, 2008). They transform schools into places "where the social and pastoral environment nurture[s] a desire to learn in students" (Blair, 2002, p. 184). Assets such as care and warmth are stockpiled to assist in helping students reach ambitious learning targets (Demaray & Malecki, 2002b; Quint, 2006; Roth & Brooks-Gunn, 2003).

CAUTIONS AND REMINDERS

The nature and quality of the principal has a significant influence on the nature of the school climate. (Stoll, Bolam, McMahon, Wallace, & Thomas, 2006, p. 235)

The benefits of participating in a caring school community may be particularly great for those students who, traditionally, have not been well served by our schools—the socioeconomically disadvantaged and socially disenfranchised. (Battistich, Solomon, Watson, & Schaps, 1997, p. 140)

Before we unpack the model of student personalization in Figure 4.1, we reintroduce some reminders, central themes that appear throughout these chapters that have special importance for student culture. We begin with the hallmark finding that leadership is the essential catalyst to ensure that a positive school culture takes root and flourishes (Barnett & McCormick, 2004; Bruggencate et al., 2012; Mukuria, 2002): "Critical to the creation of maintenance of school culture are the leadership practices of the school principal" (Barnett, McCormick, & Conners, 2001, p. 25; see also Brookover, Beady, Flood, Schweitzer, & Wisenbaker, 1979; Brookover et al., 1978; Cosner, 2011; Dinham, 2005; Hallinger & Murphy, 1985; Heck & Hallinger, 2010; Supovitz et al., 2010; Wahlstrom & Louis, 2008). Indeed, a principal's influence on the learning culture of the school may be his or her most powerful tool to influence student achievement (Blase & Kirby, 2009; Louis et al., 2010), especially in middle and high schools (Sebastian & Allensworth, 2012).

We also need to reinforce the structural law that was surfaced in earlier chapters. That is, structural changes do not predict organizational outcomes. The key is the powerful medicine that structures are supposed to carry. As has been seen more often than not, structures arrive without the medicine. Schools are left with the empty containers. This cautionary tale is especially relevant in the domain of communities of pastoral care for students because much of the reform here is structural in design, e.g., advisory periods, academies, small schools, and so forth (Iatarola, Schwartz, Stiefel, & Chellman, 2008; Patterson et al., 2007; Smerdon, Borman, & Hannaway, 2009). There is a robust if misguided sense in many schools, and by many school leaders, that these interventions by themselves will power up desired improvements in culture along with the accompanying organizational outcomes. Educators need to be vigilant about being seduced by the logic of structure.

It is instructive to recall another of our laws of school improvement here: Context always matters. "Effective practice is inevitably highly contextualized" (Battistich et al., 1997, p. 150), and "where students attend school matters" (Crosnoe, 2011, p. 56). Context holds an especially important role in the supportive student learning play (Fredricks et al., 2004; Guest & Schneider, 2003). We know, for example, that demographic factors have a robust influence on student culture (Farrell, 1990; Feldman & Matjasko, 2005; Newmann et al., 1989). Family conditions (e.g., family size, age of mother) influence school culture, sometimes for the better, sometimes for the worse (Eckert, 1989; Ensminger & Slusarcick, 1992; Rumberger, 2011). So too do neighborhood conditions (e.g., availability of social services) (Gonzales & Padilla, 1997; Murphy, 2010a). Cutting across all of these, of course, are the thick cords of socioeconomic status (SES) (e.g., occupation, income) (Eckert, 1989, Guest & Schneider, 2003; Marsh & Kleitman, 2002) and race (Balfanz et al., 2007; Bloomberg, Ganey, Alba, Quintero, & Alvarez-Alcantara, 2003; Jordan & Cooper, 2003). The unmistakable conclusion here is "that sense of community for students is negatively correlated with school poverty" (Battistich et al., 1997, p. 142), membership in racial and ethnic minority groups (Adams, 2010; Lee & Burkam, 2003), and marginalized status in society (Crosnoe, 2011).

We know that there is a varying relationship between school level and the importance of a personalized culture (Demaray & Malecki, 2002a). Community becomes especially significant in the early to mid-teen years and less so at the tail end of high school (Crosnoe, 2011; Goodenow, 1993; Ma, 2003). School SES has a strong effect on supportive learning culture, independent of family SES (Rumberger, 2011). School size has been linked to personalization as well (Bryk et al., 2010; Fredricks et al., 2004; Lee & Burkam, 2003), with small size creating opportunities for communal norms to take root, especially in schools with large percentages of students in peril (Lee & Burkam, 2003; Hattie, 2009). A more supportive community is especially important for students who have limited access to social capital outside of school (Croninger & Lee, 2001; Goddard, 2003; Murphy, 2010a), for students from low-income homes (Battistich et al., 1995; 1997), and for students who are socially and academically at risk (Battistich et al., 1997; Croninger & Lee, 2001; Darling-Hammond, Ancess, & Ort, 2002). Pastoral care "shows its strongest positive relations with student measures in the highest poverty schools" (Battistich et al., 1997, p. 144).

NORMS OF COMMUNITIES OF PASTORAL CARE FOR STUDENTS

> Schools are an essential source of social capital for adolescents. (Croninger & Lee, 2001, p. 549)

> What we need to know is the extent to which productive forms of social capital can be cultivated to promote the success of all children. (Goddard, 2003, p. 71)

The DNA of pastoral care for students, "a philosophy of caring and personalization" (Ackerman & Maslin-Ostrowski, 2002, p. 79), is contained in the norms listed on the left-hand side of the model in Figure 4.1. These elements are most powerful when they are in play at both the classroom and school levels and in both individual and group relationships. Consistent with our two-stroke engine, efforts here are designed both to deinstitutionalize the school climate and to add community assets to the culture. Four macro level norms are featured in the model, care, support, safety, and membership. Before we examine these values, however, we highlight the theme that forms the heart and soul of pastoral care.

Teacher-Student Relationships

> We need to have each student feel that his teacher is taking a special interest in him. (Farrell, 1990, p. 104)

> Student participation, engagement, and eventual success are powered by connections and relationships. (Cooper, Ponder, Merritt, & Matthews, 2005, p. 20)

> Creating relationships is the foundation for success in school reform. (Center for Teaching Quality, 2007, p. 4)

We know that positive relationships are essential to all forms of community in schools, for students, teachers, and parents (Ancess, 2003). As Bryk and colleagues (2010), Rumberger (2011), and Baker et al. (1997) remind us, these relationships are a hallmark ingredient in school improvement work, the "most powerful driving force of schools" (Ancess, 2003, p. 127). This is the case because "schools are fundamentally social institutions that depend daily on the quality of interpersonal relations with which they are imbued" (Goddard, Salloum, & Berebitsky, 2009, p. 293).

More specifically, analysts help us see that "student-teacher relationships matter for the development of children" (Adams, 2010, p. 258), that positive linkages between students and teachers are foundational for creating personalized communities for students (Ancess, 2003; Newmann, 1992;

Roth & Brooks-Gunn, 2003). These relationships are heavily responsible for establishing the educational value of classrooms. They make academic press a possibility for many students (Darling-Hammond et al., 2002; Rodriguez, 2008). Because many students "learn only from teachers promoting healthy personal relationships" (Opdenakker, Maulana, & Brock, 2012, p. 99), "the power of positive teacher-student relationships is critical for learning to occur" (Hattie, 2009, p. 118) and for students to experience academic success (Darling-Hammond et al., 2002; Goddard, 2003; Goodenow, 1993). These relationships have "far-reaching significance in terms of the various trajectories that children follow throughout their schooling experience" (Birch & Ladd, 1997). Positive connections create the social capital needed for effective work to unfold in classrooms (Adams & Forsyth, 2009; Ancess, 2003; Croninger & Lee, 2001). They provide the engine and the drivetrain to power the norms in personalized communities (Epstein & McPartland, 1976; Farrell, 1990; Patterson et al., 2007).

These positive relationships are of singular benefit for students from low-income homes and in schools with high concentrations of students in peril (Battistich et al., 1995; Marks, 2000; Murphy, 2010a). When these relationships do not exist, students are placed in a compromised position relative to learning (Rodriguez, 2008). Or as Croninger and Lee (2001, p. 569) assert, "an absence of positive social relationships and contacts with teachers denies students resources that help them develop positively." Deteriorating and negative relationships are even worse (Fredricks et al., 2004). They are "destructive to student outcomes and development" (Opdenakker et al., 2012, p. 95). In short, "relationships mediate student performance" (Ancess, 2003, p. 82; Baker et al., 1997; Crosnoe, 2011; Goodenow, 1993). We examine these relationships between teachers and students below in our analysis of the four norms of community for students.

Norm of Care

> A community orientation based in caring allows children to appraise school as a meaningful social context in which to function. (Baker et al., 1997, p. 586)

> Caring adults in a caring school community can be the hook to achievement, graduation, and a future of meaningful options, particularly where students seem not to care about school or their future, lack confidence, and are alienated or marginalized educationally or socially because of prior school experiences or because of how they learn or do not learn, or because they are members of racially, ethnically, linguistically, or economically disenfranchised populations. (Ancess, 2003, p. 8)

> Effective schools have caring relationships that are a pervasive part of the school culture. (Waxman, Padron, & Garcia, 2007, p. 141)

We know that students arrive at school ready to learn. They naturally engage in the work of schooling (see Figure 4.2, path A). As they progress, many youngsters divert from the pathway of active engagement. They pull away from school. Some of these students become passively engaged (path B). They attend school, collect Carnegie units, stay quietly at the back of the room of academic pursuits, do not work especially hard, and do not receive a quality education. These are the withdrawn and anonymous. Other youngsters exercise a more aggressive form of disengagement (path C). They move in opposition to school values and expectations. These are the resistant and the alienated. Some from each of these two groups, the passive and actively disengaged, simply withdraw from the game altogether, dropping out of school (path D). The number of students who follow each of these pathways varies by school level and critical context variables such as socioeconomic status and minority status (Crosnoe, 2011; Eckert, 1989; Farrell, 1990), and of course, the quality of student community.

We know that the actions of schools have a good deal to do with the engagement choices of students. Particularly salient here, as we reported above, are the relationships between teachers and students. Good schools keep students actively engaged by demonstrating an ethic of care and robust systems of academic and social support. Because some students in all schools are free to disengage and many students in some schools are free to do so, schools are filled with a good number of unconnected youngsters. Care and the other norms of communities of pastoral care for students close the door to disengagement and failure.

In Chapters 5 and 6, we explore norms from the perspective of teacher professional communities. Here we simply note that these professional norms are also woven into the relational tapestry between teachers and students. Included here are values such as commitment and dedication

Figure 4.2   States of Student Engagement in Schools

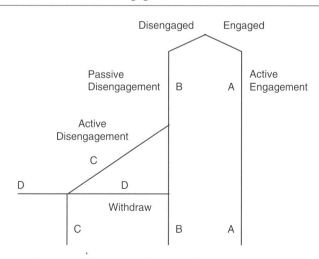

(Newmann, 1992; Phillips, 2003), sense of efficacy (Leithwood et al., 1999; Silins & Mulford, 2010), persistence (Ancess, 2003), acceptance of responsibility for student success (Wilson & Corbett, 1999), and effort (Louis, 2007).

Caring has been studied by scholars in a variety of disciplines and professions. Here the spotlight is on caring relationships between teachers culled from studies of schools that are effective in ensuring that all pupils reach ambitious targets of performance (see Table 4.1. p. 61).

Although it is much too infrequently discussed as such, students routinely remind us that a cardinal element of the norm of care is *teachers who work to the best of their ability*, who consistently bring their "A" games to the classroom—who challenge students to do their best work (Felner et al., 2007; Marks, 2000; Sanders & Harvey, 2002). Students also document what an instructional "A" game looks like. It includes working hard to make classes meaningful, and to show that meaningfulness to youngsters. It means teachers not simply going through the motions, doing their jobs, but rather demonstrating palpable interest in whether students learn or not (Fredricks et al., 2004; Newmann et al., 1992; Wilson & Corbett, 1999). Teachers who work to peak performance, acknowledge the difficulties of teaching, especially teaching students who are struggling, but they embrace those challenges, not offer excuses and justifications (Roney et al., 2007). They, according to Shouse (1996, p. 66), "appreciate the rugged demands of learning." They are firm and orchestrate structured classrooms (Ancess, 2003; Wilson & Corbett, 1999). These teachers are painstaking in their efforts to ensure that all students are brought along and successfully complete learning journeys, not jettisoned on the trip (Ancess, 2003; Wilson & Corbett, 1999). According to students, teachers accomplish this by establishing clear goals, maps, and benchmarks of success and by providing close monitoring, abundant feedback, and targeted encouragement and help (DeRidder, 1991; Wilson & Corbett, 1999). They work hard to connect with students, not simply to present information (Wilson & Corbett, 1999).

Teachers who students assess as bringing their best to the classroom day in and day out, that is, who demonstrate care, emphasize what Newmann (1981) calls authentic work. They employ varied approaches to learning and emphasize active and creative work, while ensuring that students clearly understand what they need to do, how they need to meet the challenges, and why (Fredricks et al., 2004; Wilson & Corbett, 1999). "A" game teachers make learning relevant to their young charges (Conchas, 2001; Newmann, 1981). They focus on intrinsically interesting activities (Fredricks et al., 2004; Newmann, 1992) and "tasks that are considered meaningful, valuable, significant, and worthy of one's efforts" (Newmann et al., 1992, p. 23). They also underscore collaborative activities for students and flexible use of time (Fredricks et al., 2004; Newmann et al., 1992). Teachers who routinely strive for personal excellence in the classroom put learning in perspective for youngsters and work hard to align and integrate goals, activities, and structures for learning (Battistich et al.,

1995; Marks, 2000). According to students, caring teachers demonstrate considerable imagination, live beyond the textbook, and unearth multiple pathways to accomplish work and show success (Wilson & Corbett, 1999).

Another hallmark element of caring relations in schools is the willingness of teachers to reveal *themselves to children* as persons, not solely as organizational functionaries (Adams & Forsyth, 2009; Antrop-Gonzalez, 2006; Newmann et al., 1992). They do this by opening aspects of their nonprofessional lives to their pupils, especially incidents that are relevant to the decisions and struggles that confront youngsters (Rodriguez, 2008). "The self that teachers offer is a student self rather than a career self" (Farrell, 1990, p. 25). According to Adams (2010), part of this opening process is the willingness of teachers to allow themselves to be vulnerable in front of their students. This stance "humanizes the teacher as a person" (Rodriguez, 2008, p. 765) and helps establish a frame of authenticity for student-teacher connections (Raywid, 1995). It also permits students to feel safe in sharing their "hopes, dreams, problems, and disappointments" (Reitzug & Patterson, 1998, p. 167).

Although as overlooked as teachers giving students their best, care is also fundamentally about standards and about *challenging students* to meet and exceed robust expectations (Alexander & Entwisle, 1996; Johnson & Asera, 1999; Roth & Brooks-Gunn, 2003). There is abundant evidence on this point: "Teachers who push students prove to be an important dimension to the personalized student-adult relationship" (Rodriguez, 2008, p. 772). Perhaps the essential point here is the integration of push and press with other elements of care discussed above (Murphy, 2013a), a practice labeled as "hard caring" by Antrop-Gonzalez and De Jesus (2006, p. 413) and "rugged care" by Shouse (1996, p. 48). There is an especially valuable line of research that confirms that many students, especially students in peril, will not benefit unless the elements of care and the other norms of personalization are blended (Becker & Luthar, 2002; Roth & Brooks-Gunn, 2003). When this cocktail of push and support is in place, students are able to see challenge "as coming from a place of teacher concern about the students themselves" (Patterson et al., 2007, p. 136). Challenge also means providing students with as much responsibility as they can handle (Joselowsky, 2007) and upholding a commitment to help them succeed (Wilson & Corbett, 1999). Obstacles are acknowledged but they are not accepted as explanations for lack of performance (Rodriguez, 2008; Shouse, 1996).

Challenge for students in a caring environment is laced with clear and high expectations (Newmann, 1981; Rodriguez 2008; Wilson & Corbett, 1999). Teachers ask more of students. There is strong academic and social press (Ancess, 2003; Johnson & Asera, 1999). They place higher order cognitive demands on students, moving beyond basic skills to higher order thinking (Battistich et al., 1995; Marks, 2000). They expect students "to be active interpreters of knowledge, rather than docile recipients"

(Newmann, 1992, p. 185). In schools where care is engrained in the culture, teachers provide more challenging assignments and tasks (Fredricks et al., 2004), "more complex and cognitively challenging class work" (Marks, 2000, p. 157) and greater depth of understanding (Newmann, 1981). They expect students to take intellectual risks and reward them for doing so (Cooper, 1996, 1999).

In strong communities, care is more than providing high expectations and challenge, that is, academic and social press. Caring teachers take away the possibility of passive involvement. Students cannot check out or drift through class (Ancess, 2003; Huberman et al., 2011). They are pulled into the game. No spectators are allowed. Neither are students allowed to easily accept failure. "Teachers not only believe that students [can] complete their work, they do everything possible to make that happen" (Wilson & Corbett, 1999, p. 77). In caring environments "teachers make it harder to fail than succeed" (Ancess, 2000, p. 74). They "stay on students" to complete their work (Wilson & Corbett, 1999, p. 80), requiring them to bring their "A" games to the classroom. Teachers are there to help students succeed, not simply teach subject matter. They push and pull students to the goal line (Ancess, 2003; Darling-Hammond et al., 2002; Oakes & Guiton, 1995) and acknowledge and celebrate successes along the way. Classes are rich with extra help and teacher-guided second chances (Wilson & Corbett, 1999). They are particularly adept at addressing "patterns of behaviors and performances that are unproductive and problematic" (Ancess, 2003, p. 76) for student development (Cooper, 1996).

Earlier, we argued that high-functioning communities for students close down opportunities for students to select pathways of disengagement and disaffiliation (see Figure 4.2). Here we suggest that they also preclude the selection of failure in the face of rigorous expectations and standards (Ancess, 2000; Huberman et al., 2011; Shear et al., 2008). Efforts here pivot on the positive perspective of assets-based analysis we outlined above and the concomitant to the elimination of deficit-based thinking (Antrop-Gonzalez & De Jesus, 2006; Hattie, 2009). Possibilities hold the high ground: "Youth are resources to be developed, not problems to be fixed" (Bloomberg et al., 2003, p. 50). All of this "hard care" is layered over significant opportunities for students to be successful (Antrop-Gonzalez, 2006; Strahan, 2003).

A fourth dimension of caring is *knowing students well*, a quality Ancess (2003, p. 65) refers to as "intimacy" and a condition that Bryk and colleagues (2010, p. 58) establish as "essential to the effective design of classroom lessons that advance academic learning for all." In a caring environment, teachers make efforts to learn about the youngsters they teach (Antrop-Gonzalez, 2006). They commit the time necessary for this understanding to form and grow (Ancess, 2000). Teachers know what is unfolding in the lives of their students, "socially and at home. They know their students as learners in the class and in the classes of their colleagues" (Ancess, 2000, pp. 65–66). They are cognizant of the social and cultural worlds in which their pupils live (Antrop-Gonzalez & De Jesus, 2006; McLaughlin, 1994; Rodriguez, 2008). Teachers employ this knowledge to help students learn and to pursue their personal goals (Bryk, Lee, & Holland, 1993; Newmann, 1992).

In personalized communities, caring is defined also by *students being valued* by their teachers (Battistich et al., 1995; Conchas, 2001; Scheurich, 1998). According to Reitzug and Patterson (1998), this translates into teacher efforts to connect with students on a personal level, rather than on a categorical basis (McLaughlin & Talbert, 2001). More specifically, it means that each student is accepted as a person, someone who has value as an individual and as a member of communities in the school (Ancess, 2003; Conchas, 2001; Rodriguez, 2008), someone "worthy of mentorship and guidance" (Antrop-Gonzalez, 2006, p. 288). In caring communities, being valued is conveyed through teachers being "person centered" (Hattie, 2009, p. 119). Valued status is communicated to youngsters when teachers express concern for what is happening in the world of the student and when they invest time and energy in developing and maintaining personal linkages to students (Farrell, 1990; Hattie, 2009; Wilson & Corbett, 1999). Included here is a not-so-subtle switch from seeing students as problems to seeing them as "willing and capable human beings" (Reitzug & Patterson, 1998, p. 168) who need help to address challenges in their lives. In these valued relationships there is a tendency to avoid blaming youngsters when things do not go well (Patterson et al., 2007).

In a related vein, caring is demonstrated when teachers *take interest in and invest in their students* (Galletta & Ayala, 2008; Croninger & Lee,

Table 4.1   Aspects of the Norm of Caring in Student Community

Working to the best of their ability

Challenging students

Sharing one's self as a person

Knowing students well

Valuing students

Demonstrating interest and investment

Being accessible

Seeing through the eyes of students

Establishing trustworthiness

Respecting students

Treating students fairly

Providing recognition

2001; Wilson & Corbett, 1999). This includes devoting considerable personal and professional capital into one's work with children (McDougall et al., 2003) and the development and honoring of reciprocal obligations (Antrop-Gonzalez & De Jesus, 2006). It includes being accessible to students on both academic and personal fronts (Goddard, 2003; Hattie, 2009; Noguera, 1996), "in their education and their lives" (Patterson et al., 2007, p. 128). Investment tells students that they are acknowledged for who they are as persons and for their potential (Ma, 2003; Steele, 1992). At the deepest level, it includes a ferocious unwillingness to permit students to founder or fail (Farrell, 1990). Students see "teachers as truly interested and invested in enabling [them] to succeed" (Wilson & Corbett, 1999, p. 73). They feel that adults are willing to provide personal attention (Cooper et al., 2005; Cotton, 2000; Rodriguez, 2008).

Caring means that teachers are *accessible to students* (Darling-Hammond et al., 2002; Newmann et al., 1992). A dimension of accessibility is willingness to help, an ingredient that cuts across the norms of care and support (Rutter et al., 1979). Another aspect is making time available to students, of building closeness (Birch & Ladd, 1997) in the context of warm relationships (Opdenakker et al., 2012; Strahan, 2003). Invitational threads are also woven into the fabric of accessibility (Ancess, 2003). So too are efforts to pull students into active participation. That is, accessibility means not exiting in the face of student resistance or oppositionality and not permitting youngsters to exit either (Newmann, 1981). The literature refers to this as maintaining beliefs in students through hardships and refusing to give up on students (Ancess, 2003). More aggressively, it is appropriate to think about accessibility in terms of advocacy for youngsters (Ancess, 2003). In strong, personalized communities, teachers stand up for students to ensure that conditions for success are forthcoming (Rodriguez, 2008). Students feel that their teachers are looking out for them. They are not left to pursue success on their own or only with the help of peers (Roney et al., 2007): "Teachers can be counted on to be accessible, accepting, and helpful" (Ancess, 2003, p. 68).

Another theme in the chronicle on the norm of care in personalized communities is constructed around the ability and willingness of teachers to *see things through the eyes of students* (Farrell, 1990), in popular parlance to know where students are coming from (Rodriguez, 2008). It includes a willingness to see and understand the developmental needs of students (Ancess, 2003) and to "embrace students' priorities" (p. 8). It means taking the world of students seriously (Csikszentmihalyi & Larson, 1984), remembering that things that are important to students are important regardless of whether they are important to teachers or not (Murphy, 2013a). More important, it entails efforts to adapt schooling to the needs of students, not requiring students to constantly remold themselves to fit the school (Bulkley & Hicks, 2005; Day, 2005; Quint, 2006). This in turn requires seeing children as whole and in a positive light, not as defiant and damaged (Becker & Luthar, 2002). Viewing from the perspective of students requires an active responsiveness to youngsters. It means that when the norm of care is present, teachers listen to students (Adams & Forsyth, 2009; Antrop-Gonzalez, 2006), and that students believe that they are heard (Reitzug & Patterson, 1998; Rodriguez, 2008).

As we described above, trust is the foundation for relationships (Adams & Forsyth, 2009). Thus we should not be surprised to learn that an important piece of the caring storyline is teachers *assessing youngsters as trustworthy* (Battistich et al., 1997) and students reciprocating (Adams, 2010; Antrop-Gonzalez & De Jesus, 2006). The rule here is universal: No trust, no relationship (Bryk et al., 2010; Newmann, 1981). As with other dimensions of care, we find asset-based as opposed to deficit-based assessments in our analysis of trustworthiness (Ancess, 2003). Teachers need to earn the mantle of trustworthiness from pupils. This they do by being open, reliable, honest, benevolent, and competent in the eyes of students (Adams & Forsyth, 2009).

Treating youngsters with respect is a tenth dimension in the web of care (Ancess, 2003; Antrop-Gonzalez & De Jesus, 2006; Hattie, 2009). Central points here are that teachers must give respect to receive it in return (Rodriguez, 2008) and "that for many students respect precedes engagement" (p. 767). One half of the storyline, here, is the avoidance of actions that demean or belittle youngsters (Antrop-Gonzalez, 2006; Murphy, 2010a). The other half of the narrative is the use of positive actions that demonstrate the fact that students are held in high regard (Raywid, 1995; Rodriguez, 2008). Treating students as young adults is important here (Ancess, 2003), with a sense of dignity (Leithwood et al., 1999). So too is the provision of opportunities for participation and voice. Actions that affirm students' cultural, racial, and ethnic backgrounds show respect (Gonzalez & Padilla, 1997; Noguera, 1996; Scanlan & Lopez, 2012). So too do behaviors that honor the assets students bring to the classroom more generally (Hattie, 2009).

Students possess a refined sense of equity. For that reason, care is often defined in terms of fairness, especially the perceived *fairness* of teachers in their treatment of students (Ma, 2003; Patterson et al., 2007; Wilson & Corbett, 1999). Reliability and consistency are key elements of fairness for students (Adams, 2010; Adams & Forsyth, 2009).

Finally, recognizing the link between the learning environment and motivation (Opdenakker et al., 2012), care includes students experiencing success and opportunities to receive *recognition* for that success (Csikszentmihalyi & Larson, 1984; Foster & St. Hilaire, 2003; Sather, 1999). That is, schools create a "culture of success" for students (Rodriguez, 2008, p. 776) and opportunities for acknowledgment. Newmann and his colleagues (1992, p. 22) underscore this element of care when they report that "if the school is to nurture a sense of membership, its most important task is to ensure students experience success in the development of competence."

Norm of Support

> Findings underscore the importance of interpersonal support in fostering academic motivation and achievement. (Goodenow, 1993, p. 21)

> If students are to build confidence and willingness to invest themselves, their participation in academic tasks must be accompanied by personal support from teachers. (Newmann et al., 1992, p. 22)

> Student support in all its guises was central to the outstanding outcomes achieved at schools. (Dinham, 2005, p. 352)

A second critical norm in communities of pastoral care for students is support (Battistich et al., 1995; Conchas, 2001; Goodenow, 1993). As is the case with care, it operates on two fronts. On one hand, support buffers students from events that can damage them and their success in school (Bloomberg et al., 2003; Demaray & Malecki, 2002a). Or as Jackson and Warren (2000, p. 1452) so nicely capture the idea, "social support is a possible immunity to the effects of life events." On the other hand, support unleashes a host of positive actions in the service of students. Researchers help us see that this norm of support is most critical as youngsters mature (i.e., with adolescents), with children who lack a dense web of support outside of school, and for students placed at risk by society (Croninger & Lee, 2001; Murphy & Tobin, 2011; Roth, Brooks-Gunn, Murray, & Foster, 1998). Support can best be thought of as the extension of help by teachers coupled with students' understanding that they can count on that assistance (Ancess, 2003; Antrop-Gonzalez & De Jesus, 2006; Louis & Marks, 1998). It is personalized relationships with teachers that make help seeking and the provision of assistance part of the culture (Demaray & Malecki, 2002a; Rodriguez, 2008). The starting point here is teachers "understanding that their supportive role appears to play a significant part in students' attitudes about teachers and their school experience in general" (Demaray & Malecki, 2002b, p. 314).

Support is tightly linked to the norm of care (see Table 4.2). Indeed the two share a good deal of conceptual and applied space (Roth & Brooks-Gunn, 2003). Perhaps the best way to think about the two norms is to observe that much of the ability of schools to create support is a function of caring connections between teachers and students (Rodriguez, 2008). Getting to know students and creating personal relationships are important in their own right. The maximum gain occurs, however, when teachers use these caring linkages to support the academic and social development of their students (Ancess, 2003; Croninger & Lee, 2001).

The research allows us to distill overlapping types of support in personalized student communities of pastoral care. In particular, analysts

Table 4.2   Aspects of the Norm of Support in Student Community

Providing assistance

Offering encouragement

Ensuring availability of safety nets

Monitoring

Mentoring

Advocating

highlight the importance of emotional support (Crosnoe, 2011; Demaray & Malecki, 2002a), social support (Goddard et al., 2009; Jackson & Warren, 2000), and academic support (Ancess, 2003; Antrop-Gonzalez & De Jesus, 2006).

As with each of the norms, support can be defined by its essential elements, six in total. It is useful to think of these ingredients as overlapping and intertwined strands in the web of support. The first is the *provision of assistance* in the face of student help-seeking or intuited need for such help (Adams & Forsyth, 2009; Croninger & Lee, 2001). Informal and formal counseling is often noted in the research here (Raywid, 1995). Navigational assistance is also discussed (Quint, 2006). So too is the provision of assistance with school work (Antrop-Gonzalez, 2006; Croninger & Lee, 2001). Assistance in helping youngsters master transitions in life is underscored as an especially powerful (and needed) form of aid (Jackson & Warren, 2000; Manguin & Loeber, 1996; Rodriguez, 2008).

Support includes *encouragement* as well (Balfanz et al., 2007). Mastering school is difficult work for many students and "to invest time and energy in the present young people need to believe that there is a viable future" (Joselowsky, 2007, p. 272). Teachers are in a unique position to help students see the potential for success, what Crosnoe (2011, p. 186) calls a "future orientation," when such possibilities are unclear for students (Rodriguez, 2008). Teachers can open these doors through encouragement (Newmann, 1992; Roth et al., 1998), especially around the importance of investments in academic work (Hoy et al., 1998).

Providing safety nets is a third essential aspect of student support (Cooper et al., 2005). The core idea here is to prevent students from falling through the cracks, to "go missing" and be unnoticed (Allensworth & Easton, 2005). These protections provide another backstop against disengagement and failure. Good schools build these nets and legitimize and encourage the use of the interventions found therein (Ancess, 2000). In these schools, teachers help students; they do not blame them for requiring assistance (Patterson et al., 2007).

Support also encompasses *monitoring* how well students are doing in school, socially, emotionally, and academically (Antrop-Gonzalez &

De Jesus, 2006; Gray et al., 1999; Quint, 2006), a type of "proactive troubleshooting" (Raywid, 1995, p. 53). It includes *mentoring young persons* toward success, a dimension that is especially powerful for students at risk of failure (Woloszyk, 1996).

Finally, *advocating for students* is a well-illuminated strand in the web of support (Murphy, Elliott, Goldring, & Porter, 2007; Rumberger, 2011). Here, support is defined as "personally negotiating" (O'Conner, 1997, p. 616) to ensure that students garner all the aid they require to be successful, both from the school and the larger community (Ancess, 2003; Cooper et al., 2005; Patterson et al., 2007). Collectively, support can be thought of as "responsibility for shepherding the student" (Balfanz et al., 2007, p. 232).

Before we close our discussion on the norms of care and support, it is helpful to highlight some of the concepts that make supportive and caring relationships work. The lynchpin is student access. Without contact, it is impossible to make caring and supportive relationships come to life (Reitzug & Patterson, 1998; Rodriguez, 2008). For care and support to power up attachment and subsequent student commitment and engagement, and to enhance academic and social learning, the quality and depth of interactions between students and teachers needs to increase. The time dimension here, a direct measure of students' judgments of teacher commitment (Ancess, 2003) can be addressed in a variety of ways. School expectations for student participation in teacher-facilitated academic and social activities are important. So too are teachers' intentional communications of accessibility (Ancess, 2003). Increasing the ratio of adults to students can create time for relationships to take root and develop (Noguera, 1996). Enhancing proximity between teachers and students is helpful (Opdenakker et al., 2012). Ancess (2003, p. 27) describes this as "creating regular and spontaneous opportunities for frequent contact."

Both quality and depth of care and support can be increased through an emphasis on "extended, rather than limited, role relationships" (Newmann, 1981, p. 554) (e.g., as classroom teacher, advisor, and co-curricular program sponsor). Engagement in a range of activities rather than a single function is preferable (Ancess, 2003; Newmann, 1981). Social and academic domains both can be used to enrich student-teacher relationships (Fredricks et al., 2004), and multiple dimensions within each domain provide the hooks for linkages. A focus on "guidance and friendship inside and outside the classroom" (Antrop-Gonzalez, 2006, p. 289) is helpful. Before-school, during-school, and after-school times can be turned into avenues that foster relationships in the service of personalized communities for students. Both one-on-one connections (e.g., an advisor-advisee relationship) and linkages formed in groups (e.g., a coach) can be the basis of providing care and support (Demaray & Malecki, 2002a; Woloszyk, 1996). A focus on both formal and informal interactions opens the door to the formation of teacher-student attachments that promote student engagement and success (Ancess, 2003; Joselowsky, 2007). Finally, training for teachers about the importance and content of caring and supportive norms, that is, how to establish personalized communities for students is essential (Roth et al., 1998).

So overall, the keystone issues here are a strong understanding of the interlaced strands of care and support and a blueprint that provides time for access to materialize and attachments to form. Once these pieces of the improvement narrative are well understood, there is a plethora of activities from which to forge a coherent package to deepen care and support for students in specific contexts. The cardinal rule is to begin with the norms and the subcomponents, not specific initiatives. When strategies follow norms, student community is deepened. When strategies are expected to power norm development, more often than not, community remains largely unaffected (Murphy, 1991, 2013b).

Norm of Safety

Safety for young people is paramount. (Joselowsky, 2007, p. 272)

Community is not present until members experience feelings of safety. (Osterman, 2000, p. 323)

Safety and order play a major role in securing student engagement with schooling. (Bryk et al., 2010, p. 123)

Communities of pastoral care for students are defined by a norm of safety (Christle et al., 2005), which in effective schools research is often referred to as the correlate of a safe and orderly learning environment (Cotton, 2003; Hallinger & Murphy, 1985; Robinson et al., 2008). We learn from studies across a variety of areas of interest (e.g., child development, school reform) that security needs are of major importance for youngsters (Dinham, 2005; Joselowsky, 2007) and that meeting those needs is essential for their healthy development, academically, socially, and emotionally (Baker et al., 1997; Christle et al., 2005; Rumberger & Palardy, 2005).

As was the case with the norms of care and support, positively charged and negatively charged analyses are intertwined throughout the research narrative on safety (Felner et al., 2007). The latter storyline attends to efforts to banish, or at least minimize, unsafe and damaging elements in the school culture (e.g., criminal capital, crumbling infrastructure) (Allensworth & Easton, 2005). The positive chronicle underscores actions schools undertake to promote warmth and protection (e.g., creating authentic relationships between teachers and students) (Felner et al., 2007). Collectively, these efforts create spaces in which it is safe and enjoyable for students to engage with the business of schooling and develop as persons (Antrop-Gonzalez & De Jesus, 2006; Creemers & Reezigt, 1996; Robinson, 2007). Schools become sanctuaries for students (Ackerman & Maslin-Ostrowski,

2002; Ancess, 2003). We also discover from an assortment of investigators that the norm of safety is often conspicuous by its absence in schools, especially schools serving high concentrations of students placed at risk for failure (Mendez, Knoff, & Ferron, 2002; Mukuria, 2002).

A few touchstones require resurfacing before we unpack the norm of safety. To begin with, we know that the principal plays a hallmark role in the formation of a safe, protective, warm, and orderly learning environment (Rutter et al., 1979; Valentine & Prater, 2011; Wynne, 1980). We understand that safety works well when it shares space with the norms of care and support (Clark et al., 1980; Russell, Mazzarella, White, & Mauer, 1985), when these three norms are seen as overlapping strands of the student community rope. Also, it is important to remember that relationships with teachers and peers are a major vehicle for carrying the norm of safety in schools (Ma & Klinger, 2000). Impersonality, a core element of institutionalism and hierarchy, is toxic to the formation of a protective and warm learning environment, especially for students listed on the disadvantaged side of the opportunity ledger (Quint, 2006; Scanlan & Lopez, 2012). We point out again that context (e.g., student age, school SES) is important in examining the norm of safety (Maguin & Loeber, 1996; Mendez et al., 2002). The essence of the storyline with safety, as with the other norms, is to keep underlying values on center stage. Strategies, policies, structures, activities, and so forth can work but only when they carry essential values. Finally, while "classroom management" is an important beam in the safe and orderly learning construct, we do not focus on it here. Rather, the spotlight is on schoolwide climate.

Later in this chapter, we review the evidence on the impact of safety on the academic and social learning of students. Here we simply provide an advance organizer on the linkage. We confirm that lack of safety undermines the academic function of the school (Finn & Rock, 1997; Freiberg, Huzinec, & Templeton, 2009; Wilson & Corbett, 1999). Many traditional school safety moves are also harmful to learning (Christle et al., 2005; Nichols, Ludwin, & Iadicola, 1999). On the flip side, relationship-anchored improvements in the safety of the school environment enhance academic performance (Maguin & Loeber, 1996; Smerdon & Borman, 2009).

The safety norm can be unpacked into seven overlapping and integrated elements. To begin with, safety is built on foundations of *personalization,* not a scaffolding of hierarchy. While expectations are clear, firm, and consistently enforced, actions center on students as persons not simply as occupants of the institution of school (Robinson, 2007). Inculcating the norm of safety, or what Bryk and colleagues (2010, p. 8) call norms of "civil conduct," occurs by using "soft power" (Adams, 2010, p. 265) and by engaging in "gentle schooling" (Reitzug & Patterson, 1998, p. 179). Rules, regulations, and system responses are about more than simply effective control (Wilson & Corbett, 1999). They encompass community and personalization properties such as identification and engagement (Adams, 2010; Baker et al., 1997; Bryk et al., 2010). Warmth is a hallmark ingredient in the personalization element of safety (Mendez et al., 2002). Positive expectations dominate the environmental climate (Roth & Brooks-Gunn, 2003). A protective culture is formed in large part through respectful relationships between teachers and children (Baker et al., 1997; Mendez et al., 2002; Robinson, 2007). Students are seen "as resources to be developed rather than as problems to be managed" (Roth et al., 1998, p. 427). Attention is directed to learning the values of the community, not simply learning to comply with rules (Freiberg et al., 2009). The rules in play "are based upon principles and virtues (kindness, fairness) and are connected to respect for the community" (Baker et al., 1997, p. 592).

Care is infused into the development and operation of personalization (Antrop-Gonzalez & De Jesus, 2006; Reitzug & Patterson, 1998). Support for adherence to community ideas is more important than consequences for inappropriate behavior. Appropriate behavior is defined in light of the full range of students' social and emotional needs (Antrop-Gonzalez, 2006; Mendez et al., 2002). Nourishing internal control is important (Baker et al., 1997). Students are viewed holistically, not only as violators of regulations.

Developmentally appropriate work (Mendez et al., 2002) and individualization (Cheney, Blum, & Walker, 2004) are visible in the personalization element of safety (see Table 4.3). So too is an emphasis on helping students learn to assume responsibility for their behavior (Ancess, 2003; Csikszentmihalyi & Larson, 1984; Johnson & Asera, 1999). Schools characterized by a norm of safety are adept at providing youngsters with three types of protective armor, personal, interpersonal, and group (Crosnoe, 2011).

As we touched on above, a safe environment is one in which the focus is on the _prevention_ of unwanted behavior rather than on the punishment of inappropriate behavior (Freiberg et al., 2009; Mendez et al., 2002). Early identification and treatment lie at the heart of the prevention element. That is, early screening for potential and actual discipline problems and early intervention are highlighted in preventive climates (Cheney et al., 2004; Ensminger & Slusarcick, 1992), especially efforts to damp down individual risk factors associated with disorder (St. Pierre, Mark, Kaltreider, & Aikin,

Table 4.3   Aspects of the Norm of Safety in Student Community

Personalization (noninstitutional) focus

Preventative focus

Systematic focus

Positive (nonpunitive) focus

Academic engagement

Shared development and ownership

Appealing physical space

1997). So too is early involvement of parents before problems begin to spin out of control (Mendez et al., 2002).

Prevention strategies that work well are identified in the research on safety. Generally speaking, integrating safety with the other norms of student community—care, support, and membership, receives high marks. Shaping peer cultures to support rather than contradict the values and ideals of community provides a strong platform to prevent disorder and unsafe conditions (Rutter et al., 1979). Working to understand and address causes of problems that interfere with the development of a safe climate is particularly helpful (Antrop-Gonzalez & De Jesus, 2006; Balfanz et al., 2007; Nichols et al., 1999). Keeping longer-term objectives in mind rather than only addressing immediate problems is important as well (Mendez et al., 2002). Involving parents is a wise policy (Mendez et al., 2002). Training in the area of social skills for students is a good preventative strategy (Catalano, Loeber, & McKinney, 1999; St. Pierre et al., 1997). Collaborative development of positively framed expectations for conduct with clear expectations for behavior is essential here (Fredricks et al., 2004). So too is a reliance on positive rather than negative reinforcement (Cotton, 2003; Rutter et al., 1979). Seeking external assistance for help in working on problems, real and potential, can be productive in preventing problems from mushrooming and damaging the climate of safety in a school (Cheney et al., 2004).

What should be clear from the above discussion is that while most of the time we see safety through the prisms of the institution and implementation, warm and protective schools are primarily concerned about the well-being of students and maintain a focus on prevention. Plans to bring the norm of safety to life are comprehensive and *systematic* (Mukuria, 2002). They are schoolwide in design (Cheney et al., 2004). They attend to safety at the macro level of values and the micro level of expectations in an integrated and coherent manner (Cotton, 2003; Fredricks et al., 2004; Rutter et al., 1979), allowing little room for confusion to emerge (Mukuria, 2002; Quint, 2006; Robinson et al., 2008). Systematic focus extends to development of plans as well. They are often the product of a good deal of input and collaboration (Baker et al., 2007; Mendez et al., 2002). Comprehensiveness also means that a safe and orderly learning environment is defined by consistency and coordination across teachers in the school and between teachers and administrators (Balfanz et al., 2007; Greene & Lee, 2006; Quint, 2006). Everyone in the school uses the same playbook when working with students. Systematic plans promote the use of varied methods to forge and maintain safety and warmth (Mendez et al., 2002). Finally, because "fair treatment is critical to organizational bonding" (Newmann et al., 1992, p. 21) and because fairness is an intermittent property in many schools (Bloomberg et al., 2003; Nichols et al., 1999), schools with a protective aura are attentive to equity in a cross-cutting and comprehensive manner. Fairness is deeply woven into plans and codes of action found in schools defined by the norm of safety (Mendez et al., 2002; Newmann et al., 1992; Scheurich, 1998).

Scholarship affirms that reliance on negative and exclusionary practices to create safety is often dysfunctional for the school and harmful to students (Christle et al., 2005; Mendez et al., 2002; Nichols et al., 1999). An emphasis on punitive actions, especially ones unanchored to understanding, support, and personal and social development, has been found to be uniformly ineffective in the struggle to forge the norm of safety (Antrop-Gonzalez & De Jesus, 2006; Catalano et al., 1999; Nichols et al., 1999). On the other hand, *positive,* asset-based approaches to bringing safety to life are much more likely to be productive. Especially relevant here is an emphasis on positive consequences (Crosnoe, 2011) and positive feedback to students (Mendez et al., 2002; Rutter et al., 1979).

Safety is also intricately linked to the instructional program in the school (Cheney et al., 2004; Garmezy, 1991; Murphy, Weil, & McGreal, 1986). The major lesson from the research is that both the presence and the absence of the norm of safety can be traced directly to the *quality of the instructional program.* That is, safety is as much a product of "meaningful academic work" (Baker et al., 1997, p. 592) as it is of community-building efforts. Instruction and curriculum that foster academic engagement and promote student success go a long way to creating a warm and protective climate (Catalano et al., 1999; Cheney et al., 2004; Garmezy, 1991). Good schools rely more on quality programs than control strategies in their quest for creating productive student communities (Weil & Murphy, 1982).

Research on student communities in general and the norm of safety in particular suggests a strong role for collaborative work in the formation of the architecture undergirding a climate of safety and order (Blase & Kirby, 2009; Cotton, 2003; Murphy, Weil, Hallinger, & Mitman, 1985). There is *shared development and ownership.* Plans are "achieved consensually" (Alexander & Entwisle, 1996, p. 80). Involvement begins with teachers. It extends to parents. Here, involvement in the development of codes and with the implementation of efforts to ensure safety both seem important (Cheney et al., 2004; Mendez et al., 2002). Students are a part of the action here as well (Baker et al., 1997; Mukuria, 2002). It is also essential that the fingerprints of the principal and the school leadership team be visible on the values and goals that buttress a protective environment and the implementation actions that help define the norm of safety (Cheney et al., 2004; Gray et al., 1999; Wynne, 1980). A "unified stand is critical" (Mukuria, 2002, p. 441). Collectively, shared ownership for student community and the norm of safety emerges (Murphy, 1992; Patterson et al., 2007). There is a thick strand of analysis in the literature that collective professional development for faculty is especially helpful in anchoring a shared stance on safety (Christle et al., 2005; Mendez et al., 2002).

Safety can also be traced to the *physical condition of the school,* to its well-being and appearance (Gray et al., 1999). For, as Joselowsky (2007, p. 272) astutely notes, community for young people "often begins with the physical space." Safe and orderly communities are characterized by an absence of evidence of vandalism, degenerative facilities, and crumbling infrastructure (Christle et al., 2005; Dinham, 2005; Edmonds & Frederiksen, 1978). The institutional patina of the building is lightened (Christle et al., 2005). On the positive side of the physical space narrative, safe schools are defined by cleanliness and an appealing appearance (Johnson & Asera, 1999; Wilson & Corbett, 1999). They are welcoming spaces with a positive ambience (Christle et al., 2005; Joselowsky, 2007). People care about and attend to the image of the school (Dinham, Cairney, Craigie, & Wilson, 1995; Gray et al., 1999). In safe schools, adults provide "pleasant working conditions" for their youngsters (Rutter et al., 1979, p. 195).

Norm of Membership

> It is increasingly clear that learning to high standards cannot take place if students feel no stake in the life of the school and classroom. (Joselowsky, 2007, p. 258)

> Sense of belonging and meaningful involvement in school counteracts the alienation voiced by many students. (Baker et al., 1997, p. 588)

> What is important is that pupils are actively participating in the school and feel that their contributions are valued. (Mulford & Silins, 2003, p. 183)

The core idea here is belonging, which we describe in concrete form as feelings of membership in the school (Battistich et al., 1995; Roth & Brooks-Gunn, 2003; Voelkl, 1997). Newmann (1992, p. 183) captures the power of this norm when he reports that "from the students' point of view, a basic cultural requirement for engagement is a sense of school membership—the key is school membership" (Newmann et al., 1992, p. 19). We know that a number of persons help determine whether youngsters are authentic members of their schools or mere tourists in the buildings. The literature also informs us that a number of the conditions that lead to authentic membership are under the control of the school, especially those associated with the academic program and the school culture. In short, "the organization of the school creates the possibility of belonging" (Ancess, 2003, p. 128). Effective schools develop and systematically use all available opportunities to bond young people to the central values of the school community (Roth & Brooks-Gunn, 2003; Rutter et al., 1979).

We see here again the essential cross-cutting theme of relationships between teachers and students at the center of membership work. We also uncover a critical role for peers with the membership norm, a topic we address in a special section below. As with the norms of care, support, and safety, we feature two lines of analysis on the work undertaken to foster membership for students. One attends to the removal of the negatives associated with developing belonging (e.g., working to overcome oppositional peer culture). The other is the construction of positive rungs on the membership ladder (e.g., developing opportunities for students to assume responsibility). Again, we re-emphasize the fact that there is considerable overlap among and integration of the four norms of student community. This storyline of overlap and integration also applies to the three elements of the norm of membership.

The central law of school improvement that context matters is brightly illuminated here as well (Feldman & Matjasko, 2005; Guest & Schneider, 2003). Individual-level characteristics and school, family, peer, and neighborhood contexts each exert force on whether youngsters become members of a school or not (Feldman & Matjasko, 2005; Voelkl, 1997). "The school and community in which participation takes place matters" (Guest & Schneider, 2003, p. 91) a good deal in whether students are bystanders or active citizens in the school (Freiberg et al., 2009) and whether the desired outcomes of membership materialize or not (Guest & Schneider, 2003). Finally, and consistent with our examination of the other norms, authentic membership seems to be especially important and productive for students at risk of failure (Felner et al., 2007; Murphy, 2010a; Murphy & Tobin, 2011). Indeed, "belonging could be *the* single most crucial factor in the motivation and engagement of certain categories of at-risk students" (Goodenow, 1993, p. 39). We examine the form and texture of membership through an analysis of its three defining elements: ownership, involvement, and accomplishment (see Table 4.4).

Ownership is often defined in terms of student empowerment (Joselowsky, 2007; Silins & Mulford, 2010). As Roth and Brooks-Gunn (2003, p. 175) discovered, ownership is marked by "an empowering atmosphere [that] encourages youth to engage in useful roles [and] practice self-determination." Students become "stakeholders" in the school (Joselowsky, 2007). One aspect of the ownership subtheme of membership is student agency (Joselowsky, 2007), commitment to improvement and opportunities to influence actions at the school coupled with the belief that efforts will lead to positive effects (Jackson, 2000; Reitzug & Patterson, 1998). Student voice is also a component of ownership. Students are allowed and encouraged to express themselves and their ideas (Battistich et al., 1997).

Table 4.4   Aspects of the Norm of Membership in Student Community

Ownership
Involvement
Accomplishment

Their voices are not silenced or devalued (Patterson et al., 2007; Rodriguez, 2008). Rather, they "have voice in school affairs" (Newmann, 1981, p. 553). More important, student views are heard (McLaughlin & Talbert, 2001; Patterson et al., 2007), and honored (Ancess, 2003). Educators are "physically and emotionally present in social exchanges with students" (Adams & Forsyth, 2009, p. 268). Students' perspectives are received (Reitzug & Patterson, 1998).

Ownership entails influence on the part of the owners, students in this case (Battistich et al., 1997). Schools that build powerful communities for students "maximize opportunities for students to contribute to school policy and management" (Newmann, 1981, p. 552) through both formal and informal mechanisms, assuring that students' points of view are taken into account in classroom and school decision making (Ancess, 2003; Newmann, 1981) and in the "conception, execution, and evaluation of work" (Newmann et al., 1992, p. 25) and school-based activities. Ownership includes "bringing the learner in as a full and active participant in enhancing and shaping their own learning" (Felner et al., 2007, p. 210), making youngsters "constructors of both their learning environment and learning experience" (Joselowsky, 2007, p. 265). Students with influence are "active agents in the creation of school success" (Conchas, 2001, p. 501). They own the school and their work (Ancess, 2003; Newmann et al., 1992). They are partners and producers, not simply categories or recipients (Joselowsky, 2007), tourists (Freiberg et al., 2009), or consumers (Eckert, 1989). They "take ownership of their own learning" (Levin & Datnow, 2012, p. 190).

Relatedly, ownership implies common purpose, one that "builds a sense of membership that enhances engagement in work" (Newmann et al., 1992, p. 21). It entails the opportunity to engage in meaningful and challenging activities (Roth & Brooks-Gunn, 2003)—in "authentic academic work" (Marks, 2000, p. 158)—and influence over the ways in which students engage with those activities (Newmann, 1981, 1992).

As we have noted throughout this chapter, schools in the nineteenth and twentieth centuries were heavily defined by hierarchy, bureaucracy, and institutionalism. The result was that the school (adults) had all the control and students were, to a varying extent, invisible (Weis, 1990). Schools were characterized by what Laffey (1982, p. 64) refers to as "externality," an environment in "which students feel that they are pawns to external forces." Students in these schools were often locked in a dysfunctional battle to gain some control (Crosnoe, 2011; Csikszentmihalyi & Larson, 1984; Patterson et al., 2007). In contrast, and clearly ribboned in the discussion above, the norm of membership includes autonomy, control, and choice for those who have an ownership stake in the school. Schools that promote student autonomy and responsibility enhance engagement and learning (Gonzalez & Padilla, 1997; Hattie, 2009; Rutter et al., 1979). Overly controlling environments, on the other hand, "diminish interest, preference for challenge, and persistence—all aspects of engagement" (Fredricks et al., 2004, p. 78). This two-sided rule holds at both the classroom and school levels (Battistich et al., 1997). "Community [is] inversely associated with an emphasis on the teacher as sole authority in the classroom" (Battistich et al., 1997, p. 143) whereas having students take responsibility for their learning promotes ownership (Garmezy, 1991; Joselowsky, 2007). In schools with strong student communities, youngsters are provided choice and responsibility to accomplish important work (Joselowsky, 2007; Roth et al., 1998; Rutter et al., 1979), both in terms of their own learning and development (Gurr, Drysdale, & Mulford, 2005) and the improvement of the school (Joselowsky, 2007). Opportunities for students to lead are an especially important aspect of responsibility (Jackson, 2000; Roth & Brooks-Gunn, 2003; Sather, 1999).

Ownership includes the concepts of space and place. Students in meaningful communities have their own space, and they see school as a place for them (Eckert, 1989; McLaughlin & Talbert, 2001; Weis, 1990). Such tangibleness helps students "develop a sense that they [are] an integral part of the school collective" (Cooper et al., 2005, p. 9) and feelings of inclusiveness (Eckert, 1989; Newmann, 1992).

Involvement is a second critical element that helps define membership, one that as noted above shares considerable space with ownership. It features opportunities provided by the school for youngsters to engage their "talents, skills, and interests" (Crosnoe, 2011, p. 238) in meaningful and challenging work (Newmann, 1981, 1992) and in school activities (Marsh & Kleitman, 2002; Silins & Mulford, 2010). The critical issue here according to Joselowsky (2007, p. 273) is that schools "cease treating youth engagement as an add-on to improved learning outcomes but as central to student and school success." That is, "youth engagement must be conceptualized as a guiding principle of organizational operations" (p. 270). Indeed, Ma (2003, p. 347) argues "that students' participation in school activities may be the key to their sense of belonging in school."

Schools with well-formed student communities provide a host of "participatory opportunities" (Cooper et al., 2005, p. 17) centered on chances for youngsters to contribute to the school and take positions of responsibility (Johnson & Asera, 1999; Rutter et al., 1979). Given the cardinal place of student-adult connections in fostering community, it will surprise no one to learn that opportunities to develop meaningful relationships with teachers are critical to getting students involved in schools. So too are creating chances for youngsters to participate in class and schoolwide decisions (Ancess, 2003; Battistich et al., 1995; Epstein, 1996) and school governance (Baker et al., 1997; Woloszyk, 1996). Opportunities for leadership (Harris, 2009; MacBeath, 2009; Sather, 1999) and community service are often found in schools that are characterized by high levels of student involvement, both within the school (Ancess, 2003; Raywid, 1995) and in the extended community (Antrop-Gonzalez & De Jesus, 2006; Bloomberg et al., 2003; Eckert, 1989).

Although participation in academic work is the keystone strand of involvement, a good deal of the literature also rightfully examines involvement in school activities, especially co-curricular or extracurricular programs. Schools that score well on involvement specifically and personalized community in general offer a significant range of such experiences (Leithwood et al., 2004). These schools are defined by inclusionary practices (Eckert, 1989), pulling large percentages of youngsters into extracurricular activities. Involvement here, as we discuss in detail in the last section of the chapter, is linked to improved academic and social learning (Finn & Rock, 1997; Hattie, 2009; Rumberger, 2011).

Studies on extracurricular activities provide considerable guidance to educators for planning, developing, and putting these experiences into play for students. Many of those guidelines are threaded throughout the analysis above (e.g., providing students with input about activities to be offered). The core question here has been provided by Marsh and Kleitman (2002, p. 465): "How should students spend their time for maximum academic, psychological, and social benefits to support future accomplishments?"

We know from the research that structured activities are better than unstructured ones for promoting positive outcomes (Catalano et al., 1999; Feldman & Matjasko, 2005; Hattie, 2009). Structured and organized activities trump leisure activities as well (Marsh & Kleitman, 2002). Experiences that lead to tangible outcomes are preferable (Roth et al., 1998). "Effective programs engage young people in a variety of ways, so that they are not just physically present, but intellectually immersed, socially connected, and emotionally centered" (Joselowsky, 2007, p. 260). Activities that nurture collaboration and cooperation and those that engender teamwork among students (Conchas, 2001) are generally preferable to those featuring competition (Cooper, 1996). Guest and Schneider (2003) also report that activities that foster identity and positive recognition are linked to valued outcomes. They also help us see that identity interacts with social context. That is, "activity-based identities are given meaning by school community value systems" (p. 90).

Experiences that lead to success for students from active engagement are desirable (Feldman & Matjasko, 2005). So also are programs in which peers from one's social network participate (Feldman & Matjasko, 2005) and ones where there is a strong match with the interests of the students (Eggert, Thompson, Herting, & Nicholas, 1995). Staff characteristics matter (Roth et al., 1998). Activities shepherded by strong and supportive leaders are more productive than those that are run by adults who are less committed to the programs (Roth et al., 1998). We know that getting parents on board can be an important asset in encouraging and maintaining involvement (Gonzalez & Padilla, 1997; Rumberger, 2011). Continuity of program participation is important. This includes the length of participation and the regularity of engagement (Feldman & Matjasko, 2005; Roth et al., 1998). A combination of activities from different domains (e.g., academic clubs, sports teams) is often preferable to a single concentration (Joselowsky,

2007; Roth et al., 1998). Except at the extreme end of the continuum, deeper participation, with active engagement, leads to the realization of valued ends (Feldman & Matjasko, 2005; Marsh & Kleitman, 2002). Experiences that cover "more of the contexts in which adolescents live" (Roth et al., 1998, p. 438) are desirable. "Multiple opportunities for multiple forms of access and interaction across various members of the school community" (Ancess, 2000, p. 605) provides the operational structure here.

Researchers also help us see that to be most beneficial, activities that promote involvement should be aligned with and integrated into the school culture and core school operations (Joselowsky, 2007; Marsh & Kleitman, 1992). "More comprehensive and sustained programs" (Roth et al., 1998, p. 440) lead to more positive outcomes. Within the context of the findings above, research allows us to say a few things about the types of activities that are most productive in fostering membership and community. Both academic and sports programs have been shown to produce positive outcomes (Guest & Schneider, 2003; Marsh & Kleitman, 2002), although, not surprisingly, academic activities have larger impacts on achievement (Hattie, 2009). School-related activities consistently lead to more favorable outcomes than out-of-school experiences (Marsh & Kleitman, 2002).

Finally, analysts confirm that *accomplishment* is a keystone element in the norm of authentic membership (Baker et al., 1997; Crosnoe, 2011; Farrell, 1990). Two aspects of success are important. The first is a feeling of personal accomplishment (Baker et al., 1997; Dinham, 2005; Johnson & Asera, 1999). The second is the belief that if one's efforts are worthwhile, they make a meaningful contribution to the school community (Battistich et al., 1995; Csikszentmihalyi & Larson, 1984). Schools facilitate reaching both goals by centering on student competencies rather than student problems (Roth et al., 1998). Indeed, research confirms that competency building is an essential ingredient in student community (Battistich et al., 1995; Dinham, 2005; Roth et al., 1998).

Educators exert considerable influence on students' sense of competency and success in the school by creating a plethora of ways to recognize, honor and celebrate, and reward active engagement and achievements (Battistich et al., 1995; Jackson & Warren, 2000; Wynne, 1980) across academic, behavioral, and community fronts (Blase & Kirby, 2009; Cotton, 2000). Recognition from others whose opinions matter is implicated in strengthening students' commitment, engagement, and learning.

Student-Student Relationships

The average adolescent probably learns more from peers than from any other category of people. (Eckert, 1989, p. 184)

Peer pressure [is] far more powerful than teacher reinforcement. (Farrell, 1990, p. 111)

To this point in the chapter, the focus has been on teacher-student relationships and how these personal connections can foster the growth of powerful norms that mark highly productive student communities. Concomitantly, it is essential to acknowledge that peer relationships are equally critical in the narrative of press and support for the formation of these norms, and ultimately student social and academic learning. That is, "peers exert a powerful influence on adolescents. They influence students' social and academic behaviors, attitudes toward school, and access to resources (social capital) that may benefit their education" (Rumberger, 2011, p. 175). Indeed, although remarkably understated and generally insufficiently acknowledged, they, not teachers, define the informal aspects of schooling (Crosnoe, 2011; Smerdon et al., 2009) in which the formal aspects grow or atrophy (Eckert, 1989; Farrell, 1990). Major lines of research converge on this conclusion: "Few things matter more [than] peer relations on how young people turn out" (Crosnoe, 2011, p. 206). That is "the social structure of the student cohort dominates virtually all aspects of life in the institution, choices in all domains are restricted not so clearly by adult judgment as by peer social boundaries" (Eckert, 1989, p. 12).

Analysts show us how life changes for young persons as they advance into their teens. More and more time is spent with peers (Csikszentmihalyi & Larson, 1984; Farrell, 1990; Goodenow, 1993). In turn, "teacher influence and proximity decreases over time" (Opdenakker et al., 2012, p. 113). The centrality of parents in the lives of youngsters is reduced as well (Eckert, 1989; Lee & Burkam, 2003) As adolescents "redirect psychic energy away from members of one's family [and teachers] to one's peers" (Csikszentmihalyi & Larson, 1984, p. 130), they increasingly begin to see themselves through their peers, that is "peers serve as a looking glass for teenagers trying to figure out who they are and where they fit in the world" (Crosnoe, 2011, p. 56). It is to peers that they begin to turn for the majority of their feedback (Hattie, 2009), for validation (Smerdon et al., 2009), and for sense of identity (Eckert, 1989). It is friends rather than adults to whom they often turn for information, guidance, and emotional support (Csikszentmihalyi & Larson, 1984). For many youngsters, "the peer group is the major source of morals and values" (Farrell, 1990, p. 4) and often "the most important resource for resilience (Crosnoe, 2011, p. 177).

Given the reality that the academic domain of the school has a limited pull on students (Newmann et al., 1992), that schooling for adolescents "is often far more about navigating a social terrain that may or may not place value on education and academic achievement" (Crosnoe, 2011, p. 9), we should not be surprised to learn that peer relationships have significant potential to enhance or undercut the formal domain of schooling (Eckert, 1989; Newmann et al., 1992; Steele & Aronson, 1995). The narrative here is similar to the one we discussed about engagement and disengagement based on Figure 4.2. More specifically, a very sturdy line of research confirms that peer culture (the informal domain of education) can reinforce the academic values of the school or it can pull youngsters to different, often noncompatible (e.g., we do not kill ourselves here) or oppositional (e.g., the degradation of academic work and relationships with teachers' values) and subsequent behaviors (e.g., blowing off classes) (Goddard & Goff, 1999; Maguin & Loeber, 1996; St. Pierre et al., 1997). Crosnoe (2011, p. 76) refers to this later option as "antiacademic and antiadult attitudes and orientations" and Farrell (1990, p. 143) talks about "deviant universes." This impressive line of research is clear in its assessment that if "counterproductive norms are operating among students, any academic reform task becomes exceedingly difficult" (Smerdon et al., 2009, p. 210) and academic achievement is significantly compromised (Eckert, 1989; Opdenakker et al., 2012). Students in this scenario end up rejecting the authority of the school, privileging the norms of the peer community, and "pursu[ing] their primate activities on the fringes of the official activity" (Eckert, 1989, p. 88). We also know that the tendency to move in the direction of oppositional culture is more evident for students placed at risk by society and its schools (Dishion, Poulin, & Barraston, 2001; Farrell, 1990; Murphy, 2010a).

On the other hand, in scenario number one above, peer culture can turn out to be a distinctly valuable resource for youngsters and their schools. If a student community that brings young people into alignment with the academic success values is nourished and grown, good things accrue to students in terms of social and academic outcomes. Below, we discuss what the research reveals about creating a positive peer culture. Here we simply reinforce the cardinal message: "Changes in peer context are critically important to individual student outcomes" (Felner et al., 2007, p. 15). To create productive communities for students, educators need to work to ensure that the various peer cultures reinforce rather than undermine the values the school holds for youngsters. Dishion and colleagues (2001, p. 90) make this point quite explicitly when they assert "that adults' role in structuring, managing, and attending to children's peer contexts is perhaps the most critical for promoting health and reducing risks." That is, it is not sufficient to work on individual teacher-student relationships. Teachers and administrators also need to actively shape student-student relationships in the service of nurturing positive communities for students.

Research in this area reveals tangible pathways for educators to create isomorphism between the formal and informal dimensions of schooling, or what Feldman and Matjasko (2005, p. 197) call the "integration of school and peer contexts." Many of these can be distilled from the elements of the four core norms of personalized community examined above. For example, developing opportunities for collaborative work; providing students with voice in classroom and school decision; establishing multiple ways for students to lead their colleagues; and carving out place, space, and autonomy for youngsters all assist in the formation of positive peer cultures (Battistich et al., 1997; Conchas, 2001; Hoy et al., 1998). Pursuing multiple avenues to bring and hold essential values front and center is a wise strategy (Bryk et al., 2010; Goddard, 2003), especially values about social interactions (Eckert, 1989). Inviting and encouraging youngsters to participate in school-sponsored activities, that is, shaping friendships is good policy as well, both in regular and extracurricular programs (Crosnoe, 2011; Newmann, 1981). So too is providing training in how to use peer support networks (Eckert, 1989). Special attention to peer relationships when assigning youngsters to academic interventions can be helpful here (Demaray & Malecki, 2002a). Conscious attention by teachers and administrators to issues of race can do much to help build productive student-student relationships. The research also highlights the power of honoring different cultures and ethnicities and deliberately mixing youngsters by class and race (Conchas, 2001; Murphy, 2010a), helping break down formal and informal patterns that foster prejudices and social inequalities (Conchas, 2001; Crosnoe, 2011). Considerable attention to student-student relationships when students move across levels and grades can pay dividends to the bank of school community. The operant rule is that inclusiveness is almost always a good idea (Antrop-Gonzalez, 2006; Galletta & Ayala, 2008; Scanlan & Lopez, 2012).

INSTITUTIONAL AFFILIATION AND IDENTITY

> Students' feelings of acceptance and support, combined with the feeling that they are making important contributions to the group, help to create and maintain feelings of identification with, and commitments to, the group and acceptance of its expressed goals and values. (Battistich et al., 1995, p. 629)

> An important link connects social experiences in high school to academic progress, and that link is personal and interpersonal development. (Crosnoe, 2011, p. 48)

> Feelings of belonging in school have been found to be associated with levels of engagement, persistent effort in schoolwork, and academic motivation, including expectations for success and general school motivation and interest. (Voelkl, 1997, p. 297)

In this section, we turn to the initial outcomes that accrue when schools create communities of pastoral care for students, environments defined by personalized relationships and marked by care, support, safety, and membership. We examine three intermediate results, social integration, psychological well-being, and learning dispositions, collectively often described in terms of human and social capital (Feldman & Matjasko, 2005). As we see in Figure 4.1, these factors are critical to the development of strong engagement with and in school which, in turn, is essential to student academic and social learning. We address these last two links of our model in the final sections of the chapter.

Before we lay out the narrative on institutional and social integration, we want to spotlight an essential point that appears in various places throughout this volume. Specifically, we find that the effects of pastoral care are especially powerful for students placed at risk by society for failure in schools (Battistich et al., 1995; Feldman & Matjasko, 2005; Marsh & Kleitman, 2002)—socioeconomically disadvantaged students, youth of color, second-language children, students historically underserved by schools, and youngsters in schools with high concentrations of students from low-income families. We also want to remind the reader of the reciprocal, interrelated nature of the variables in our model. Overlap among the elements, what we call shared spaces, is the norm.

Social Integration

Identification represents the extent to which a student has bonded with school and incorporated it as a significant part of his or her self-concept and lifestyle. (Voelkl, 1997, p. 296)

Students who experience the school as a caring and supportive environment in which they actively participate and have opportunities to exercise influence will feel attached to the school community and will, therefore, come to accept its norms and values. (Battistich et al., 1995, p. 649)

Feelings of not fitting in might not only pose risks to mental health and general well-being, but also undermine educational attainment. (Crosnoe, 2011, p. 90)

We know from the research that both academic proficiency and positive school culture promote integration (Catalano et al., 1999; Croninger & Lee, 2001; Ma, 2003). Our focus here is on the second element in the integration equation, culture. Studies regularly report that a culture defined by norms of care, support, safety, and membership helps attach or bond young people to school (Battistich et al., 1997; Crosnoe, 2011; Voelkl, 1997). These bonds, in turn, lead to a cascade of other important effects (e.g., enhanced self-esteem, greater motivation), all of which presage engagement and learning (see Figure 4.1).

Pastoral care leads first to student identification with the school, what Eckert (1989) labels as a merging of the personal and institutional. Scholars describe this state in a variety of ways: membership (Eckert, 1989; Gonzalez & Padilla, 1997), belonging (Battistich et al., 1995; Fredricks et al., 2004), integration (Scanlan & Lopez, 2012), affiliation (Newmann, 1981, O'Conner, 1997), attachment (Alexander et al., 1997; Conchas, 2001), inclusion (Ma, 2003; Voelkl, 1997), connection (Feldman & Matjasko, 2005; Roth & Brooks-Gunn, 2003), fitting in (Crosnoe, 2011), and acceptance (Goodenow, 1993). Underlying these various markers for identification is a sense of being part of the school, of being valued by the institution and by peers, of "feeling oneself to be an important part of the life and activity of the class" (Goodenow, 1993, p. 25) and school—"of feel[ing] personally accepted, respected, included, and supported in the school" (Ma, 2003, p. 340). It is about affinity (Conchas, 2001).

Muted pastoral care, on the other hand, is an invitation to weak student identification with and/or possible disaffiliation with the school, "an absence of highly developed feelings of valuing and belonging" (Voelkl, 1997, p. 296). Students in such schools are often portrayed as "just passing through" (Eckert, 1989, p. 65). Rather than being bonded to the school, they are independent actors, ones who often feel a sense of disconnection and alienation toward teachers and peers (Antrop-Gonzalez, 2006; Newmann 1981). They display what Farrell (1990, p. 112) calls "absenting behavior," a "culture that is dominated by the private as opposed to the institutional" (Eckert, 1989, p. 172). Separation and exclusion are elements of disidentification. So also are estrangement, detachment, and isolation (Newmann 1981)—"emotional and physical withdrawal" (Voelkl, 1997, p. 294).

Identification (or disidentification) impacts commitment to the school and a sense of obligation to those at the school (Gamoran, 1996). Positive identification helps build a sense of legitimacy around the school and a valuing of the institution (Fredricks et al., 2004; Goodenow, 1993). According to Voelkl (1997, p. 296), the idea of valuing schooling

> include[s] the recognition of the value of the school as both a social institution and a tool for facilitating personal advancement. That is, the youngster regards school as a central institution in society and feels that what is learned in class is important in its own right and that school is instrumental in obtaining his or her personal life objectives . . . the belief that schoolwork is both interesting and important.

Valuing also leads to a "commitment to and identification with the goals of the institution" (Eckert, 1989, p. 103); its values and purposes (Ancess, 2003; Baker et al., 1997; Marsh & Kleitman, 1992); its norms and practices (Battistich et al., 1995, 1997; Voelkl, 1997); "the means it prescribes for members to pursue goals" (Newmann et al., 1992, p. 20), that is, its structures, policies, and practices (Hallinan & Kubitschek, 1999); and its sanctioned outcomes (Marsh & Kleitman, 2002, Voelkl, 1997). In schools with strong pastoral care, "students become invested in the operations of the classroom" (Freiberg et al., 2009) and school (Marsh & Kleitman, 2002).

Psychological Well-Being

Social psychological theories on the formation of self-image have suggested that a person's self-image is formed through interaction with others and that one's view of oneself changes with the positive and negative feedback provided in social exchange. (Hallinan & Kubitschek, 1999, p. 46)

Aspects of youth identity are shaped *in relation* to schools and teachers. (Weis, 1990, p. 116)

All of the correlations among self-concept and support reveal a significant relationship between how students perceive themselves and their competencies and the social support they perceive from those around them. (Demaray & Malecki, 2002a, p. 235)

Researchers also document strong linkages between a community of care and belonging and the psychological health of students (Feldman & Matjasko, 2005; Ma, 2003) and conclude that the relationship is reciprocal in nature (Ma, 2003). These scholars remind us that the work here is two-pronged, the creation of pathways to positive psychosocial characteristics (e.g., self concept) and the development of fortifications to protect against negative life events that could undermine mental health (Jackson & Warren, 2000).

We know that the major quest for youngsters is for personal identity (Csikszentmihalyi & Larson, 1984; Farrell, 1990), what Crosnoe (2011) calls identity work and Feldman and Matjasko (2005) talk about as learning to understand oneself. Analysts also document that identity and self-esteem are tightly yoked. Each student's self-concept is forged in good measure through the sense of community he or she feels at school, by the relationships forged with teachers and peers (Battistich et al., 1997; Guest & Schneider, 2003; Marsh & Kleitman, 2002). That is, students "come to an understanding of their own social worth by seeing how they are treated by others" (Crosnoe, 2011, p. 139). Supportive communities help nourish the formation of healthy self-concept and stronger self-esteem (Demaray & Malecki, 2002a; Pounder, 1999), thus positively shaping the nature of students' developmental pathways (Feldman & Matjasko, 2005) and consequently, prosocial attitudes and actions (Battistich et al., 1997; Rothman & Cosden, 1995). Nonsupportive communities for students, on the other hand, can lead to reduced self-esteem, nonproductive developmental pathways, and counterproductive attitudes and behaviors (Crosnoe, 2011). These behaviors and attitudes, in turn, are related to engagement and school success (Finn & Rock, 1997; Mulford & Silins, 2003; Rumberger, 2011)—for better or worse.

Communities of belonging and support are associated with student sense of expectancy and self-efficacy (Battistich et al., 1995; Goodenow, 1993; Scanlan & Lopez, 2012), concepts that are "among the most robust predictors of academic achievement" (Scanlan & Lopez, 2012, p. 607). Personalized student community also promotes a sense of control and autonomy (Ancess, 2003; Goodenow, 1993). Caring environments "ignite agency" (Rodriguez, 2008, p. 774) as well (Felner et al., 2007; Fredricks et al., 2004), providing students with what Csikszentmihalyi and Larson (1984) depict as internalized standards of performance. Communities of pastoral care strengthen students' internal locus of control (Marsh & Kleitman, 1992). That is, as Osterman (2000, p. 329) in her seminal review reminds us, "autonomy develops most effectively in situations where children and teenagers feel a sense of relatedness and closeness rather than disaffiliation from significant adults." Autonomy is not about isolation and private space "but, instead, refers to the individual's sense of agency or self-determination in a social context" (p. 329).

Related dynamics of a healthy self also grow in positive student communities. We know, for example, that self-confidence is often augmented in schools characterized by authentic membership and support (Croninger & Lee, 2001; Farrell, 1990; Goodenow, 1993). Caring and support are also welded tightly to feelings of competence (Laffey, 1982; Osterman, 2000; Silins & Mulford, 2010) and resilience (Crosnoe, 2011; Gonzalez & Padilla, 1997).

Dispositions Toward Learning

Student community [is] consistently associated with a positive orientation toward school and learning, including attraction to school, task orientation toward learning, and educational aspirations. (Battistich et al., 1997, p. 143)

Research has proven the significant effects of teacher-student relationships on student motivations. (Opdenakker et al., 2012, p. 96)

A thick line of research has established that pastoral care influences students' orientation toward school and learning and promotes the development of positive educational values and attitudes (Battistich et al., 1995; Sweetland & Hoy, 2000; Osterman, 2000) and subsequent achievement-related behaviors (Adams & Forsyth, 2009; Goodenow, 1993). Students in safe and caring environments are more likely than peers in communities of low pastoral care to find value in school (Adams & Forsyth, 2009) and have "a positive orientation toward school" (Osterman, 2000, p. 331). These youngsters often have a greater interest in school and like school and classes more than students in communities assessed as low in support and belonging (Birch & Ladd, 1997; Gonzalez & Padilla, 1997; Osterman, 2000). They identify with their schools more and invest more in their learning (Ancess, 2003; Marsh & Kleitman, 2002). Community also exerts a strong shaping force on "prosocial attitudes, beliefs, and behaviors, including concern and respect for peers and teachers, conflict resolution, acceptance of out groups, [and] intrinsic prosocial motivation and behavior" (Osterman, 2000, p. 334). The obverse of the research-themed storyline above is true as well. Weak communities in which students have impersonal connections with teachers and perceive a lack of pastoral care produce negative orientations toward school (Osterman, 2000). They nurture values and attitudes that often lead to counterproductive coping strategies (Crosnoe, 2011; Eckert, 1989; Farrell, 1990), ones that undercut meaningful engagement and social and academic learning (Demaray & Malecki, 2002b; Hattie, 2009; Ma, 2003).

Motivation is the most examined learning disposition in the literature on student community. Here scholars routinely find that pastoral care is highly associated with student motivation to work and to succeed in school (Barnett & McCormick, 2004; Bryk et al., 2010; Opdenakker et al., 2012):

> A positive school climate—where students and adults know each other well and where adults express care and concern for students' well-being, intellectual growth, and educational success—is a key motivational element in the learning process for adolescents. (Quint, 2006, p. 19)

> Students' motivation is enhanced in schools in which they feel cared for, supported, valued, and influential—schools that they experience as communities. (Battistich et al., 1995, p. 19)

According to Battistich and associates (1995, 1997), personalized community motivates students to adopt and honor school classroom norms and values and enhances the desire to acquire competence. Motivation is important, in turn, because it impacts engagement and social and cognitive outcomes (Battistich et al., 1995; Hattie, 2009; Opdenakker et al., 2010).

Studies have also shown that sense of support and belonging forged in relationships with teachers and peers is correlated with student commitment to the school and the work they do there (Ancess, 2003; Baker et al., 1997; Battistich et al., 1995). Self-confidence is impacted by pastoral care (Ancess, 2000; Wilson & Corbett, 1999). With high pastoral care, students become more invested in their academic achievement (Ancess, 2000); demonstrate a greater appetite for learning (Felner et al., 2007; Munoz, Ross, & McDonald, 2007), that is, "greater interest in challenging instructional activities" (Johnson & Asera, 1999, p. 100), and exhibit more "academically oriented forms of agency" (Conchas, 2001, p. 501). Community grows the important disposition of future orientation (O'Conner, 1997). In particular, educational aspirations are shaped by pastoral care (Laffey, 1982; Marsh & Kleitman, 2002).

Community nourishes possibility and hope (Eckert, 1989; Farrell, 1990; Rodriguez, 2008). Students ensconced in a strong climate of safety and care are likely to develop a robust sense of industry and a robust work ethic, a commitment to and feeling of accomplishment in undertaking schoolwork, and a commitment to learn the adaptive skills (Demaray & Malecki, 2002b) and master "the habits of work necessary for school success" (Ancess, 2003, p. 21). In particular, students in such school environments demonstrate greater self-directedness (Birch & Ladd, 1997; Farrell, 1990) and exercise more leadership (Demaray & Malecki, 2002b). They are willing to take risks in the service of learning (Goodenow, 1993), exercise meaningful "pursuit in the demands and struggle for quality performance" (Ancess, 2003, p. 41), and assume responsibility for their work (Ancess, 2003; Birch & Ladd, 1997; Silins & Mulford, 2010). Students in positively anchored cultures learn to take and display pride in their efforts and their accomplishments (Marsh & Kleitman, 2002).

ENGAGEMENT AND LEARNING

No manner of school reform will be successful until we first face and resolve the engagement problem. (Hattie, 2009, p. 32)

Engagement can result from a variety of antecedents in the context, both social and academic, at both the school and classroom levels. (Fredricks et al., 2004, p. 83)

Engagement in learning activities and in the broader school environment are important antecedents of school achievement. (Finn & Rock, 1997, p. 221)

When we examine the model of community of pastoral care for students, we see that everything examined to this point is designed to impact the variable most proximal to learning, student engagement. As Conchas (2001, p. 480) succinctly captures this essential reality, "institutional mechanisms mediate school engagement," that is, "changing students' experiences within schools can enhance engagement" (Newmann et al., 1992, p. 17). More specifically, we note that powerful relations, robust norms, and social integration and self-development promote active engagement, while the absence of these cultural ingredients leads to disaffiliation and disengagement. We also learn, and explore in the next section, that there is a moderate to strong link between engagement and student academic success, one that has the power to trump aptitude (Laffey, 1982).

Engagement

Effective schools are defined by high levels of student engagement. In these schools, teachers work to make the option of disengagement difficult to impossible for youngsters (Ancess, 2003). To strengthen schools, it is essential, therefore, that increasing student engagement be relocated to the center stage of the school improvement production (Datnow, Park, & Kennedy, 2008; Hattie, 2009; Joselowsky, 2007; Newmann, 1981) and that we work to deepen our understanding of this pivotal construct (Fredricks et al., 2004; Marks, 2000). We turn to that work shortly. However, we revisit recurring reminders before we do so. It is essential to remember that both academic press and pastoral care are central pathways toward active student engagement, pathways that regularly intertwine. Our focus in this chapter is on the second avenue, creating communities of pastoral care. Our discussion of academic press is limited to the points where the two pathways cross and/or travel together. As is the case with the other pieces of the model, context matters with engagement. There are, for example, nuances associated with level of schooling, at risk status, gender, and so forth (Fredricks et al., 2004; Galletta & Ayala, 2008; Laffey, 1982). Also, while we do not continuously highlight the fact in our unpacking of engagement, leadership is an essential catalyst in fostering this deep commitment. Our goal is to enrich the toolbox of ways for principals to accomplish that work.

Definition

We define student engagement in academic work as the student's psychological investment in and effort directed toward learning, understanding, or mastering the knowledge, skills, or crafts that academic work is intended to promote. (Newmann et al., 1992, p. 12)

We define school disengagement as a higher order factor composed of correlated subfactors measuring different aspects of the process of detaching from school, disconnecting from its norms and expectations, reducing effort and involvement at school, and withdrawing from a commitment to school and to school completion. (Balfanz et al., 2007, p. 224)

As with a good number of the elements in our model, engagement is not directly observable. It needs to be inferred from observations, observations informed by knowledge and influenced by judgments (Newmann et al., 1992; Rumberger, 2011). It has a manipulable or malleable quality absent from many of the context variables that surround and interact with the model (e.g., gender). However, as Fredricks and associates (2004) explain in their keystone review, like other elements of the model (e.g., self-concept) engagement is a theoretically and conceptually messy construct.

Research provides different lenses to think through the idea of student engagement in school, all of which illuminate the multidimensional nature of the construct (Fredricks et al., 2004; Marks, 2000). One of the most important is place of action: inside classrooms, outside the classroom but inside the school, and outside regular school activity (i.e., extracurricular experiences) (Finn & Rock, 1997; Rumberger, 2011). Another approach is to define engagement by its intensity and/or duration (Fredricks et al., 2004). Finn and Rock (1997) explore levels of engagement, with level one signifying compliance and level two representing active initiative taking, what Alexander and team (1997) designate as procedural versus psychological engagement and others label procedural versus substantive commitment. All emphasize the fact that active engagement is required if youngsters are to reap the benefits of schooling (Fredricks et al., 2004). At other times, engagement and disengagement are defined in terms of its components—which are generally coupled to level—such as participation, investment, and commitment (Fredricks et al., 2004). It is best, perhaps, to think of engagement as both ways of acting and states of mind (Alexander et al., 1997), often described in the literature as behavioral and emotional engagement, with the former dimension picking up involvement and the latter incorporating the affective responses of youngsters to schooling.

Fredricks and associates (2004) provide us with the richest conceptual map of engagement, one that is scaffolded on three core pillars: cognitive engagement, emotional engagement, and behavioral engagement. Cognitive engagement attends to issues of self-regulation. The focus here is on metacognition and cognitive strategy use and investment in learning. It "includes flexibility in problem solving, preference for hard work, and positive coping in the face of failure" (p. 64). Emotional engagement according to these scholars is often cast in terms of student identification with school, including an assortment of "emotions related to the school, schoolwork, and the people at the school" (p. 66). Finally, for Fredricks and colleagues and other scholars of student engagement (Alexander et al., 1997; Balfanz et al., 2007; Voelkl, 1997), behavioral engagement includes general and specific actions, including work-related and conduct actions such as putting forth effort, attending, participating, paying attention, and demonstrating persistence. More specifically, they define behavioral engagement in three ways.

> The first definition entails positive conduct, such as following the rules and adhering to classroom norms, as well as the absence of disruptive behaviors such as skipping school and getting in trouble. The second definition concerns involvement in learning and academic tasks and includes behaviors such as effort, persistence, concentration, attention, asking questions, and contributing to class discussion. A third definition involves participation in school-related activities such as athletics or school governance. (p. 61)

A Model of Engagement

Earlier, we introduced pathways of engagement and disengagement in schooling (see Figure 4.2). Here we delve more fully into disaffiliation and disengagement, what we hold to be the most critical problem in education today, in general and even more so for subordinate minorities (Fredricks et al., 2004; Steele, 1992, 1997) and students from low income (Murphy, 2010a) and working class homes (Eckert, 1989; Farrell, 1990; Weis, 1990)— students who are least likely to fit the existing model of schooling and most likely to have cultural norms and values that are at odds with the prevailing expectations and norms of schooling (O'Conner, 1997; Voelkl, 1997). We use Figure 4.3 to supplement the earlier discussion.

We start with the fact that engagement and disengagement are two sides of a continuum (Newmann et al., 1992). The job of the school is to get and keep students at the farthest right-hand side of that continuum, full and meaningful engagement in the classroom and the school, "arranging conditions so that people expend energy in ways that enhance engagement with work" (Newmann, 1981, p. 548). As suggested above, the roots of disengagement (or engagement) in schools can be traced to conditions in the larger world of childhood and adolescence, to the alignment between this larger world and the focus and methods of schooling, and to actions specific to schools. At times, schools cause disengagement. More often than not, however, they fail to ameliorate or exacerbate nascent disaffiliation (Baker et al., 1997), either by ignoring the realities of the larger world in which youngsters operate or ineptly (often thoughtlessly) attempting to force students to fit into prevailing school models (e.g., demonstrating unawareness of or rejecting cultural norms and values of working class and minority cultures) (Crosnoe, 2011; Murphy, 2010a; O'Conner, 1997). We also build on Laffey's (1982) sage advice and employ multiple indicators to measure engagement. In terms of an advance organizer, we note that the model in Figure 4.3 is designed to provide a comprehensive profile of commitment and effort featuring indicators across the various categories we discussed above (e.g., places, types, components).

Figure 4.3   Levels of Engagement and Disengagement in Schools

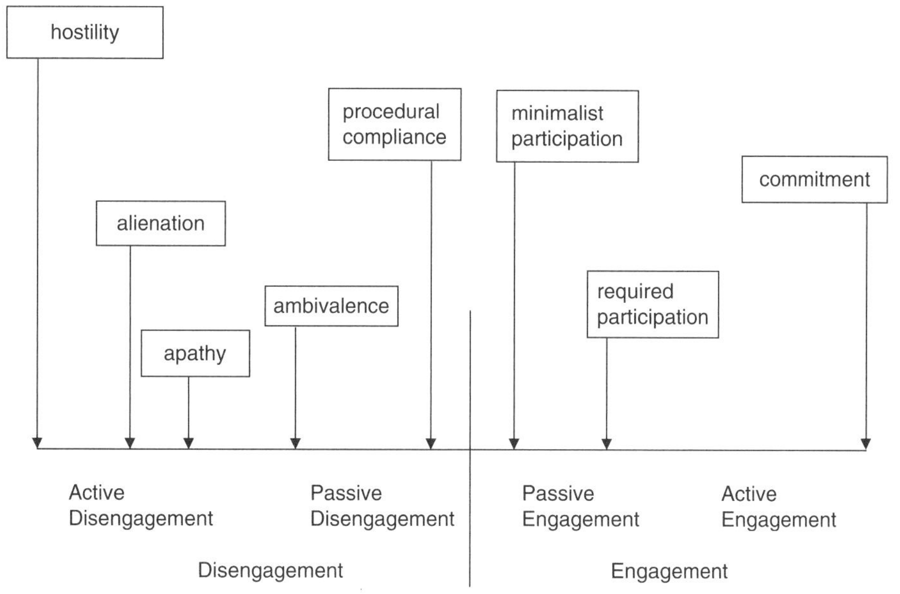

The model is heuristic. It shows "levels" of engagement on a continuum, from active disengagement to active engagement. The categories represent overlapping bands on that continuum. On the positive side of the line, we refer to the lowest level of engagement as "minimalist participation." At this point, students are investing very little in schooling, "doing just enough." Minimal effort, involvement, and psychological investment are evident (Eckert, 1989; Newmann et al., 1992; Weis, 1990). This is a marginal form of engagement, overlapping with "procedural compliance" on the disengagement side of the line. They share the gene of passivity, with students "doing what they are told but not consciously doing anything at all" (Weis, 1990, p. 32). The middle point on the engagement side of the continuum is best thought of as "required participation," where more than minimum is invested by students. Students exert sufficient energy to meet classroom and school expectations. Students appear to be "on task" here. There is involvement but little psychological investment. The high point on the engagement continuum is "commitment." At this level, we see active involvement and meaningful investment in learning on the part of students. Active involvement

> involves psychological investment in learning, comprehending, or mastering knowledge, skills, and crafts, not simply a commitment to complete assigned tasks or to acquire symbols of high performance such as grades or social approval. (Newmann et al., 1992, p. 12)

Five levels define disengagement, "the emotional and physical withdrawal of students from school" (Voelkl, 1997, p. 294), rungs on the ladder of disaffiliation representing degrees of "students' feeling of not belonging in school and not valuing school and school related behaviors" (p. 294). We examine them from passive to active withdrawal. We see first "procedural compliance" which we argue is the modal point of student engagement with schooling today, a reality that is both troubling and sobering for those in the schooling business (Newmann et al., 1992; Voelkl, 1997; Weis, 1990). As we revealed above, it shares space with minimalist participation. Students here work to "get by" (Weis, 1990). They are not especially interested in the goals of the school (Csikszentmihalyi & Larson, 1984) and demonstrate very little interest in their education (Crosnoe, 2011; Weis, 1990). They have mastered the art of appearances, however. They have learned how to get along by going along. By and large, they "do not engage in overt or calculated rejection of school" (Weis, 1990, p. 18) or its values and norms. They participate in the form but not the substance of education (Eckert, 1989; Farrell, 1990). Here, as Weis (1990, pp. 32–33) documents, engagement "plays itself out largely in student participation in the maintenance of the appearance of order and a willingness to hand something in in order to pass courses." There is adherence to school routines and little more than perfunctory effort

(Ancess, 2003; Newmann et al., 1992). "Students just sit in class and do what they are told" (Weis, 1990, p. 30).

On the next two rungs down the ladder of engagement, we see "ambivalence" and "apathy." They overlap and share a few defining elements with procedural compliance as well. The key difference between them and their lethargic cousin is that some active resistance to schooling, to its goals, values, norms, procedures, and ways of operating, begins to appear. Going along to get along is supplemented at times by even less positive and more negative energy, push back on school routines and structures, although more implicit and less subversive than we find further down the continuum (Crosnoe, 2011; Farrell, 1990).

"Alienation" represents a still more robust form of disengagement. It includes withdraw of personal agency and withdraw from accepted forms of community in school (Ancess, 2003), a deepening estrangement (Newmann, 1981). The resistance gene is enriched and becomes increasingly explicit (Eckert, 1989). School goals and values are not simply rejected but often trampled upon. The most vigorous form of disengagement is "hostility." Getting by and going along to get along are rejected as personally demeaning actions. Counterproductive (from the schools' perspective) values formed on "ways of being" at school are on display (Crosnoe, 2011; Eckert, 1989). Controlled battles with teachers are engaged, and sometimes sought out. Maladjustment becomes a viable protective faction in the short term (Jackson & Warren, 2000). "Delinquent" subcultures often materialize based on this hostility to school (Eckert, 1989).

Community and Engagement

Students in schools with more elements of communal organization show higher engagement and greater gains in engagement over time. (Fredricks et al., 2004, p. 73)

The social psychology of a school can have profound effects on student engagement. (Bryk et al., 2010, p. 59)

Investigatory work that backward maps from student success is quite informative at this point of the narrative. It demonstrates that engagement does indeed occupy a keystone position in the framework of student learning. That is, it establishes the validity of the right-hand side of the model in Figure 4.1. This scientific analysis confirms the validity of the left hand side of the model as well. That is, a positive culture for youngsters is shown to be a central catalyst in fostering student engagement, especially for students from lower SES families (Felner et al., 2007; Ma & Klinger, 2000; Rumberger, 2011). Research helps us see that each of the earlier pieces of the model in Figure 4.1 (e.g., safety) enhances student connections to school and that collectively they provide a powerful platform for active engagement (Marks, 2000). Communities of pastoral care for students make weak engagement and disengagement difficult options for youngsters to select (Ancess, 2003).

To begin, we learn that the quality of student relationships with teachers is "significantly associated with students' active engagement in schools" (Goodenow, 1993, p. 23): "School culture that prioritizes relationships can significantly mediate academic engagement" (Rodriguez, 2008, p. 768). Scholars also illustrate a parallel connection between peers and student engagement (Fredricks et al., 2004). Peers push and pull friends toward commitment to school goals, values, and norms, investment and effort that helps foster communities of care and membership, communities that ratchet up student engagement in school (Fredricks et al., 2004).

Turning to the norms of personalized culture that unfold in the context of student-teacher and student-student relationships, researchers confirm a strong, positive linkage between care and engagement (Baker et al., 1997; Ma, 2003; Quint, 2006). They also substantiate an association between students' perceptions of teacher support and active investment and involvement in the classroom, in school, and in extracurricular activities (Battistich et al., 1995; Conchas, 2001; Goodenow, 1993); with all three types of engagement reviewed by Fredricks and colleagues (2004)—cognitive, emotional, and behavioral; and in both the academic and social support categories (Balfanz et al., 2007; Demaray & Malecki, 2002a). There is evidence of a viable connection between the norm of safety and order and a variety of indices of student engagement as well (Bryk et al., 2010). In schools characterized by a lack of order, disengagement flourishes (Bryk et al., 2010). Finally, an abundance of research draws empirical links between membership (belonging) and student engagement (Fredricks et al., 2004), as reflected in investment, effort, and commitment (Goodenow, 1993; Ma, 2003; Osterman, 2000).

A nearly identical theme is evident in the research narrative on the intermediate outcomes displayed in Figure 4.1. Each of the three mediating variables here can enrich or diminish student effort and identification with the school. Social integration has a vibrant association with student engagement (Gonzalez & Padilla, 1997; Newmann, 1992; Voelkl, 1997). We reported above that pastoral care enhances self-concept. Here we add that self-concept, as reflected in measures of competence (Fredricks et al., 2004), "student appraisals of personal skillfulness" (Laffey, 1982, p. 62), and agency (Fredricks et al., 2004; Rodriguez, 2008), is powerfully linked with student engagement. Finally, studies substantiate that the enhancement of learning dispositions such as motivation (Goodenow, 1993; Hattie, 2009; Opdenakker et al., 2012), orientation toward school (Bruggencate et al., 2012; Crosnoe, 2011; Marks, 2000), and persistence (Voelkl, 1997) deepen student engagement.

Learning

School community is significantly related to a large number of desirable outcomes for students. (Battistich et al., 1997, p. 146)

Engagement in meaningful and interesting work and the percep-tion of being cared about and valued provide children with a sense of belonging to the school community which allows them to achieve to their potential. (Baker et al., 1997, p. 590)

Getting Started

The research is consistent and firm in demonstrating a relationship between communities for students and their success in school (Battistich et al., 1997; Demaray & Malecki, 2002b; Rodriguez, 2008), especially in terms of academic and social learning (Allensworth & Easton, 2005; Goodenow, 1993; Rodriguez, 2008). That is, "different school cultures can indeed distinguish consequences for student outcomes" (Witziers et al., 2003, p. 416). At times, these connections are drawn for single elements of the model in Figure 4.1 (e.g., the norm of safety, learning dispositions) (Croninger & Lee, 2001; Lee & Burkam, 2003; Newmann et al., 1989) and in other cases for clusters of the elements (Gamoran, 1996) consistent with the core notion of community, "exchanges of social resources enhance the effectiveness not only of individual actions but also collective actions" (Lee & Burkam, 2003, p. 362). There are also spillover effects here to pro-fessional communities for teachers and communities of engagement for parents.

In some of the research of interest here, the engagement piece of our model is implicit, it remains unhighlighted in the story of student com-munity and learning outcomes. Other studies do, however, throw a bright spotlight on student commitment and effort with engagement operating as the summative catalyst to power final valued outcomes. Fredricks and team (2004, p. 61) make this point explicitly when they conclude "that engagement, once established, builds on itself, thereby contributing to increased improvements in more distal outcomes of interest." Analyses in these studies uncover strong associations, for better or worse, between engagement and academic and social-emotional student development (Bruggencate et al., 2012; Feldman & Matjasko, 2005; Finn & Rock, 1997; Marks, 2000). As highlighted in other sections of this chapter, there is also a good quantity of solid scientific evidence that pastoral care and engage-ment are of particular significance for students in peril, that is, for children from low-income households, for youngsters from subordinated minor-ity groups, and for students on the wrong side of the achievement gap (Croninger & Lee, 2001; Felner et al., 2007; Rumberger, 2011).

Before we explore the specific outcomes that are influenced by engage-ment, it is beneficial to revisit a few key points and introduce the impor-tance of variability in connections between engagement and learning. On the first issue, it is important to once again remind ourselves that it is both academic and social support and press interlinked that carry us to the goal of strong learning outcomes. We also resurface the importance of reciproc-ity and interactiveness throughout the model. Here that means that while strengthened, student engagement produces better student outcomes, better outcomes, in turn, enhance engagement—and the earlier variables in the model as well (e.g., the norm of membership, sense of self).

It is also important to re-acknowledge that our understanding of engagement is comprised of multiple concepts or components, components that can have different effects on various outcomes. And components themselves are often comprised of multiple elements. For example, as discussed above, engagement can occur in three places, classrooms, the school extending beyond the classroom, and extracurricular venues. Extracurricular activities, in turn, include diverse offerings such as sports, academic and nonacademic clubs, student government activities, and so forth. Effects on academic and social outcomes are not the same for each type of activity. Some of these activities are more valuable for one type of outcome, that is, social learning rather than academic learning or vice versa. Within each outcome, there can also be variation. For example, on the matter of academic achievement, engagement in sports may produce stronger results in literacy than mathematics (Leitner, 1994), while the opposite may hold for active participation in school governance. We note also that engagement effects on outcomes are not linear (Marsh & Kleitman, 2002). There is often an optimal amount of participation, a sweet spot if you will. A surfeit of engagement will often produce deteriorating effects.

Finally, it is necessary to direct attention to the meaning of outcome effects. Such effects are almost always registered in terms of enhancements of the outcomes under scrutiny (e.g., better student attendance, higher graduation rates). Our understanding is broader. Positive effects also include breaking downward spirals of achievement and socioemotional states. As Felner and team (2007, p. 215) discovered, this "preventive effect" is essential in the chronicle of communities of pastoral care for students.

Socioemotional and Academic Outcomes

The primary function of schooling is to create positive possibilities for students, an outcome that is often not met, especially in schools with large numbers of students from minority, low-income, and working-class homes (Eckert, 1989; McLaughlin & Talbert, 2001; Weis, 1990). The most important avenue schools have to achieve this goal is to help students reach ambitious targets of social and academic learning. This, of course, is the essential rationale for fostering and nurturing communities of pastoral care for students.

Social learning. On the socio-emotional dimension, pastoral care is associated with both personal and social adjustment (Ancess, 2003). Included here are outcomes such as prosocial values and reasoning (Baker et al., 1997; Battistich et al., 1997), emotional well-being (e.g., mental health and psychological adjustment) (Feldman & Matjasko, 2005; Felner et al., 2007), satisfaction with school (Baker et al., 1997), and effective social skills (Demaray & Malecki, 2002a).

When attending to social-emotional outcomes, scholars focus heavily on what Guest and Schneider (2003, p. 89) and Birch and Ladd (1997, p. 78) respectively call "social adjustment" and "school adjustment." This concept can be partitioned into three subareas. The first is the well documented power of a cooperative culture to reduce behavioral risks, risks often linked to limited sense of community membership, or what Crosnoe (2011, p. 128) refers to as "not fitting in socially." Particularly salient here, according to Crosnoe (2011, p. 103), is the link between positive culture and the prevention of "coping responses that are self-protective in the short term but are problematic, even disastrous, in the long term," that is, counterproductive coping strategies such as depression and withdrawal.

A second, and related, function is the ability of community to "constrain and prevent delinquent behavior" (Maguin & Loeber, 1996), to damp down misbehavior (Felner et al., 2007; Osterman, 2000; Rumberger, 2011). For example, in her comprehensive review of student community, Osterman (2000) reports that pastoral care is negatively correlated with student use of illegal drugs and delinquency. Similar conclusions on behavioral problems have been documented by others as well (Bloomberg et al., 2003; Catalano et al., 1999; Goddard & Goff, 1999), including Demaray and Malecki (2002a, p. 235) whose "results provide strong evidence to suggest that there is a negative relationship between the amount of social support students perceive and the amount of problem behavior in which they are engaging." Research affirms also that damping down misbehavior extends to attendance issues, such as skipping classes, and truancy (Felner et al., 2007; Fredricks et al., 2004; Quint, 2006).

The third aspect of social and school adjustment addresses the ways by which positive student community nurtures the development and growth of social skills. Marsh and Kleitman (2002) highlight effects on character and social adeptness. Feldman and Matjasko (2005, p. 191) note that pastoral care leads to stronger community engagement later in life.

Academic outcomes. Two overlapping academic outcomes are linked to communities for students in the research, best captured under the broad heading of "positive academic behaviors" (Croninger & Lee, 2001, p. 565). The first is attainment. The second is achievement.

Attainment. One set of data here are collected in the two-sided ledger of dropping out and graduation. Investigators report vibrant linkages between pastoral care in general and these two indices of effectiveness. It is widely documented that anemic amounts of community, defined by relationships, norms, institutional affiliation, and engagement, are highly associated with students not finishing high school (Balfanz et al., 2007; Farrell, 1990; Ma, 2003)—college as well (Braxton, Hirschy, & McClendon, 2011).

Students who are engaged in school, whether in the academic arena or the social arena, are more likely to attend, to learn, and eventually to finish high school; students who are disengaged are not. Research studies have measured engagement in several ways, but no matter how it is measured, the level of engagement predicts dropping out. (Rumberger, 2011, p. 168)

Conversely, through the chain of action presented in Figure 4.1, the presence of supportive communities promotes graduation (Alexander et al., 1997; Balfanz et al., 2007; Croninger & Lee, 2001). Relationships are linked to school completion, reducing the likelihood of leaving school early by nearly half (Croninger & Lee, 2001). The community norms and intermediate outcomes in Figure 4.1 are also implicated in the narrative of school completion (Croninger & Lee, 2001; Fredricks et al., 2004; Lee & Burkham, 2003; Osterman, 2000; Patterson et al., 2007; Rumberger, 2011). So too is the critical bridging variable of student engagement, with "dropping out consistently linked to disengagement" (Balfanz et al., 2007, p. 225) and "engagement leading to higher retention rates" (Bruggencate et al., 2012, p. 703). We close with the recognition that the three aspects of school and social adjustment—reducing behavioral risks, constraining misbehavior, and developing social skills, are deeply intertwined (Balfanz et al., 2007). They are also tightly linked to the indicators of achievement we explore below.

A sibling of high school graduation is "academic progress," how effective students are in earning the academic credits they need to be successful, including promotion between grades, what Crosnoe (2011, p. 106) refers to as "the accumulation of valued academic credentials." We find here again that there are quite meaningful associations between communities of pastoral care (i.e., relationships, norms, institutional affiliation, engagement) and academic progress (Balfanz et al., 2007; Patterson et al., 2007). According to Crosnoe (2011), the long-term effects of interfering with progress starting in the early grades is of special concern.

A third measure of attainment addresses college enrollment. As with the other two indicators of attainment, academic progress and high school graduation, communities rich in positive relationships of care and support open doors to college. Students with less productive relationships with their teachers and peers and those who are marginalized and/or disengaged in high school are less likely to enroll in institutions of higher education.

Academic achievement. Not surprisingly, although there are some cautions in the literature about tunnel vision (Csikszentmihalyi & Larson, 1984), most of the findings on outcomes of communities for students are in the domain of academic achievement. While the storyline here is not completely cloudless (see Battistich et al., 1995; Bryk et al., 2010; and Quint, 2006 for some cautionary notes), the cumulative weight of the evidence leads to the conclusion that there are robust connections between the early pieces of the model in Figure 4.1 and academic achievement (Hoy et al., 1998; Roney et al., 2007) and, not surprisingly given the discussion above, that there is an even stronger bond between the final two pieces of the model, engagement and achievement.

Focusing in on relationships, a good deal of research connects "familial-type environments" (Antrop-Gonzalez, 2006, p. 289) and academic success (Conchas, 2001; Sebastian & Allensworth, 2012; Sweeney, 1982). Theorists have posited and researches have documented that strong relationships help, indirectly, students learn more than when those relationships are absent, or worse, negative (Ancess, 2003; Hattie, 2009; Leithwood et al., 2010). Closeness matters for student learning (Birch & Ladd, 1997). Relationships "constitute a form of social capital that is of value in children's academic success" (Goddard, 2003, p. 59). In a parallel manner, analysts also confirm that there are vibrant indirect linkages between the norms that define student-teacher and student-peer relationships and academic success. Care (Adams & Forsyth, 2009; Antrop-Gonzalez, 2006; Ma, 2003), support (Balfanz et al., 1997; Conchas, 2001), safety (Newmann et al., 1989; Robinson et al., 2008; Wilson & Corbett, 1999), and membership (Crosnoe, 2011; Ma, 2003; Voelkl, 1997) are each implicated in this finding. The same conclusion holds for the intermediate outcomes, each of which—social integration (Marsh & Kleitman, 2002), self-concept (Hallinan & Kubitschek, 1999; Rothman & Cosden, 1995), and learning dispositions (Hattie, 2009; Marsh & Kleitman, 1992)—is associated with academic success.

Turning to the last link in the model, we uncover a familiar theme. The benefits of education require activities that "elicit and maintain involvement" (Laffey, 1982, p. 62). When this occurs, scholars uniformly demonstrate "a positive correlation" between engagement and "achievement-related outcomes" (Fredricks et al., 2004, p. 70). This finding holds for all types of children (Feldman & Matjasko, 2005; Osterman, 2000; Voelkl, 1997), or as Marks (2000, p. 155) says, "across diverse populations." Of course, the obverse is true as well, "lack of engagement adversely effects student achievement" (Marks, 2000, p. 155). Returning to the positive side of the ledger, we find evidence that engagement that fuels achievement may induce "a positive self-confirming cycle supportive of continued engagement" (Balfanz et al., 2007, p. 230) and aspirations for further achievement (Guest & Schneider, 2003; Marsh & Kleitman, 2002). We also uncover confirmatory evidence that these positive gains in academic performance stretch across a variety of assessments, for example, grades, scores on standardized tests, and measures of deeper understanding (Crosnoe, 2011; Fredricks et al., 2004; Voelkl, 1997).

CONCLUSION

The focus of this volume is productive school culture, culture that enhances student and academic learning. We address culture through the lens of community, creating communities of pastoral care for students, communities of professionalism for teachers, and communities of engagement for parents and those in the extended school environment. In this chapter, we explored what a community of pastoral care looks like and how it functions. The heart of this narrative is seen in Figure 4.1. We turn in the next two chapters to exploring communities of professionalism for teachers.

5

Communities of Professional Practice for Teachers

It is important not only to help individual staff members become technically more effective, but deliberately to build the collective schoolwide ethos. (Newmann, Rutter, & Smith, 1989, p. 221)

The future of schools depends on the successful implementation of the learning organisation paradigm which requires the full participation and involvement of teachers. (Silins & Mulford, 2004, p. 462)

An increasing body of research suggests that real change in schools requires the development of strong professional communities. (Spillane & Louis, 2002)

At the heart of this volume is the assertion that great schools build powerful educational programs and learning cultures and that principals play an essential role in the construction processes (see Figure 1.1). In the last chapter, we focused on culture for students, culture reflected in communities of support. In this part of the book, we address professional culture, culture reflected in collaborative communities of professional practice. In the balance of this introductory section, we discuss the "seed-bed" from which professional culture is growing as well as what some of the flowers look like when they have emerged. We provide definitions and list well-known frameworks of the components of professional learning communities. The bulk of the chapter is then devoted to presenting and unpacking our model of community of professionalism for teachers. We integrate a discussion of the logic of how community works with the essential ingredients of the model.

ROOTS OF PROFESSIONAL LEARNING CULTURE

> PLC seems to have emerged from a variety of sources. (Stoll, Bolam, McMahon, Wallace, & Thomas, 2006, p. 233)

Seedbed Changes in Education

Professional culture in schools has been deepened and enriched by two of the deep alterations in the foundation of schooling that we examined in Chapter 2. Absent shifts in how we think about learning and the organization of schooling, the seeds of community would never grow. You will remember that at the technical core level, there has been a discernible shift from teaching to learning. Also, behaviorally anchored understandings of learning and transmission models of teaching are being replaced, or at least joined, by social learning and constructed models of instruction. We also examined how the organizational scaffolding of schooling is being rebuilt using different materials. Management slabs taken from the bureaucratic quarry are being replaced with stone taken from the quarry of community (Beck & Foster, 1999; Scribner et al., 1994).

Concepts From Other Fields

Four bodies of work have given substance and shape to the concept of professional communities of practice in education. All are anchored on social understandings of learning and community-grounded perspectives of organization. One is the emergence of the importance of "social capital," an idea generally attributed to James Coleman (see Penuel, Riel, Krause, & Frank, 2009; Spillane, Hallett, & Diamond, 2003). A second is the theory of "learning organizations," first formally fleshed out by Senge in 1990 (see Mitchell & Sackney, 2006; Vescio et al., 2008). A third is the expanding body of knowledge on the importance of "teams" in highly effective organizations (Pounder, 1999). The last is the development of the concept of "communities of practice," a framework forged by Lave and Wenger in the 1990s (Wenger, 1998, 2000).

DEFINITIONS AND MODELS

Communities of practice are groups of people informally bound together by shared expertise and passion for a joint enterprise. (Wenger & Snyder, 2000, p. 139)

Communities of practice consist of members who share values and interests, who engage in shared activity, and who produce shared resources in the process. (Printy, 2008, p. 190)

Definitions

There are a variety of definitions of professional community in play in the educational research and development worlds (Saunders, Goldenberg, & Gallimore, 2009). While there is no universal definition (Morrissey, 2000), there is, fortunately, a great deal of overlap in the various perspectives (Stoll et al., 2006). We highlight three representative definitions below.

A joint effort to generate new knowledge of practice and the mutual support of each other's professional growth. (McLaughlin & Talbert, 2001, p. 75)

A group of people sharing and critically interrogating their practice in an ongoing reflective, collaborative, inclusive, learning-oriented, growth-promoting way. (Stoll et al., 2006, p. 223)

A professional community, therefore, is one where teachers participate in decision making, have a shared sense of purpose, engage in collaborative work and accept joint responsibility for the outcomes of their work. (Harris, 2003, p. 321)

Numerous terms are used in the research and development branches of the educational family to capture the idea of shared work toward a common vision (Dufour & Eaker, 1992), almost all of which do justice to core ideas such as a focus on the human aspect of schooling (Curry, 2008), "common enterprise" (Levine & Marcus, 2007, p. 122), and shared responsibility (Curry, 2008)—community of teachers (Grossman et al., 2001), teacher learning community (McLaughlin & Talbert, 2001), inquiry communities (Cochran-Smith & Lytle, 1999), discussion networks (Bidwell & Yasumoto, 1999), communities of practice (Penuel et al., 2009), communities of knowing (Craig, 2009), community of instructional practice (Spillane, Halverson, & Diamond, 2001), professional learning communities (Dufour & Eaker, 1998), communities of commitment (Ancess, 2003), professional communities (Curry, 2008), communities of continuous inquiry and improvement (Stoll et al., 2006), and so forth.

These collectives take a variety of forms in schools. The full school may become a "macro-professional community" (Curry, 2008, p. 737). Schools may also have "micro-professional communities" (p. 737) such as critical friends groups, department and grade-level groups, action research teams, study groups, inquiry groups, learning teams, and so forth (Ermeling, 2010; Mullen & Hutinger, 2008). They can extend beyond the school as well (Spillane et al., 2003). We know that these communities can be naturally occurring (see Wenger, 1998) or designed by leaders in the organization (Printy, 2008). They can form, or be created, around curricular content, problems, functions, unit of work, and so forth (Saunders et al., 2009). Individuals can and often are members of multiple communities of practice (Palincsar et al., 1998; Wenger, 2000). It is important to remember through all this description that professional community "is not a thing, it is a way of operating" (Morrissey, 2000, p. 23).

Existing Frameworks

Analysts from various branches of the educational family (e.g., educational leadership, teaching and learning, special education) over the last quarter century have committed themselves to understanding and spreading professional communities. Some of the seminal work here has been provided by Seashore Louis and Kruse, Little, Hord, Newmann, Grossman, Dufour, and McLaughlin and Talbert. In Table 5.1, we outline the essential elements of professional learning communities as uncovered by these and other scholars.

Table 5.1   Core Elements of Communities of Professional Practice

Authors	Elements
Ancess (2003)	• common ethos and vision • caring and caregiving • will and capacity for struggle • mutual accountability • reciprocity • mutual interest • attachment • commonality • ownership • shared values • common experience • sense of belonging • mutual concern and support • ownership • habits of cooperation

Authors	Elements
Battistich, Solomon, Watson, and Schaps (1997)	• collegiality • involvement • shared goals and values • caring and support
Hord (1997)	• shared values and vision • collective learning • supportive conditions • shared leadership • shared practice
Bryk, Sebring, Allensworth, Luppescu, and Easton (2010)	• social learning • collective responsibility • collaboration • public work • critical dialogue
Grossman, Wineburg, and Woolworth (2001)	• sense of shared identity • shared values • common language • control
Kruse, Seashore Louis, and Bryk (1995)	• shared values • reflective dialogue • deprivatization of practice • focus on student learning • collaboration
Leithwood, Louis, Anderson, and Wahlstrom (2004)	• client oreintation • knowledge focus • inquiry and reflection • personal connections
Mulford and Silins (2003)	• shared norms and values • deprivatization of practice • collaboration • critical reflective dialogue • continuous learning • evidence-based dialogue
Newmann, King, and Youngs (2000)	• shared goals for student learning • collaboration • collective responsibility • influence • professional inquiry

(Continued)

Table 5.1   (Continued)

Authors	Elements
Rowan and Miller (2007)	• trust and respect • critical discourse • collaboration
Spillane, Halverson, and Diamond (2001)	• trust • collaboration • obligation
Wenger (2000)	• sense of joint enterprise • mutuality • shared repertoire of resources
Youngs and King (2002)	• shared goals for student learning • collaboration • inquiry • influence

MODEL AND THEORY OF ACTION: THE ESSENTIAL ELEMENTS

> The theory of action underlying the development of teacher communities is that the fostering of these kinds of communities will instigate improvements in the quality of instruction, which will lead to enhanced student learning. (Supovitz & Christman, 2003, p. 1)

> Learning communities are grounded in two assumptions. First, it is assumed that knowledge is situated in the day-to-day lived experiences of teachers and best understood through critical reflection with others who share the same experience. Second, it is assumed that actively engaging teachers in PLCs will increase their professional knowledge and enhance student learning. (Vescio et al., 2008, p. 81)

Based on the extensive work completed in this area over the last two decades, we have forged a model to explain how professional culture comes to life in communities of practice. Our model is contained in Figure 5.1. On the *what* side, a professional learning culture is characterized by six core elements. It is these ingredients that define professional learning culture and produce the social control and social capital needed to promote teacher learning and foster the growth of professional norms (Bidwell & Yasumoto, 1999; Spillane, Halverson, & Diamond, 2001).

On the *how* side, we see that a community of practice works by adding capital to the school. One dimension of this capital is knowledge. Thus professional community promotes learning, intellectual capital (e.g., deeper content knowledge, enriched pedagogical skills). The other dimension is professional cultural capital. A community of practice deepens professional norms and accompanying attitudes (e.g., commitment). Note also that the capital accumulating in both of these areas is of two types, that accruing to individuals (i.e., human capital) and that accruing to the group (i.e., social capital). Both are important. However, it is the emphasis on social capital development that distinguishes practice communities from many other reforms.

Increased capital, in turn, leads to changes in the ways teachers conduct their work with students. Practice is improved in two core fields of action, classroom climate and instruction. More effective instruction and an enhanced climate lead to better learning outcomes for students.

In the balance of the chapter, we explore the model in Figure 5.1 in considerable detail. Before we do so, however, it is important to draw attention to the interrelated, reciprocal nature of the framework. For example, while professional norms influence teacher practice and student outcomes, they also influence the essential elements of community (King, 2001; Olivier & Hipp, 2006; Tschannen-Moran & Barr, 2004). In short, energy flows in both directions in the model across the columns, left to right and right to left (Bryk et al., 2010; Levine & Marcus, 2007; MacBeath, 2009), what Goddard and team (2000, p. 483) call "reciprocal causality" and Heck and Hallinger (2009, p. 681) refer to as "mutually reinforcing constructs." We note that energy flows among concepts within each

Figure 5.1   Communities of Professional Practice for Teachers

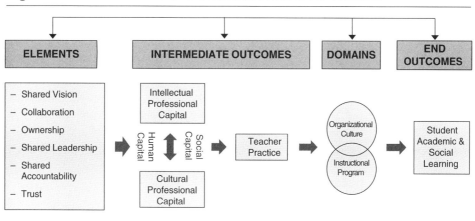

column as well. For example, in the "elements" column, shared accountability shapes shared values and collaborative work. Energy flows up
and down the model as well as in both directions across the framework.
Communities of practice are, to use the language of Strahan (2003, p. 130),
"spirals of reform activities."

> Teachers work collaboratively to identify priorities for school
> improvement and initiate conversations about instruction. As
> they do so, they target areas for instructional improvement and
> coordinate their efforts to implement shared instructional strate-
> gies. These coordinated efforts enhance student achievement and
> strengthen the professional learning community. Consequently, the
> school provides more social support for learning; school culture
> grows more collaborative; and teachers develop strong collective
> efficacy. (p. 130)

It is also important to acknowledge that professional community
provides an integrative framework. It is not so much a reform as it is a
caldron for the infusing and mixing of professional norms and for pushing change efforts into the collaborative work of teachers (Huberman
et al., 2011; Stoll et al., 2006)—"a verb rather than a noun" (Grossman
et al., 2001, p. 68). Finally, a number of analysts report that well-functioning
professional communities have fusion-like properties. Once set in motion,
they have a self-generating dynamic, what Newmann and colleagues
(1989, p. 224) refer to as an "interactive, progressive cycle" and Tichy
and Cardwell (2004, p. 7) call a "virtuous teaching cycle." The father of
communities of practice makes this point explicitly when he reports that

> the strength of communities of practice is self-perpetuating. As
> they generate knowledge, they reinforce and renew themselves.
> That's why communities of practice give you not only the golden
> eggs but also the goose that lays them. (Wenger & Snyder, 2000,
> p. 143)

Shared Vision

> Shared values are an important characteristic of professional com-
> munities. (Visscher & Witziers, 2004, p. 789)

> Without a core of shared beliefs about institutional purposes, prac-
> tices, and desired behaviors, the other elements of professional
> community cannot emerge. (Kruse et al., 1995, p. 29)

At the broadest level, vision is about moral purpose and possibilities (Auerbach, 2007; Barnett et al., 2001; Day, 2005), concepts forged from values and beliefs that define the instructional program and shape school climate in ways that enhance student learning (Creemers & Reezigt, 1996; Dinham, 2005; Siu, 2008). Mission is the bedrock of school improvement with large (Dufour & Eaker, 1992; Fullan, 1982, 1993, 2002) and professional communities specifically (Kruse et al., 1995; Louis, Dretzke, & Wahlstrom, 2010). Schools do not progress well without it (Borman, 2005; Leithwood, 2005; Riester et al., 2002). Indeed, "without a shared vision . . . the various trajectories of learning that occur may have little synergy or coherence and thus may not have a powerful positive impact on teaching and learning" (Levine & Marcus, 2007, p. 134). Below, we examine three levels of vision: mission, goals, and expectations.

Mission

Researchers have harvested important clues about how mission serves school improvement. Mission influences the instructional program and the learning climate, which, in turn, shape the behaviors of teachers and students (Murphy, 2013b). As Mitchell and Sackney (2006) found, because schools are loosely coupled systems (see Cohen, March, & Olsen, 1972; Meyer & Rowan, 1975; Weick, 1976) they lack clear goals. In such situations, there is a natural tendency for effort to splinter and for community to lay fallow, effects only exacerbated by the frenetic nature of schooling. Mission begins to tighten systems by establishing the boundaries in which "schooling" occurs (Murphy, Hallinger, & Mesa, 1985a). Mission coheres means (Louis & Miles, 1990, 1991; Morrissey, 2000) and ends (Hallinger & Heck, 1998; Louis et al., 2010) around shared values and beliefs (Levine & Marcus, 2010; Silins & Mulford, 2004).

It is important to note that not all school missions harness equal amounts of energy (Barnett & McCormick, 2004; Mitchell & Sackney, 2006; Scheurich, 1998). From our analysis, we distill eight core ideas that anchor the strong missions that help define professional culture, those that consistently direct the school into productive channels of collaborative work. To begin with, the mission needs to convey *a sense of hope,* to open the door of possibility (Brookover et al., 1979; Murphy, 1996; Olivier & Hipp, 2006). As Leithwood and colleagues (Leithwood, Jantzi, & Steinbach, 1999; Yu, Leithwood, & Jantzi, 2002) instruct us, missions should be inspirational. They need to convey a palpable sense that through collective engagement, conditions (e.g., low levels of success, disaffiliation) are malleable and that improvement is possible, even likely (McLaughlin & Talbert, 2001; Oakes & Guiton, 1995; Scheurich, 1998).

Table 5.2   Core Elements of Mission in Effective Schools

Sense of hope
Norm of commitment
Asset-based thinking
Student focus
Academic anchoring
Outcome focus
Norm of continuous improvement
Norm of collective responsibility

In addition, as indicated in Table 5.2, mission in teacher communities should address *commitment to success* (Bryk et al., 2010; Louis & Miles, 1991; Timperley, 2009) and to the work that such commitment entails (Blair, 2002; Olivier & Hipp, 2006; Riehl & Sipple, 1996). This encompasses the understanding that second best is insufficient (Dinham, 2005; Raywid, 1995; Southworth, 2002) and the conviction that the school can and will improve (Bryk et al., 2010; Riester et al., 2002; Strahan, 2003). In a related vein, mission should reflect the belief that all students will be success-ful (Eilers & Camacho, 2007; Gurr, Drysdale, & Mulford, 2005; Lezotte, Hathaway, Miller, Passalacque, & Brookover, 1980). That is, no one is permitted to fail. The embedded understanding is that schooling is the game changer for students (Bryk et al., 2010; Cotton, 2003; Raywid, 1995), a conviction and moral imperative about success (Dinham, 2005; Edmonds, 1979; Raywid, 1995).

Relatedly, mission should reflect *asset-based thinking* about students and the larger community (Auerbach, 2007, 2009). As Edmonds (1979) and Brookover and colleagues (1977, 1978, 1979) reported at the begin-ning of the modern era of school improvement (see also Purkey & Smith, 1983), this third core idea pushes back against the deficit-based thinking often found in struggling or failing schools and schools with large num-bers of students placed at risk (Murphy, 2010a; Rutter et al., 1979; Scanlan & Lopez, 2012). It is anchored on the belief that all students are capable of learning, that the school does not underestimate the abilities and effi-cacy of children (DuFour & Eaker, 1992; Goldenberg, 2004; Lezotte et al., 1980). Assets-based thinking means not accommodating instruction to preconceived assumptions of limitations but rather conducting schools in ways that change students' abilities and interests (Murphy, 1989; Oakes & Guiton, 1995). Optimism rather than pessimism holds the high ground (Edmonds, 1979; Theoharis, 2007). Problems and failure are not attrib-uted to children and their families (McDougall et al., 2007; Murphy, 1992;

Theoharis, 2007). Deficiencies are not assumed (Blair, 2002). Negative attitudes are conspicuous by their absence (Cooper, 1996). Constraints are recognized, but they are challenged as impediments to success (Gurr et al., 2005; Leithwood et al., 1999; Murphy, 2013a). Schools push back on resistance to norms of success proactively, not reactively (Cotton, 2003; Crum & Sherman, 2008; Murphy, 1996).

Student focus is the fourth core element in mission. Student-centered values hold the high ground in schools with strong cultures of professionalism (McLaughlin & Talbert, 2001). The spotlight is on children and youth (Eilers & Camacho, 2007), what is in the best interests of students (Gurr et al., 2005; Johnson & Asera, 1999). Concretely, that means developing professional culture that features ideology (Blair, 2002; Caldwell, 1998; May & Supovitz, 2006) in context of the specific youngsters in the school (Leithwood et al., 1999).

Fifth, a mission in a school with strong professional community is *academically anchored* (Hoy, Hannum, & Tschannen-Moran, 1998; May & Supovitz, 2011; Venezky & Winfield, 1979). Mission highlights student learning (Blase & Blase, 2004; Orr, Berg, Shore, & Meier, 2008) and academic success (Dinham, 2005; Hallinger, Bickman, & Davis, 1996). An academically anchored mission focuses the community on the instructional program (Cotton, 2000; Murphy, Beck, Crawford, Hodges, & McGaughy, 2001; Supovitz et al., 2010). Teaching and learning hold center stage and better instruction is job one (Collins & Valentine, 2010; Gurr et al., 2006).

Learning-community schools have *outcome-focused* missions (Supovitz & Poglinco, 2001). These outcomes feature measures of student learning in general (Leithwood, 2005) and provide markers of student achievement in particular (Hallinger & Heck, 1998; Timperley, 2009; Waters et al., & 2003). Missions in schools with robust teacher communities highlight the idea of *continuous improvement* (Ancess, 2003; Crum & Sherman, 2008; Jackson, 2000). Norms of complacency are challenged. Risk taking is promoted and there is an appetite for change (Blair, 2002; Foster & St. Hilaire, 2003; Louis & Miles, 1991). Finally, when strong professional culture is in place, mission carries the seeds of *collective responsibility* (Edmonds, 1979; Huberman et al., 2011). A culture of accountability emerges (Barker, 2001; May & Supovitz, 2006) replacing traditions of externalizing responsibility (Bryk et al., 2010; Spillane, Diamond, Walker, Halverson, & Jita, 2001; May & Supovitz, 2006). Success is a collective endeavor of the community (McLaughlin & Talbert, 2001).

Goals

Our analysis suggests the goals for teacher professional communities should be defined by critical markers. The most essential of these is a focus on the academic domain in general and on student learning in particular (Barnes et al., 2010; Spillane, Halverson, & Diamond, 2001). Robinson and associates (2008) remind us that goals are most productive when they are specific, not generic.

Supovitz and Poglinco (2001, pp. 3–4) make this point as well, concluding that while generic goals can be a starting point, the "exponential value comes from a marriage of intensive organizational focus on instructional improvement with a clear vision of instructional quality." Barnett and McCormick (2004) call this a "task focus," and Strahan (2003) refers to it as a specific "stance about learning." Goldenberg (2004) weighs in, arguing that the critical issue is establishing a clear notion of what the school is attempting to accomplish is explicit. Thus "academic focus" and "learning stance" are essential (Blase & Kirby, 2009; Brewer, 1993; Robinson et al., 2008). They positively impact student achievement (Barnes et al., 2010; McDougall et al., 2007; Silins & Mulford, 2004). Robinson (2007) drives these points home when she asserts that academic goal focus needs to become an explicit dimension of school culture with large and professional communities of practice in particular.

Implicitly and explicitly, other cardinal elements can be discerned in analyses of academic learning focus. We discover, for example, that goals are best when the spotlight is on students (Leithwood et al., 1999; Rutherford, 1985; Wimpelberg, 1986), when there is a children first perspective and when student achievement is the central theme (Clark et al., 1980; Robinson et al., 2008; Wynne, 1980). Researchers also inform us that the goals that are found in well-functioning professional communities are challenging but achievable (Cotton, 2003; Leithwood & Jantzi, 2005) and apply to all students (Louis & Miles, 1991; Murphy 1990). Goals that work well are meaningful to the community (Dinham, 2005; Leithwood & Jantzi, 2000b; Murphy et al., 2001). Meaningfulness includes knowledge of, internalization of, and group ownership of goals (Blanc, Christman, Liu, Mitchell, Travers, & Bulkley, 2010; Goldenberg, 2004; Supovitz & Poglinco, 2001).

Almost every study of school improvement has concluded that goals need to be clear and concrete (Blase & Kirby, 2009; Goldenberg, 2004; Ogden & Germinario, 1995), not abstract or subject to interpretation (Brewer, 1993; Gray et al., 1999; Robinson, 2007). They should provide "stakes in the ground" indicating the destination for the learning community and the way to travel (Murphy, Elliott, Goldring, & Porter, 2007). Parsimony and simplicity are desirable (Lomotey, 1989; Newmann et al., 2001). Scholars also report that goal clarity in productive professional communities directs the allocation and development of human and financial resources (Gray et al., 1999; Huberman et al., 2011; Wilson & Corcoran, 1988). Recent studies of teaching communities have also identified the importance of tailoring goals to the specific needs of students in a given school (Ancess, 2000; Wohlstetter, Datnow, & Park, 2008). Short-term goals that move the school to larger ends are desirable (Cotton, 2003) as they permit staff to experience reinforcing, short-term wins (Bryk et al., 2010; Johnson & Asera, 1999). It is important, however, that these short-term wins derive from and support the more encompassing mission of the school (Leithwood & Montgomery, 1982; Robinson et al., 2008).

Analyses across time also reveal important insights about the ways in which goals are forged in schools with robust professional cultures. One critical discovery is the importance of a process that fosters ownership of goals (Leithwood, Day, et al., 2006). What is particularly important is the creation of ownership of the work to reach goals and responsibility for the results of those efforts, a recurring theme in our analysis of a culture of professionalism (Leithwood, Jantzi, & McElheron-Hopkins, 2006; Murphy, 1992). Wide participation of community stakeholders and reliance on hard data to arrive at decisions should also define goal development (Datnow, Park, & Kennedy, 2008; Murphy, 1990).

We close this part of our analysis with a note on what that research tells us about how goals function to improve student learning in schools characterized by a culture of professionalism. At a fundamental level, goals adhering to the description above provide tangible meaning to the school mission (Bryman, 2004; Leithwood, Louis, Anderson, & Wahlstrom, 2004; Supovitz & Poglinco, 2001). In so doing, they solidify community action around shared values and purpose (Leithwood & Jantzi, 2000b; Robinson, 2007). As such, they help people see more clearly. They keep a professional community from becoming distracted by separating the really important work from the balance of activity (Goldenberg, 2004; McDougall et al., 2007). Effort becomes more focused and more productive (Louis & Miles, 1991). Goals also serve as a powerful mechanism for organizational cohesion (Goldring & Pasternack, 1994; Robinson, 2007), helping teachers collectively to coordinate action (Bryk et al., 2010; McDougall et al., 2007; Robinson et al., 2008).

Strong goals can be powerful motivators for staff (Datnow et al., 2008; Geijsel et al., 2003; Leithwood, Jantzi, & McElheron-Hopkins, 2006), encouraging educators to reach for higher standards (Ancess, 2000; Barnett & McCormick, 2004). Goals have been shown to have an energizing effect (Leithwood et al., 1999; Newmann, 1992). They also have the potential to strengthen professionalism by helping dismantle the wall between teaching and school administration (Lomotey, 1989; Murphy, 2005). Shared work, in turn, can strengthen commitment and responsibility (Hallinger & Heck, 1998; Youngs & King, 2002).

Expectations

Expectations are the third layer of school vision. They make even more concrete the understandings of performance for professional teacher communities (Day, 2005; Mulford & Silins, 2003). They create a platform to bring goals to life (Goldenberg, 2004). They are both a measure of (Brookover et al., 1979) and a method to develop academic press in the school (Edmonds & Frederiksen, 1978; Goldenberg, 1996).

Over the last 35 years, researchers have shown that high expectations widely shared have important organizational consequences (Miller, 1995; Magnuson & Duncan, 2006; Shannon & Bylsma, 2002). Most important, they differentiate between more and less effective schools, with higher academic expectations linked to better outcomes, outcomes defined in terms of student learning (Bryk et al., 2010; Christle, Jolivette, & Nelson, 2005; Rutter et al., 1979). They work in part by helping to shape school culture in general and professional norms and organizational learning in particular (Brookover et al., 1978; Hallinger & Heck, 1998; Leithwood et al., 1999). Expectations have their largest impact on children on the wrong side of the achievement gap, especially children from low-income families (Hughes, 2003; Meehan, Cowley, Schumacher, Hauser, & Croom, 2003; Murphy, 2010a).

Expectations help professional communities define understandings of quality in concrete terms (Leithwood & Jantzi, 2000a). According to Leithwood and colleagues (1999, p. 69) who have examined this issue in considerable depth,

> expectations of this sort help teachers see the challenging nature of the goals being pursued in their school. They may also sharpen teachers' perceptions of the gap between what the school aspires to and what is presently being accomplished. Done well, expressions of high expectations also result in perceptions among teachers that what is being expected is also feasible.

High expectations convey in tangible fashion the hard work and improvement required by a community of teachers to create a school where all youngsters reach ambitious targets of performance (Barnett & McCormick, 2004). They can energize community to keep student improvement in the spotlight (Leithwood et al., 1999; Leithwood, Day, et al., 2006; McLaughlin & Talbert, 2001). At the heart of the success equation here are consistency and repetition of expectations (Blase & Kirby, 2009; Kochanek, 2005) that mediate the work of professional communities of learning (Hallinan, 2001; Hughes, 2003).

Collaboration

> Learning communities are characterized by a collaborative work culture. (Mitchell & Sackney, 2006, p. 628)

> The notion of professional communities implies that teaching is a joint effort. (Visscher & Witziers, 2004, p. 789)

> Productive communities are those whose members refine their practice in collaboration with close teaching colleagues. (Printy, 2008, p. 200)

We continue our analysis of what Horn (2005, p. 230) refers to as the "conceptual infrastructure" of teacher community by turning the spotlight on collaboration. Ermeling (2010, p. 386) defines collaboration as a "joint productive activity where participants assist each other to solve a common problem or produce a common product." Because it is more tangible than other elements of community (e.g., vision, trust) and often provides the backdrop on which the elements come to life, it occupies disproportionate space in the community of practice narrative. For collaboration to be productive, shifts in how teachers think about, talk about, and go about their work are required (Cotton, 2003; Drago-Severson, 2004; Levine & Marcus, 2010). It rests on the understanding that what teachers do outside their classrooms is as important as what unfolds inside those settings (McLaughlin & Talbert, 2001; Stoll et al., 2006) and that collective work done well can accelerate their learning and the achievement of their students (Heck & Hallinger, 2009; Supovitz, 2002).

An assortment of researchers have crafted robust frameworks to expose the dimension of collaboration. For example, for McLaughlin and Talbert, (2001, p. 41) "teachers are mutually engaged in teaching; they jointly develop their practice; and they share a repertoire of resources and history." For Printy (2008, p. 199), the following are all important pieces of collaborative effort: "the range of activities available for participation, the quality of members' participation as legitimate or peripheral, the rules for social interaction of members, and the joint understanding of the work that brings individuals together." More generally, Wenger (1998, 2000) describes collaboration as an algorithm of events, commitments, membership, and tasks. From our analysis, we assert that the power of professional communities of practice can be measured by how well the subelements of engagement—purpose, structure, focus, and nature—adhere to known quality criteria. More concretely, we find that effective collaboration is mutual, purpose-driven work. It is learning centered and instructionally focused. It is driven by the tenets of evidence-based inquiry. And it is directed to improved teacher practice and student achievement via teacher learning.

Purpose of Engagement: Improvement

Effective collaboration is defined by clear purpose, "persistently working toward detectable improvements" (Ermeling, 2010, p. 378). The work itself is the avenue to improvement, not the outcome (Ermeling, 2010). Effectiveness plays out in the application of a teacher's learning practice (Cochran-Smith & Lytle, 1999). What Wenger (1998, 2000) refers to as the "purpose of shared enterprise" (1998, p. 45) pivots on clear measures of outcomes benchmarked against expectations (Louis, 2007) or common goals (Johnson & Asera, 1999) and compelling direction (Fullan, 2002).

Structure and Organization of Engagement: Mutuality.

"Work together" is most usefully elaborated as an array of specific interactions by which teachers discuss, plan for, design, conduct, analyze, evaluate, and experiment with the business of teaching. (Little, 1982, p. 338)

Mutuality provides the structure or frame of collaboration, the process of joint work (Johnson & Asera, 1999; Supovitz et al., 2010). It is grounded on the understanding that relationships are the heart and soul of community (Bryk et al., 2010; Gronn, 2009; Sergiovanni, 1994). One of the fathers of communities of practice, Wenger, talks about "mutual engagement" (2000, p. 229) and "shared enterprise" (1998, p. 45). Colleagues in education refer to mutuality as group practice, changing a roster of individuals into a collaboration of "relational cultures" (Drago-Severson, 2004, p. 40), "joint enterprise" (Young, 2006, p. 538), and "joint identity" (Grossman et al., 2001, p. 63) featuring a "culture of collaboration" (Southworth, 2002, p. 88), "collective engagement" (Visscher & Witziers, 2004, p. 786), and a "process of participation" (Horn, 2005, p. 211). In this chapter, we focus on understanding the dynamics of shared enterprise. In Chapter 6, we turn the spotlight on the barriers to the development of collaborative work and the "mechanisms that enhance and extend the art of working collaboratively" (Olivier & Hipp, 2006, p. 513).

Mutuality according to Printy (2008) requires that members be advantaged by access to the resources of the group and that they add to that capacity (Heller & Firestone, 1995; McLaughlin & Talbert, 2001). It is about "enabling a rich fabric of connectivity" (Wenger, 2000, p. 232). It is about making shared engagement, peer support, mutual assistance, and joint enterprise a generalized condition in schools (Goldenberg, 2004; Kruse et al., 1995; Newmann et al., 2000), about working and learning together (Olivier & Hipp, 2006; Stein & Coburn, 2008). Mutuality is essential because it "provides a point of convergence for teachers' inquiry—the joint enterprise for community of practice" (McLaughlin & Talbert, 2001, p. 122). It underscores needed job-centered learning (Drago-Severson, 2004; Olivier & Hipp, 2006) and, as shown in the model in Figure 5.1, fosters capacity development (Clark et al., 1999). Shared enterprise features what Louis and Marks (1998, p. 538) refer to as "the quality of relationships among group work members." Collegial support and general norms of teamwork and joint engagement are paramount under conditions of mutuality (Grossman et al., 2001; Phillips, 2003). Without mutuality, purpose of engagement cannot be fulfilled (Levine & Marcus, 2010).

Mutuality and its family members, participation, engagement, and joint activity, are dependent, of course, on opportunities to work together, on "enabling structure and supportive organizational context" (Fullan, 2002,

p. 15) or "knowledge space" (Hattie, 2009, p. 264). These opportunities, as we detail in Chapter 7, are often conspicuous by their absence in schools and require the strong hand of leadership broadly defined. Of course, this means that there needs to be something on which time to plan, work, and learn together makes sense (Johnson & Asera, 1999; Wenger, 2000), "some intersection of interest, some activity" (Wenger, 2000, p. 232), what Ermeling (2010, p. 386) refers to as "common ground to talk." Without this, there can be no authentic joint exchange (Beck & Foster, 1999).

Creating structure for productive joint enterprise requires attending to an array of issues. Most important, there is the need to establish the *domain* of collaboration (Wenger & Snyder, 2000). We know also that thought must be devoted to what Wenger (2000) refers to as the *types of activities* that will ground the collaborative. Important here is ensuring that both formal and informal mechanisms are engaged (Ancess, 2003; Fullan & Ballew, 2002; Olivier & Hipp, 2006)—and in a coordinated and synchronized manner (Drago-Severson, 2004). The *size* of groups is important and the question of how much to align with existing organizational arrangements (e.g., departments, grade levels, teaching teams) needs resolution (Wenger, 1998, 2000). Thus the topic of *boundaries* is important, including how these demarcations are managed (Penuel et al., 2010; Wenger, 2000). So too is the fluidity and *stability* of collaborative work teams (Curry, 2008; McLaughlin & Talbert, 2001), what Wenger (2000) describes as rhythms of the work. *Amount of time* to work and the *regularity of exchanges* merit consideration. So too does the *life span* of a work group (Leithwood et al., 1999; McLaughlin & Talbert, 2001). The topic of how teachers become members of collaborative teams also must be addressed. Contrary to normal practice in education, self-selection receives high grades in the general literature as a *mechanism of selection* (Wenger, 1998). Also important is how much of one's *professional identity* is committed to and defined by collaborative work (Wenger, 2000). Finally, the research informs us that *how work is structured* and the *tools employed* to guide the work make valuable contributions to how well joint enterprise is conducted (Curry, 2008; Levine & Marcus, 2010; Saunders et al., 2009). The *concreteness of the work* and the *collaborative organizational form employed* (e.g., book clubs, joint lesson planning) are quite relevant as well (Vescio et al., 2008). We delve deeply into these topics in the following chapter.

The research carries us one level deeper in thinking about collaboration, to the criteria for judging the authenticity of joint work. Issues here include the presence or absence of reciprocal influence (Kruse et al., 1995), density of ties (Wenger, 2000) and mutual dependence (Beck & Foster, 1999; Young, 2006). Measures of the amount of the teaching-learning process (i.e., the work of classrooms) that is made open for inspection helps determine authenticity (Grossman et al., 2001; Horn, 2005), that is, how much of the work becomes "public" (Printy, 2008; Young, 2006). The depth of sharing can reveal a good deal about the validity of collaboration

(Harris, 2009; Wenger, 2000; Young, 2006). The "fingerprint" test for joint construction work is useful here. How many members of the collaborative actively contributed to the work? How many are mere spectators? Authenticity can also be determined in part by the robustness of the leadership displayed by members in the collaborative (Murphy, 2005). The extent to which teachers change their practice is a key criterion (Printy, 2008; Visscher & Witziers, 2004).

Focus of Engagement: Student Learning

> Growth of the school-based professional community is marked by conversations that hold practice, pedagogy, and student learning under scrutiny. (Kruse et al., 1995, p. 30)

Structure is an essential dimension of community. But as Ancess (2003, p. 4) cautions, "achievement of community requires more than the space for developing commodity." More specifically, "what collaboration is designed to focus on will have significant implications for what teachers can and can't learn from work with colleagues" (Levine & Marcus, 2010, pp. 392–393). For example, researchers report that simply addressing logistical issues and nonlearning conditions does not translate into robust collaboration and community nor result in the intermediate or summative outcomes seen in Figure 5.1.

On the positive side of the storyboard, analysts have uncovered productive foci for collaborative work. To begin with, it is clear that the center of gravity should be the *classroom* (Goldenberg, 2004; Gray et al., 1999; Hayes et al., 2004) and on challenges of work there. Educational concerns trump nonacademic issues (Murphy et al., 2001; Printy, 2008). Attention flows to the core technology (Mulford & Silins, 2003; Newmann et al., 2001; Useem et al., 2003). That is, interactions should be anchored in issues of *learning and teaching* (Supovitz et al., 2010; Useem, Christman, Gold, & Simon, 1997) and be deep and ongoing.

Not surprisingly, given the above comments, there is near universal agreement that the focus of collaborative engagement should be on *students* (Ancess, 2003; Ermeling, 2010; McLaughlin & Talbert, 2001). Both for teachers to mature into a productive community and to power up learning, students need to be at the center of collaborative work (Goldenberg, 2004; Grossman et al., 2001; Kruse et al., 1995). Becoming more specific, these analysts find that the focus should be on student academics (Olivier & Hipp, 2006; Saunders et al., 2009): "A collective focus on *student learning* is central to professional community" (Louis & Marks, 1998, p. 539), especially analyses of student learning needs, problems, and progress (Halverson et al., 2007; Vescio et al., 2008; Visscher & Witziers, 2004).

Backward mapping from student learning, the focus of this collective engagement is *instructional practice* embedded in specific curricular domains (Curry, 2008; Visscher & Witziers, 2004; Young, 2006), collaboration to strengthen the school's instructional program (Bryk et al., 2010; Hubermann et al., 2011; Supovitz & Poglinco, 2001), and the pedagogical skills of each teacher (Gurr et al., 2006; McLaughlin & Talbert, 2001; Young, 2006). Vescio and colleagues (2008, p. 85) succinctly summarize the research on this issue as follows: "Findings reinforce the importance of persistently pursuing an instructional focus as teachers engage in their work in learning communities." As discussed above, *problems of practice* focus is privileged in highly productive collaborative work (King, 2001; Levine & Marcus, 2010; McLaughlin & Talbert, 2001). The spotlight is on specific, observable, malleable practices that are described with transparency, clarity, and concreteness (Little, 1982; Mitchell & Sackney, 2006). Finally, as we explain more fully below, a particular type of shared instructional practice is routinely discussed in the research on teacher communities in general and collaboration particularly, *evidence-based analysis* (Blanc et al., 2010; Cosner, 2011; Strahan, 2003), a condition that Visscher and Witziers (2004, p. 798) refer to as the "sine qua non for the development of professional communities."

Method of Engagement: Reflective Inquiry

> Teachers participating in inquiry use a variety of forms of evidence and data to conduct their study of a problem and learn to rely on this evidence both to better understand the problem, as well as to inform their decisions about what is working and what actions need to be tried next. (Ermeling, 2010, p. 378)

So far, we have examined three of the four core ingredients of collaboration (purpose, structure, and focus), remembering that collaboration itself is one of the six essential elements of professional communities. We now turn to the final ingredient of shared enterprise, the ways in which productive communities operate. To maintain consistency with colleagues who have researched this domain, we describe the method of engagement as reflective practice. According to Stoll and her team (2006, pp. 222–227):

> *Reflective professional inquiry* includes: "reflective dialogue" conversations about serious educational issues or problems involving the application of new knowledge in a sustained manner; "deprivatization of practice," frequent examining of teachers' practice, through mutual observation and case analysis, joint planning and curriculum development; seeking new knowledge; tacit knowledge constantly converted into shared knowledge through interaction; and applying new ideas and information to problem solving and solutions addressing pupils' needs.

We parcel the research on "method of engagement" into two overlapping concepts: inquiry and evidence-based practice.

On the first topic, in dissecting collaboration scholars consistently highlight professional practice informed by individual and group reflection (Grossman et al., 2001; Louis et al., 2011; Supovitz, 2002). Indeed, inquiry is generally presented as a hallmark "method" or "stance" that defines shared enterprise in communities of practice (Grossman et al., 2001; King, 2001; Visscher & Witziers, 2004). The concept travels under a variety of different names in the literature—reflective inquiry, reflective discussions, group inquiry, sustained inquiry, inquiry-oriented practice, reflective practice, collegial inquiry, and so forth. It means, according to Drago-Severson (2004, p. 18), "reflecting on one's assumptions, convictions, and values as part of the learning process," the investigation and critical assessment of practice, research, and logic (King, 2001). That is, it is a "stance" that honors the interrogation of knowledge, skills, and dispositions around instructional practice (Levine & Marcus, 2007). Its purpose is to forge joint understanding of and shared practices in the service of student learning (Ermeling, 2010; Kruse et al., 1995; Mitchell & Sackney, 2006). Productive inquiry in professional communities of practice is analytic, dynamic, continuous, and constructivist in nature (Horn, 2005; King, 2001; Little, 1982).

Reflective inquiry has as much to do with dialogue, or what Horn (2005, p. 229) calls "conversational involvement," as it does with patterns of thinking (Ermeling, 2010; Stoll et al., 2006; York-Barr & Duke, 2004). Indeed, it is reasonable to add conversation to the methods of engagement label, what Wilson and Berne (1999, p. 200) nicely capture with the term "narrative of inquiry." Grossman and her colleagues (2001, p. 59) maintain that teacher communities create an "invitational conversational climate," a reflective based constructed dialogue, what Cochran-Smith and Lytle (1999, p. 280) nail with the idea of "teacher learning through talk." It is in these continuous professional conversations that reflections become visible for inspection (Curry, 2008), venues in which feedback can be provided and debated (Kruse et al., 1995).

Two aspects of dialogue in the service of building collaboration are routinely highlighted in the research on professional culture. The public nature of conversations is consistently seen as essential (Horn, 2010; Young, 2006), what Levine and Marcus (2010) describe as detailed and open representations. This public stance centered on student work is especially productive (Goldenberg, 2004). A good deal of recognition is also awarded to the openness of collaborative exchange, an idea that Horn (2010, p. 255) beautifully captures as "a willingness to reveal and work at the limits of one's knowledge." Dialogue is not merely an act of civility. Difficult conversations unfold in collaborative work (Drago-Severson, 2004; Huberman et al., 2011). Critique is expected (Grossman et al., 2001; Silins & Mulford, 2004; Wilson & Berne, 1999). "Questioning and challenging colleagues" (Horn, 2010, p. 234) is normal. Concerns and doubts are to be aired, "difference, debate, and disagreement are viewed as the foundations"

(Stoll et al., 2006, p. 227) of reflective inquiry. In addition, there is solid evidence that formalizing collaborative conversations in education can be helpful (Beachum & Dentith, 2004; Horn, 2010; Levine & Marcus, 2010). There is a strong sense that "protocol-guided conversations" (Curry, 2008, p. 742) enhance the public and critical aspects of collaborative dialogue (Curry, 2008; Horn, 2005; Levine & Marcus, 2010).

Collegial dialogue is half of the method or stance on engagement. The other half, based on the findings of Levine and Marcus (2010) and Penuel and colleagues (2006, p. 527) that "the effectiveness of collaboration depends on what kinds of interactions take place," is evidence-based practice (Fullan & Ballew, 2002; Grossman et al., 2001; Johnson & Asera, 1999). This means that not only is there critical, collegial exchange, but the conversations are anchored in knowledge and data, especially support for ideas and more important evidence of impact on one's students (Ermeling, 2010; Hattie, 2009; Young, 2006).

In highly productive collaboratives, considerable attention is devoted to the "visible and explicit cause-effect connections between instructional decisions and student outcomes" (Ermeling, 2010, p. 379). "Analysis and interpretation of some form of student learning data" (Cosner, 2011, p. 789) is the grist for collaborative dialogue (Visscher & Witziers, 2004). As was the case for inquiry, researchers find that tools such as protocols and artifacts to guide evidence-based collaboration can assist greatly in the work (Horn, 2005). More concretely, Felner and his team (2007, p. 217) list five dimensions of collaboration in which inquiry and evidence-based work are especially productive.

> (a) curriculum coordination and integration; (b) coordination of student assessments, assignments, and feedback; (c) work together in engaging parents; (d) coordinate together the development of common performance standards; and (e) work as a team to integrate their efforts with other building resources (e.g., counselors, librarians, reading/special education specialists, etc.)

Ownership and Responsibility

Ownership

> Another shared belief among teachers that is associated with trust is perceived teacher influence on instructional decisions. Tschannen-Moran (2001) found that faculty trust was stronger in schools where teachers believed their instructional ideas influenced school decisions. Teacher influence over decisions in the operating core of schools empowers teachers to take ownership of teaching and learning, a core feature of professionally organized schools. (Adams, 2010, p. 263)

Collaborative initiatives are not likely to have a significant impact on the classroom unless schools organize in ways that involve teachers in decisions that are tied to the needs of learners and the teaching learning process. (Pounder, 1999, p. 319)

One of the essential reasons that collaborative communities of professional practice work is because they operationalize the cardinal understanding that teachers are fundamental to school improvement. One of the most important ways they do this is by helping teachers assume ownership of their school and their labor (Levine & Marcus, 2007; Raywid, 1995; Supovitz & Poglinco, 2001). The engine that powers this sense of empowerment is best described as "shared involvement." Our analysis suggests that three broad concepts are in play in a reciprocal and integrative manner: authority, influence, and leadership. We examine the first two here and leadership because it is a distinct element in our model in a separate section below.

To begin with, we know that collaborative communities of professional practice provide teachers with considerable professional *authority* (Barker, 2001; Vescio et al., 2008). This influence can be defined on the one hand by what is absent, the privileging of hierarchical and bureaucratic systems and procedures over professional knowledge (Adams, 2010; Ancess, 2003). On the other hand, professional authority is characterized by what is present, collective, knowledge-based autonomy for the work necessary to ensure that all youngsters are successful, including organizational support for ideas and decisions crafted by communities (Beachum & Dentith, 2004; Crum & Sherman, 2008; Dannetta, 2002). Riester and team (2002) deconstruct this autonomy in terms of freedom and openness. It is important to emphasize that this is a type of group control and influence not the isolation and privacy masquerading as autonomy in many schools (Kruse et al., 1995). It is a collective sense of agency (Gurr et al., 2006). Professional authority is also about voice, providing teachers with meaningful forums and pathways to express their professional ideas (Brooks, Scribner, & Eferakorho, 2004; Supovitz, 2002; Vescio et al., 2008).

Communities of practice also drive improvement because they create pathways to enhance teacher *influence* over important issues in the school (Bryk et al., 2010). They manufacture ownership by featuring "collaborative, cooperative, and consultative decision making" (Silins & Mulford, 2004, p. 448) and by creating abundant opportunities for that decision making to occur (Pounder, 1999). Teachers in communities of practice are empowered to act in the best interests of children (Kruse et al., 1995; Sweetland & Hoy, 2000). "Additionally, decisional power in learning communities is more collective than positional" (Adams, 2010, p. 274). Administrative leadership is more inclusive, facilitative, and person directed than managerial or institutional (Bryk et al., 2010; King, 2001; Leithwood et al., 1999).

Researchers document that empowerment can stretch across a good deal of the school landscape, including domains such as goals, organizational operations, professional learning, and classroom instruction (Newmann et al., 2000; Sweetland & Hoy, 2000). They caution that professional communities are most interested in exercising influence over decisions that impact learning and teaching and that affect the work that they do with their students (Leithwood et al., 2004; Levine & Marcus, 2010). Investigations also document that these are the areas with the highest payoff for student learning (McDougall et al., 2007).

Although it is visible in the framework that anchors this chapter (see Figure 5.1), it is worth making explicit that ownership is valued because it promotes desired outcomes, both intermediate and summative. That is, ownership fuels the development of other productive professional norms such as efficacy and persistence and adds to the school's stock of human and social capital (Blase & Kirby, 2009; Eckert, 1989; Leithwood, Steinbach, & Jantzi, 2002). As predicated by our model, these intermediate outcomes are linked to positive academic outcomes for students (Dannetta, 2002; Heck & Marcoulides, 1996).

Accountability

There is broad agreement in the literature that members of a PLC consistently take collective responsibility for student learning. (Stoll et al., 2006, p. 226)

Teacher communities foster collective responsibility and internal accountability. (Curry, 2008, p. 736)

Professional communities of practice are places where teachers hold themselves collectively accountable for school, team, and student success (Ancess, 2003; King, 2001; Printy, 2008), a norm often absent in many schools (Grossman et al., 2001; Riester et al., 2002). That is, in most schools, teachers "generally are neither granted authority or held accountable for their decisions" (McLaughlin & Talbert, 2001, p. 138). In schools with a robust professional culture, however, there is a shared sense of responsibility (Penuel et al., 2010; Raywid, 1995; Youngs & King, 2002), one that has a positive influence on student learning (Pounder, 1999).

Collective responsibility at one level means being accountable for the functioning and success of the school (Desimone, 2002; Raywid, 1995; Supovitz, 2002). Included here is responsibility for working to reach school goals and accountability for the success or failure of those efforts (Ancess, 2003; Goldenberg, 2004).

At a second level, collective control refers to teachers assuming responsibility for the instructional program, for improving the quality of instruction and curriculum across the school and in their teams (Coldren & Spillane, 2007; Eilers & Camacho, 2007).

> The school as a community is responsive and responsible to individual school community members for establishing and sustaining those organizational, pedagogical, and relational conditions that produce the performance standards and outcomes that have been promised. (Ancess, 2003, p. 12)

It means being on point for upholding the ethos of the school (Ancess, 2003) and community work norms (Grossman et al., 2001; Kruse et al., 1995). As Grossman and team (2001, p. 57) remind us, there is also a responsibility for meaningful participation: "In community, ideas are public property, their pursuit a communal responsibility. Group members can be held accountable for contributing their individual insights to the larger group." Shared accountability holds that problems are community property (Curry, 2008). It also suggests that each person is responsible for the learning of others in the community (Riester et al., 2002; Southworth, 2002; Youngs, 2007).

At the third and deepest level, collective accountability entails holding the community responsible for the results of their work (Darling-Hammond et al., 2002) and the success of students (McDougall et al., 2007; McLaughlin & Talbert, 2001; Wilson & Berne, 1999), especially academic achievement. In communities of practice, ownership of student learning is nested in the group (Ancess, 2003; Curry, 2008; Huberman et al., 2011).

Shared Leadership

> Professional community is also frequently associated with shared leadership. (Wahlstrom & Louis, 2008, p. 463)

> Sharing leadership is a fundamental principle and dynamic of learning communities. (McLaughlin & Talbert, 2001, p. 121)

The Backdrop

The fifth element of practice communities underscores teachers assuming greater leadership in the school, an idea like learning community itself that is captured in a variety of overlapping terms: collective, distributed, parallel, collaborative, pluralized, and so forth (Spillane, 2005; Spillane, Camburn, & Pareja, 2009). As with many of its sister elements, while widely trumpeted over the last few, shared leadership is not thickly embedded in schools (Beachum & Dentith, 2004; Sherrill, 1999; Spillane & Louis, 2002). The primary reason for this has been highlighted throughout this volume. Over the last century, with the development of an organizational architecture of institutionalism, leadership has become equated with formal authority and roles (Crowther & Olsen, 1997; Murphy, 2005). This understanding gave rise to conceptions of leadership that were tightly bound to domains of responsibility with the assignment of leadership in classrooms to teachers and schoolwide leadership to principals (Clift, Johnson, Holland, & Veal, 1992; Crowther et al., 2002; Murphy, 2005). The significant point here is not that teachers were unconnected to leadership but that their leadership was rarely acknowledged outside the realm of the classroom, teachers' role-based field of authority and influence as historically defined (Harris, 2003; Hulpia et al., 2009; Robinson, 2008).

Because the work of teachers in terms of role and authority "has been seen as being composed of interactions with students in classes" (Griffin, 1995, p. 30), the expectation has been hardwired into the structure and culture of schools "that the only job of teachers is to teach students and to consider the classroom, at best, as the legitimate extent of their influence" (Urbanski & Nickolaou, 1997, p. 244): "The formal authority of teachers in schools remains carefully circumscribed. They exert extensive control over teaching in their classrooms and departments, but their formal influence rarely extends beyond that" (Johnson, 1989, p. 105).

This preoccupation with the hierarchical organizational system with its tenets of separation of management (leadership) from labor, chain of command, and positional authority has led to the crystallization of (1) forms of schooling in which teachers are placed in traditional roles (Kowalski, 1995) and "teacher leadership is clearly not a common contemporary condition" (Barth, 1988, p. 134)—models in which "few people have viewed these educators as a group in the same way as other leaders, i.e., principals" (Hatfield, Blackman, & Claypool, 1986, p. 20; Smylie, Conley, & Marks, 2002) and (2) a profession in which "teachers, even those who are already leaders, do not see themselves as leaders" (Hart & Baptist, 1996, p. 87). As a consequence, "there are almost no mechanisms by which teachers can emerge as leaders for the purposes of leading work on teaching, even when they have been acknowledged as exemplary classroom teachers" (Little, 1987, p. 510).

The perspective on leadership in communities of practice is distinctly different. It begins with the belief that "the false assumption that teaching is for teachers and leading is for administrators has operated to the inutility of public schools for a long time" (Suleiman & Moore, 1997, p. 6), that the sole emphasis on principals at the core of educational leadership is ill-conceived (Crowther et al., 2002) and has real costs in terms of schooling outcomes. More positively, practice communities anchor on the proposition that shared leadership is essential to school improvement (Killion, 1996; Murphy, 2005; Whitaker, 1997), that "genuine, long-lasting school change initiatives must derive from and involve teachers" (Kelley, 1994, p. 300), and that without teachers' "full participation and leadership, any move to reform education—no matter how well-intentioned or ambitious—is doomed to failure" (Lieberman & Miller, 1999, p. xi). In short, communities of practice challenge the underlying assumptions about existing roles for teachers and school administrators (Barth, 2001). Or, as Louis and her team (2010, p. 332) capture it, "increasing teachers' involvement in the difficult task of making good decisions and introducing improved practice must be at the heart of school leadership."

The scaffolding for leadership in professional communities arises in part from the stockpile of material on leadership roles but is inclusive of more than traditional administrative roles. That is, practice communities advance beyond the view of "educational leadership as the domain of either a particular stratum of the educational system or the individuals within that stratum" (Crowther & Olsen, 1997, p. 6). For communities of professional practice to function effectively, it is important that leadership be seen as an organizational property and a dynamic of the community itself, understandings that permit the concept of shared leadership to be positioned on center stage in the leadership play (Ackerman & Maslin-Ostrowski, 2002; Jackson, 2000; Katzenmeyer & Moller, 2001).

Concept and Rationale

The work of leading in schools involves multiple individuals and differs by the type of activity or function. (Hulpia et al., 2009, p. 1030)

Distributed leadership concentrates on engaging expertise wherever it exists within the organization rather than seeking this only through formal position or role. (Harris, 2004, p. 13)

We acknowledge at the outset that the topic of shared leadership is cloaked in some ambiguity (Firestone & Martinez, 2007; Smylie et al., 2002). Part of this is attributable to the reality that it is hardly a fully developed area (Crowther & Olsen, 1997; Murphy, 2005; Silva, Gimbert, & Nolan, 2000). Some is due to the broad array of ideas housed under the shared leadership mantle (Murphy, 2005). More can be traced to the fact that it is an "emergent property" (Hulpia et al., 2009, p. 1014) and takes on different coloring in varied contents (Spillane et al., 2009; York-Barr & Duke, 2004).

To begin with, as we explained above, teacher leadership is marked by an assortment of different names—"names that mean different things in different settings and refer to a broad array of actions" (Miller, Moon, & Elko, 2000, p. 5). This variety is compounded by the fact that "when educators speak or write of teacher leadership they rarely define what they mean" (O'Hair & Reitzug, 1997, p. 67). Confusion about meanings of teacher leaders abound (Katzenmeyer & Moller, 2001) and the work of teacher leaders is often ill-defined (Johnson & Hynes, 1997; Murphy, 2005). The consequence is, of course, a significant measure of ambiguity connected with the term (Crowther et al., 2002), the use of the term "without a clear definition of what it means" (Childs-Bowen, Moller, & Scrivner, 2000, p. 28) and the near absence of "systematic conceptual definitions . . . of the variable in the [research] literature" (Smylie, 1996, p. 543). As Moller and Katzenmeyer (1996) remind us, the lack of anything approaching a "clear definition of teacher leadership also impedes its development" (p. 5) and results in roles that remain unclear.

The rationale for shared leadership is threefold. Most important, and consistent with the model in Figure 5.1, it is held that collective leadership facilitates the promotion of student learning by enhancing the quality of classroom practice, practice that is strengthened by enriching teacher knowledge and deepening professional capital (Robinson, 2008; Stoll et al., 2006). Second, there is a strong sense that shared conceptions of leadership more accurately reflect the reality of what occurs in schools (Bryk et al., 2010; Hulpia et al., 2009; Spillane et al., 2009). That is, leadership is indeed distributed in schools, and schools need to capitalize on that reality (Supovitz, 2008). Third, there is a nearly universal understanding that no single person or small cadre of administrators can lead today's complex schools alone (Hulpia et al., 2009; O'Donnell & White, 2005; Walker, 2009). In particular, the new world of schooling has "highlighted constraints on the principal's time, educational expertise, and moral authority for assuming sole responsibility for leading school improvement" (Heck & Hallinger, 2010, p. 137). As a consequence, as a field, school administration is turning to shared models of leadership (Hulpia et al., 2009; York-Barr & Duke, 2004).

We close our discussion of the conceptual backbone of shared leadership by highlighting its essential ingredients. The calculus of influence here is expertise in and around the core technology of schooling (Anderson, Moore, & Sun, 2009; Snell & Swanson, 2000; Wilson, 1993) and "general expertise as teachers" (Firestone & Martinez, 2009, p. 79). As Timperley (2005, p. 211) so aptly records, "Expertise rather than formal position should form the basis of leadership authority and this type of leadership often resides within the larger professional community of teachers." According to Harris (2004, p. 14), "leadership means multiple sources of guidance and direction, following the contours of expertise." In addition, influence is earned, not allotted (Grossman et al., 2001). Or as Yu and associates (2002, p. 372) observe, in a context of shared leadership "power is attributed by organizational members to whomever is able to inspire their commitment and collective aspirations." Personal and professional relationships matter deeply (Firestone & Martinez, 2007; Harris, 2003; Keedy, 1999).

Shared leadership means permeable boundaries between teachers and administrators (Ancess, 2003; Timperley, 2005). Fluidity is privileged (Hayes et al., 2004; York-Barr & Duke, 2004). It is an emergent property of the professional community (Gronn, 2009; Hulpia et al., 2009; Robinson, 2008). Shared leadership is "opportunistic, flexible, responsive, and context specific" (Jackson, 2000, p. 70). As Spillane (Spillane and Louis, 2002) has shown across his cardinal lines of work in this area, distributed leadership is task dependent, varying from activity to activity (Moller & Eggen, 2005; Smylie et al., 2002; Timperley, 2005). It is organic and informal (Brooks et al., 2004; Mulford & Silins, 2003). It is more a process than a fixed characteristic (Anderson et al., 2009; Gronn, 2009; Silins et al., 2002). It is more about leadership than leaders (Jackson, 2000; Sykes & Elmore, 1989). It aggregates up to more than the sum of its part (Leithwood, Mascall, Strauss, Sacks, & Yashkina, 2009).

Before we turn to pathways by which shared leadership comes to life in professionally anchored schools, a few cautions are in order. Shared leadership does not represent the demise of principals nor a "threat" to school administration. Leadership is not a zero-sum game but rather an expandable source of capital (Conley, 1991; Leithwood & Jantzi, 2006). Leadership density is good for schools (Harris, 2004; McDougall et al., 2007). The best state of affairs is "broader and deeper capacity to lead in schools" (Heck & Hallinger, 2009, p. 684).

It is also important to remember that shared leadership is ends-driven work. It is not an outcome in itself (Gurr et al., 2005; Timperley, 2005). Indeed, "there is little point in teachers exercising more influence over one another if the content of their leadership does not deliver benefits for students" (Robinson 2008, p. 249). Simply sharing leadership is likely to be insufficient as well. More than assumptions need to be put in place (Leithwood et al., 2009). For example, we know that shared leadership is often nothing more than shared work, with very limited additional influence (Murphy, 2005). We also know that teachers do not necessarily seek out colleagues with the greatest expertise (Timperley, 2005). Finally, a variety of scholars remind us that research on shared leadership is still relatively new (Hulpia et al., 2009; Spillane & Louis, 2002). In particular, specifics on how teachers influence colleagues in ways that enhance student success are quite limited.

Routes to Shared Leadership

Teacher leadership essentially refers to the exercise of leadership by teachers, regardless of position or designation. (Harris, 2003, p. 316)

The methods of distributed leadership are diverse. (Moller & Eggen, 2005, p. 34)

Over the last 20 years, researchers, developers, and practitioners have spent considerable time thinking about ways in which shared leadership has, is, and can be operationalized. On the research front, important frameworks have been crafted by Gronn, Harris, Louis, MacBeath, Smylie,

Spillane, and others. At the broadest level, scholars differentiate between leadership exercised by teachers in formal positions (e.g., department chair, math coach) and those without formal positions (e.g., a teacher stepping forward to informally mentor a new colleague) (Brooks et al., 2004; Louis et al., 2010; Silins & Mulford, 2004). They also distinguish between leadership performed on a consistent and situational basis (Supovitz et al., 2010). Harris (2004, p. 15) underscores "top down" and "bottom up" ways to collectivize leadership, with the former dependent on the principal and the latter "occurring organically and spontaneously from the activities of teachers working together." In this latter case, as MacBeath (2009, p. 50) reminds us, "leadership is taken rather than given. It is assumed rather than conferred." Robinson (2008), in turn, helps us see that shared leadership unfolds through two pathways, distribution by task and distribution by influence.

Specific models of the operationalization of shared leadership in dense professional cultures have been forged by many of the seminal figures in the area. Gronn (2009) discusses additive and holistic perspectives. Spillane, Diamond, and colleagues (2001) examine three sharing pathways, division of labor, coperformance, and parallel performance. Harris (2004, p. 18) in turn, refers to "involving others in decision-making, allocating important tasks to teachers and rotating leadership responsibilities within the school." And MacBeath's (2009, p. 44) model highlights six methods of sharing leadership: "formally, programmatically, strategically, incrementally, opportunistically, and culturally."

Building on the foundations laid by these researchers as well as our own analyses in this area (Mayrowetz, Murphy, Seashore Louis, & Smylie, 2009; Murphy, 2005; Smylie, Mayrowetz, Murphy, & Louis, 2007; Murphy, Smylie, Mayrowetz, & Louis, 2009), we think about bringing shared leadership into life through four overlapping bands, collective leadership by teachers: (1) participating in decision making, (2) assuming formal roles in the school, (3) shepherding tasks and functions; and (4) engaging with colleagues in the work of improving instruction for a group of students (e.g., second grade children).

The core idea here is leadership capacity or leadership density (Sergiovanni, 1991a), a concept that analysts have shown is connected to effective schools (Leithwood, Day, et al., 2006; Leithwood, Jantzi, & McElheron-Hopkins, 2006; Murphy & Datnow, 2003a). Robinson and her colleagues (2008, p. 668) capture this idea when they report from their research "that what matters is the frequency of various instructional leadership practices rather than the extent to which they are performed by a particular leadership role." One metaphor to employ here is "energy." In the current system of schooling, the power plants are fueled by gas and coal (e.g., authority). To make the energy production system more effective, new forms of fuel are added to the system (e.g., classroom-based expertise). New, more informal transmission lines are built as well to add overall capacity.

A second way to think about density is through the use of a web, a web of leadership. One objective here is to weave additional threads into the web. A second is to create more connective tissues across the threads. The third goal is to thicken each thread and piece of connective tissue. In this way, a web that was sparsely defined becomes quite dense. The sources of leadership increase. There is also greater overlap in the leadership work, less siloing, and enhanced coordination (Mayrowetz & Weinstein, 1999; Murphy, 2005).

Teacher involvement in governance decision making overlaps considerably with the learning community element of "participation" and the accompanying norm of "ownership" that we described in detail earlier. So here we only reinforce that this involvement does create opportunities for teachers to exercise leadership that are unavailable in schools with weak professional cultures (Gray et al., 1999; Hayes et al., 2004; Wahlstrom & Louis, 2008). Or as Brooks and team (2004, p. 9) explain, "participation in school-level policymaking activities constitutes a partial operational definition of teacher leadership" (see also Beachum & Dentith, 2004; Blair, 2002; Grubb & Flessa, 2006).

The second pathway to shared leadership is the creation of new roles for teachers (Hatfield et al., 1986; Murphy, 2005; Wasley, 1991). Initiatives here are undertaken using institutional blueprints. Two overlapping designs are featured in the role-based pathway: career-based approaches and expanded leadership structures (Firestone & Martinez, 2009; Little, 1995; York-Barr & Duke, 2004). While the concepts of differentiated staffing and *career-based models* of teacher leadership enjoy an extensive history (Christensen, 1987; Fessler & Ungaretti, 1994), they became central characters in the school reform play in the mid-1980s with the release of the Holmes Group (1986) and Carnegie Forum (1986) reports. Career approaches to teacher leadership attack "the unstaged nature of . . . teaching" (Rowley, 1988, p. 16). They create "upward movement" (McLaughlin & Yee, 1988, p. 26), "vertical progress" (Fessler & Ungaretti, 1994, p. 220), and "staged careers" (Johnson, 1989, p. 95). These strategies provide "a hierarchical, institutionally structured notion of a career" (McLaughlin & Yee, 1988, p. 26)—as opposed to the existing "horizontal" (p. 25) and "incredibly flat career structure" (Berry & Ginsberg, 1990, p. 617)—one that is "individually constructed and experienced" (McLaughlin & Yee, 1988, p. 26). Career ladders "differentiate roles for teachers as they move up a ladder of responsibility and leadership" (Fessler & Ungaretti, 1994, p. 220). For example, the Holmes Group (1986) proposed the development of a three-phase career of instructor, professional teacher, and career professional (pp. 8–9). The Association of Teacher Educators (1985, cited in Christensen, 1987) developed a model that "includes the steps of teacher, associate teacher, senior teacher, and master teacher" (p. 101).

Efforts to *broaden leadership structures,* in turn, focus on connecting teachers to new or expanded roles, roles that appear as nodes on the organizational chart (Camburn et al., 2003; Goldstein, 2004; Pounder, 1999).

The focus is less on the "hierarchically arrayed positions" (Broyles, 1991, p. 3) that define career-based efforts to develop teacher leadership and more on establishing "a richer pool of professional opportunities" (p. 3) for teachers, on "enlarg[ing] teachers' roles and responsibilities beyond their regular classroom assignments" (Smylie & Denny, 1989, p. 4; Blanc et al., 2010; York-Barr & Duke, 2004). For example, Fessler and Ungaretti (1994) assert that "modest adaptations of role structures that provide opportunities for teacher leadership include the creation of such positions as team leaders, grade-level leaders, and chairs of staff development committees" (p. 220). Efforts here include reenergizing "existing legitimized leadership roles for teachers" (Conley, 1997, p. 336), such as the department head (Little, 1995), as well as bringing new leadership roles on line, such as school reform facilitators (Berends, Bodilly, & Kirby, 2002; Datnow & Castellano, 2002; Smylie et al., 2002).

A third avenue to expand teacher leadership beyond the classroom is to turn over tasks and assignments to teachers (Murphy, 2005; Robinson, 2008; Spillane, Diamond, et al., 2001). Here, we see leadership not in terms of roles but rather as a "set of functions to be performed" (Mayrowetz & Weinstein, 1999). These assignments can be either led by a single teacher or shared across staff (Goldstein, 2004; Grossman et al., 2001; Timperley, 2005). Leadership here often finds expression in professional teams as teachers lead colleagues in addressing particular challenges (Caldwell, 1998; Silins & Mulford, 2004), e.g., an action research team to study and provide recommendations about student personalization. These teams can be arrayed on a continuum from ad hoc (e.g., how to address the transition from a K–6 to a K–8 school) to more ongoing (e.g., the intermediate-grades data analysis team) (Blase & Kirby, 2009; Harris, 2004).

Related to the third approach is a fourth pathway that energizes a small cluster of teachers to lead inquiry-based efforts to improve learning for a specific group of students. Community-inquiry leadership strategies direct our "attention away from individual and role-based conceptions of leadership" (Smylie et al., 2002, p. 172). There is a shift in focus to "the importance of teaching context and organizational development of schools" (Odell, 1997, p. 121). As a consequence, "teacher leadership is not experienced in isolation but rather is linked with development in schools" (Zimpher, 1988, p. 54). Attention is directed to the "exercise of leadership on the part of those who do not necessarily hold power or authority by virtue of their formal position" (Frost & Durant, 2003, p. 174).

Analysts of this pathway explore how leadership functions are "carved out by multiple individuals in different roles in redundant, mutually reinforcing" (Smylie et al., 2002, p. 173) ways. They "redefine teacher leadership as a fundamental principle and function of the teaching role" (Forster, 1997, p. 86). Teacher leadership is formulated as "more than a role; it is a *stance,* a mind-set, a way of being, acting, and thinking as a learner within a community of learners" (Darling-Hammond, Bullmaster, & Cobb, 1995, p. 95).

The idea of the school as a ground of inquiry (Lieberman & Miller, 1999) trumps hierarchy. Institutional and structural (McLaughlin & Yee, 1988) issues and "organizational and production metaphors" (Livingston, 1992, p. 14) are pushed into the background (Gronn, 2009; Sergiovanni, 1994). In this fourth approach to teacher leadership, "teachers assume leadership naturally as part of a more professional conception of work" (Darling-Hammond et al., 1995, p. 88): "Teacher leaders . . . emerge as a matter of course in informally structured positions along with a communitarian social system for schools" (Odell, 1997, p. 121). The calculus shifts from filling roles to "creat[ing] an interactive community of teachers collaborating for improvement and experimentation in their schools" (Boles & Troen, 1996, p. 48), to establishing work cultures (Fullan, 1994; Spillane & Louis, 2002) and "community-related approach[es] to enhancing teaching and learning" (Griffin, 1995, p. 37).

As should be clear from the analysis presented above, the scope of work in the inquiry pathway is different than in the role-based pathways. In latter designs, we observed that the scope of work was quite focused and limited to designated teacher leaders, that it was circumscribed and possessed an exclusive quality. In the inquiry-based design, there is acknowledgment that all teachers can carry leadership responsibility (Hart & Baptist, 1996; Murphy, 2005). Teacher leadership "becomes a more normative role for all teachers in the school" (Odell, 1997, p. 121).

Consistent with this analysis, we find that inquiry-based strategies work tends to be natural and informal (Murphy, 2005; Odell, 1997). They are emergent and voluntary (Katzenmeyer & Moller, 2001; Lieberman, 1992; Wasley, 1991). Teachers "assume leadership naturally as part of a more professional conception of teaching work" (Darling-Hammond et al., 1995, p. 88). Work is collaborative and collective rather than individualistic and competitive (Fay, 1992a, 1992b; Mitchell, 1997; Spillane & Louis, 2002). Leadership is seen as an essential component of a consequence, "the 'normal' role of the teacher is expanded" (Darling-Hammond et al., 1995, p. 87). The web of relationships in schools with inquiry-anchored teacher leadership designs is richer and more complex.

Teacher Leadership Work

> With a remarkable consistency, teacher leaders identified their roles primarily in terms of helping and supporting fellow teachers within their buildings. (Smylie & Denny, 1989, p. 7)

When we draw an analytic magnet across the scholarship on teacher leadership tasks, activities, functions, and roles, most of the work clusters into two broad related categories: helping teacher colleagues and facilitating school improvement. In the first domain, which is in many ways foundational for the second, teacher leaders work to develop and maintain positive *working relations with their peers* (Ainscow & Southworth, 1996;

Murphy, 2005). They become mechanisms for empowering colleagues (Berry & Ginsberg, 1990; Snell & Swanson, 2000), laboring diligently to actualize what Ainscow and Southworth (1996) label the "principle of participation" (p. 233), namely, "drawing together the staff" (p. 234) and "facilitat[ing] collaboration on activities and encourag[ing] information sharing" (Hatfield et al., 1986, p. 16).

Perhaps the central dynamic of providing help and support for teacher colleagues is role modeling (Doyle, 2000). These teachers lead by example (Ainscow & Southworth, 1996). They endeavor to "create and sustain a collaborative and collegial atmosphere" (Doyle, 2000, p, 16), "a trusting atmosphere where fellow teachers can try new teaching practices" (p. 15). They promote change (Harrison & Lembeck, 1996). Or more specifically, they "positively influence the willingness and capacity of other teachers to implement change in the school" (Leithwood, Steinbach, & Ryan, 1997, p. 5)—and they confront the barriers that stand in the way of change efforts (Crowther et al., 2002; Smylie et al., 2007).

While teacher leaders exercise an array of responsibilities in *facilitating school improvement*, three broad domains stand out: administrative tasks, staff development activities, and curricular and instructional functions. To begin with, over the years, researchers have consistently reported that administrative tasks are a central element of teacher leadership (Leithwood et al., 1997; York-Barr & Duke, 2004). On the one hand, given the central place of administrative work in school-level leadership in general, this conclusion is neither surprising nor troubling. On the other hand, as is the case with principal leadership, when administrative responsibilities consume teacher leaders or become disconnected from "educational" leadership, either from the natural turn of events or from the manipulations of formal school leaders, this conclusion is more problematic (Murphy, 2005; Wasley, 1991). A key dimension of the management domain of teacher leadership work, then, is using administration in the service of enhanced learning and teaching and improved organizational performance.

Katzenmeyer and Moller (2001) report that much teacher leadership has to do with the professional development of colleagues. Indeed, teacher leadership for school improvement comes to life when teachers assume responsibility for professional development (Firestone & Martinez, 2007; Spillane & Louis, 2002; Supovitz & Turner, 2000). Here, teacher leaders take on the tasks of "identify[ing] school and individual teacher growth needs, identifying available resources to assist in meeting those needs" (Fessler & Ungaretti, 1994, p. 216), "offering professional learning experiences, and evaluating the outcomes of teacher development" (Childs-Bowen et al., 2000, p. 30). They are often active in educating preservice teachers (Fessler & Ungaretti, 1994; Troen & Boles, 1994), inducting new teachers (Leithwood et al., 1997) and serving as mentors to new faculty and peer coaches to more experienced colleagues (Katzenmeyer & Moller, 2001; Murphy, 2005). These educators also lead by (1) exercising influence over decisions about professional development and by facilitating professional learning opportunities (Katzenmeyer & Moller, 2001); (2) as noted earlier, modeling the importance of professional development through their own actions (Harrison & Lembeck, 1996; Smylie et al., 2007); and (3) engaging in informal counseling (Doyle, 2000).

Finally, teacher leaders often assume responsibilities for and perform tasks designed to strengthen the school's curricular and instructional program and learning and teaching in classrooms (Boles & Troen, 1996; Spillane & Louis, 2002; Wasley, 1991). They often provide curricular help in particular subject domains and leadership of instructional programs (Hart, 1990).

Teacher Leader Skills

Teachers who have a wide array of skills, broad knowledge, a healthy attitude about service to others, and enthusiasm and willingness to serve have the greatest success as leaders. (Killion, 1996, p. 69)

Researchers regularly report that in addition to pedagogical and curricular expertise, teacher leaders are characterized by skills in four areas: visioning, interpersonal activities, collaborative work, and management skills. Snell and Swanson (2000) maintain that vision is "essential for teacher leadership, for without a vision of the goals toward which one is striving . . . one cannot be effective in achieving them" (p. 10). One aspect of visioning, according to Crowther and his associates (2002), is the facility to articulate "clear views [about] a better world" (p. 11) for education and for youngsters. Another component is an "understanding of school and district operations" (Harrison & Lembeck, 1996, p. 113), the capacity to "acquire an appreciation for teachers, principals, and the community as a whole" (Killion, 1996, p. 69). Thus vision includes a distinct strand of local insight, "matching local needs and capabilities" (Lieberman, Saxl, & Miles, 1988, p. 158) and adding challenges in context (Katzenmeyer & Moller, 2001).

"Strong interpersonal skills" (Snell & Swanson, 2000, p. 3) are also at the core of teacher leadership (Berry & Ginsberg, 1990; Childs-Bowen et al., 2000). Indeed, Lieberman (1987) asserts that "the key skills of people who play these [teacher leadership] roles turn out to be in the areas of social interaction" (pp. 402–403), and Yarger and Lee (1994) aver that the "ability . . . to work with colleagues distinguishes effective teachers of teachers from effective teachers of children" (p. 229). "These interpersonal skills, in interaction with personal characteristics, allow teacher leaders to earn the trust and respect of their peers and to guide and influence a colleague's instructional activities and decisions . . . and to collaborate with their colleagues on instructional improvement" (p. 229).

Indispensable elements here include communication skills (Moller & Eggen, 2005), especially the capacity "to communicate proactively, confidently, assertively" (Crowther, 1997, p. 12), and clearly with adults (Yarger & Lee, 1994). One important proficiency is the ability to bring out the best in others. For example, in her landmark study on teacher work, Rosenholtz (1989) found that "teacher leaders suggest and inspire ideas and discourse, drawing others upward to higher places" (p. 66). Adeptness at solving problems, resolving conflicts, negotiating rough terrain, and leading diverse participants to shared decisions is often found in the interpersonal toolkits of teacher leaders (Murphy, 2005). Teacher leaders also exhibit skills in creating trust (Lieberman, 1987).

Closely linked to the engagement of interpersonal capabilities is the third skill domain, collaborative proficiencies, an element of learning communities that we examined above.

Administrative skills incorporate a final set of proficiencies that define teacher leaders (Boles & Troen, 1996; York-Barr & Duke, 2004). Lieberman et al. (1988) hold that to manage work, teacher leaders need a "blend of skills, including managing time, setting priorities for work, delegating tasks and authority, taking initiative, monitoring progress, and coordinating the many strands of work taking place in their schools" (p. 158). Often featured here are skills in confronting and overcoming troublesome barriers, both structural and human (Crowther, 1997; Miller et al., 2000), and in building supportive structures (Lieberman et al., 1988) to accomplish important ends. Skills in securing and using resources often characterize teacher leaders (Miller et al., 2000). Lieberman and her colleagues (1988, p. 155) also confirm that a set of skills they label "organizational diagnosis—an understanding of the school culture and the ability to diagnose it—is critical if a leader is to have the basis for knowing how and where to intervene to mobilize people to take action and begin to work together" (p. 155).

Trust

If teachers cannot trust each other, they cannot work together effectively to create systemic change. (Louis, 2007, p. 19)

It is essential that efforts to improve struggling schools include a focus on building and maintaining trust in schools. (Goddard, Salloum, & Berebitsky, 2009)

The latent agency of trusting relationships makes the formation of trust an important process for school leaders to understand. (Adams, 2010, p. 256)

Even more so than with the other elements and norms of professional community, relational trust is difficult to corral and hold in place. It has its own space and is the catalyst for the growth and effective functioning of the other elements of teacher community (e.g., collaboration) (Cosner, 2009; Mitchell & Sackney, 2006; Scribner et al., 1999). As such, it occupies an essential place in the equation to promote learning and the formation of a professional culture (Silins et al. 2002; Useem et al., 1997). In their landmark analysis of Chicago elementary schools, Bryk and his associates (2010, p. 202) concluded that trust is "both a lubricant for organizational change and a moral resource for sustaining the hard work of school improvement," a type of "social glue" (p. 140). Without trust, "relationships and respect are compromised and mistrust exerts a corrosive influence" (MacBeath, 2005, p. 353). Efforts unravel and "meaningful organizational learning is frustrated" (Useem et al., 1997, p. 57). The doors to professional community and school improvement rarely open in its absence (Bryk et al., 2010; Firestone & Martinez, 2009; Mulford & Silins, 2003).

Numerous studies have shown that "trust plays a key role in obtaining valued future outcomes" (Goddard et al., 2009, p. 295) such as professional norms (Bryk et al., 2010; Bryk & Schneider, 2002; Bulkley & Hicks, 2005; Louis et al., 2010), teacher learning (Bryk et al., 2010; Bryk & Schneider, 2002; Goddard et al., 2009), productive work (Cosner, 2009; Useem et al., 1997), change (Bryk et al., 2010; Bryk & Schneider, 2002; Wahlstrom & Louis, 2008), and student achievement (Bryk et al., 2010; Bryk & Schneider, 2002; Goddard et al., 2009; Leithwood, 2008). Relational trust, researchers find, is an especially significant coordinating mechanism in institutions like schools that have high task complexity (Adams, 2010; Adams & Forsyth, 2009) and in organizations where nonrelational "gluing" strategies are difficult to use (Kochanek, 2005). We also know now that the connections between trust and outcomes are even more powerful in difficult times and in schools working with underserved children (Bryk et al., 2010; Bryk & Schneider, 2002; Goddard et al., 2009).

Trust is defined in slightly different but clearly overlapping ways in the research literature. For example, Louis (2007, p. 27) informs us that trust can be viewed as "confidence in or reliance on the integrity, veracity, justice, friendship, or other sound principle, of another person or group." Two seminal lines of work on trust dominate the school improvement research literature. One is by Hoy and his colleagues, especially Forsyth (Adams & Forsyth, 2009), Goddard (Goddard et al., 2009), and Tschannen-Moran (Tschannen-Moran & Barr, 2004). The other is by Bryk and assorted colleagues (Bryk et al., 2010; Bryk & Schneider, 2002). Hoy and his associates describe five essential attributes of trust: benevolence, honesty, openness, reliability, and competence. Bryk and team anchor trust on four pillars: respect, competence, personal regard for others, and integrity. In their foundational work on communities of practice, Louis and Kruse (Kruse et al., 1995; Louis et al., 2010) explain trust in terms of four ingredients: integrity, concern, competence, and reliability. Looking across these hallmark analyses and research that followed, we cull four major themes from the chronicle on mutual trust: openness, competency, integrity, and caring.

All work on trust underscores the need for *openness*, without which the other themes lay fallow. Openness is defined as a willingness to disarm, to dismantle the barriers erected to protect against the potential harm from relationships. Analysts refer to this as a willingness to assume the posture of vulnerability (Adams, 2010; Dirks & Ferrin, 2002) "under the conditions of risk and interdependence" (Robinson, 2007, p. 18; Fullan & Ballew, 2002).

Integrity encompasses a number of core ideas. Consistency between words and actions is important, as is honesty (Bryk et al., 2010; Robinson, 2007). Also lodged here are transparency and authenticity (Hoy et al., 1998; Leithwood, 2008). Reliability is found on center stage in most reviews of integrity, what Raywid (1995, p. 59) refers to as a "sense of reciprocity." Ethics is often contained here as well, specifically the commitment and practice of working in the best interests of children and families (Beck & Murphy, 1996; Bryk et al., 2010; Louis, 2007).

Competence is the keystone to the interpersonal framework that supports and energizes trust (Wenger, 2000). Wahlstrom and Louis (2008) describe this as the ability of colleagues to do what is needed (also Rumberger, 2011). Bryk and associates (2010) concur portraying competence as the knowledge, skills, and capacity to deliver required assistance.

Care lies at the heart of relational trust as well (Hattie, 2009; Louis, 2007; Yu et al., 2002). It is conveyed in the research on teacher professional community as a sense of inclusiveness (Stoll et al., 2006) and a concern one for the other (Raywid, 1995). Care encompasses attention to mutual support (McLaughlin & Talbert, 2001; Mulford & Silins, 2003). Central also is the demonstration of personal and professional respect (Curry, 2008; Drago-Severson, 2004; Robinson, 2007), "a basic regard for the dignity of others" (Kochanek, 2005, p. 7) and a willingness to hear what others are saying and weigh it seriously (Kochanek, 2005). Bryk and team (2010, p. 138) characterize this as "a genuine sense of listening." Analysts conclude that caring in communities of practice requires "the assumption of good faith" (Grossman et al., 2001, p. 62) about the motives and actions of others, and extending legitimacy to those others (Printy, 2008). It implies safe space to work and learn (Grossman et al., 2001; Hattie, 2009), "protected public space" (Ancess, 2003, p. 10), a willingness to take risks with and for others (Fullan & Ballew, 2002; Robinson, 2007), reducing the climate of vulnerability (Fullan & Ballew, 2002; Kruse et al., 1995) and a tone of civility and respect in communal interactions (Bryk et al., 2010; Mulford & Silins, 2003; Penuel et al., 2010). It encompasses a commitment to extend effort and support beyond what is normally expected or required (Bryk et al., 2010; Kochanek, 2005).

Before moving to the impact of professional culture, it is productive to pause for two reminders about this sixth element that helps define communities of practice. We know that trust can flow from different sources. For example, trust can be lodged in institutional policies and regulations or negotiated contracts (Kochanek, 2005). Our focus here is on a different taproot, social, interpersonal, or relational trust (Bryk et al., 2010). We also want to be clear that these deepening relationships among teachers do not gainsay the need for a strong hand for those in formal leadership positions (Bryk et al., 2010; Murphy, 2005).

MODEL AND THEORY OF ACTION: IMPACT OF COLLABORATIVE COMMUNITIES OF PROFESSIONAL PRACTICE

> Research provides evidence that strong professional learning communities can foster teacher learning. (Borko, 2004, p. 6)

> Communities of practice offer a pathway to improved teacher quality and educational change. (Printy, 2008, p. 190)

> The social capital formed in schools when coworkers are active participants in the building's "civil society" is a critical ingredient for organizational effectiveness. (Useem et al., 1997, p. 72)

The model in Figure 5.1 shows that teacher communities are designed ultimately to enhance student academic and social learning. Our framework also reveals that the connection between community and student learning is indirect, or mediated (Supovitz & Christman, 2003; Visscher & Witziers, 2004). It also reminds us of the reciprocal connections among the pieces of the narrative. That is, community powers professional learning and learning, and in turn, deepens community (Osterman, 2000; Stoll et al., 2006).

The initial effect in the model is twofold: greater learning (knowledge capital) and enhanced professional norms (professional capital). Augmentation of capital results in more effective instructional practice, which, in turn, leads to greater student learning. We explain this chain of linkages in detail below.

Intellectual and Professional Capital

> Distributing leadership across an increased number of people in an organization has the potential to build capacity within a school through the development of the intellectual and professional capital of the teachers. (Timperley, 2005)

Intellectual Capital

To develop expertise, teachers need ongoing ways of expanding their knowledge and improving their skills. Research increasingly suggests that the most effective way is to develop professional learning communities. (Rumberger, 2011, p. 224)

The notion behind a community of practice is that it provides a context that fosters learning and development. (Palinscar et al., 1998, p. 10)

Communities of inquiry provide cauldrons for the formation of "funds of knowledge" (Palinscar et al., 1998, p. 17), of human and social capital (Penuel et al., 2009; Spillane, Halverson, & Diamond, 2001; Wigginton, 1992) that is used to improve the education of children (Ancess, 2003). That is, communities of practice exist to promote teacher learning (Darling-Hammond et al., 1995; Grossman et al., 2001). They provide "the basic building blocks of a social learning system" (Wenger, 2000, p. 229), participation in which is a catalyst for learning (Connolly & James, 2006; Mullen & Hutinger, 2008; Wenger, 1998). Although the research here is insufficient to advance dramatic claims, it does strongly suggest that professional cultures with the norms discussed above become productive venues for teachers to learn and develop together (Franke, Carpenter, Levi, & Fennema, 2001; Grossman et al., 2001), to enhance the knowledge and skills of teachers (Harris, 2009; Smylie & Denny, 1989; Spillane & Louis, 2002). In communities of professional practice, researchers find that educators become a "profession of learners" (Silins & Mulford, 2004, p. 448) and "communities of knowledge" (Craig, 2009, p. 601), a "source of energy to push a trajectory of learning" (Levine & Marcus, 2007, p. 133). There is also a growing body of knowledge that these communities provide a more robust method of learning than the more traditional forms of professional development to which teachers are exposed (Grossman et al., 2001; McLaughlin & Talbert, 2001).

At the core of the professional community concept is the understanding that "thought, learning, and the construction of knowledge are not just influenced by social factors but are, in fact, social phenomena" (Palinscar et al., 1998, p. 6). Learning is considered in social terms (Horn, 2005; Stein & Coburn, 2008; Wenger, 1998), as a social process (Wenger, 2000). In schools "teachers learn through situated and social interactions with colleagues who possess distributed expertise and with whom they have opportunities for sustained conversations related to mutual interest" (Curry, 2008, p. 738). Learning is site based and job embedded (Ermeling, 2010; Horn, 2010), or situated (Wenger, 1998). Learning is also constructed (Mullen & Hutinger, 2008). It is work that does not feature the transmission of knowledge but rather the "active deconstruction of knowledge through reflection and analysis, and its reconstruction through action in a particular context" (Stoll et al., 2006, p. 233).

Community-based learning fosters both individual and group learning, with a special emphasis on the creation of collective knowledge (Harris, 2009; Ingram, Seashore Louis, & Schroeder, 2004). Learning in professional communities covers a wider spectrum of developmental work as well. Most prominently, it includes the broad range of informal exchanges, "not just those that deliberately and systematically set out to improve practice" (Horn, 2005, p. 230). It emphasizes what Wenger (2000) refers to as the ongoing experience of work.

In schools with strong professional cultures, learning is also a reciprocal process (Heck & Hallinger, 2009), "the learning that results from the participation feeds back into the community and impacts subsequent participation" (Printy, 2008, p. 189). Learning in communities of inquiry is about expertise. In addition, as a social phenomenon learning is about reconstructing professional culture (Printy, 2008; Wenger, 1998), what Grossman and associates (2001, p. 12) portray as a "transformation of the social setting in which individuals work." Finally, there is evidence that the teacher learning in professional communities is more transformative and more thoroughly internalized than knowledge acquired in more traditional formats (Levine & Marcus, 2007; Wenger, 1998).

Professional Capital

Professional communities provide settings in which teacher professionalism is able to flourish. (Eilers & Camacho, 2007, p. 617)

Collaborative working conditions can lead whole departments to shared norms, values, and orientations. (Levine & Marcus, 2010, p. 389)

As we illustrate in Figure 5.1, teacher communities produce professional as well as knowledge capital. They are continually adding new fibers in the professional tapestry, repairing torn threads, and enriching existing strands. Communities transform the meaning of school as a place (Goldenberg, 2004). We examine these strands of rebuilding in three overlapping clusters: (1) changes in occupational norms, (2) reinforcement to the core elements and norms of community presented above, and (3) creating powerful professional values and attitudes. Before we do so, two points need to be made explicit. First, no one has crafted nonleaky containers to capture these "fundamental shifts." Second, as we have explained throughout these chapters, action throughout the framework in Figure 5.1 is interactive and reciprocal. Energy and influence move in all directions in a "cyclical pattern" (King, 2001, p. 24). For example, core elements and norms lead to teacher learning and professionalism. Each, in turn, strengthens the elements of community (e.g., shared accountability). Likewise, learning influences professional culture and culture impacts learning (Adams, 2010; Olivier & Hipp, 2006; Saunders et al., 2009).

In Chapter 7, we expose the *organizational norms* of schools and explain how they can constrain the development of professional culture. Here we simply note that as professional culture gains a foothold in schools, it begins to alter the long-standing ways in which teaching unfolds. We know, for example, that for over a century, teaching has been primarily a private affair. With the development of community, this deeply entrenched norm of privacy is no longer dominant (Bulkley & Hicks, 2005; Louis, Marks, & Kruse, 1996; Webb, 2005). In communities, teaching practice is made "public through peer observations, review of student work and teacher curriculum, collaborative planning and problem solving, and team teaching" (Ancess, 2003, p. 12).

Schools are also defined by norms of autonomy and isolation. Teachers work alone and sink or swim accordingly (McLaughlin & Talbert, 2001). With its emphasis on collaboration, interaction, and interdependence (Palinscar et al., 1998) professional culture undermines these well-established occupational norms, "counteract[ing] the fragmentation of work" (Newmann et al., 1989, p. 223) and "breaking down the barriers that isolate teachers" (Scribner et al., 1999, p. 136; Lieberman et al., 1988).

Professional culture with its ethic of constructive feedback and critique also assails the deeply-etched organizational norm of civility in schools, where civility is defined as an unwillingness to confront problems and a penchant to withdraw in the face of conflict. Finally, we see in narratives of professional community the displacement of the norm of separation between administration and teaching, the one that holds that administrators lead and teachers teach. There is a softening of this boundary (Sykes, & Elmore, 1989; Wahlstrom & Louis, 2008).

Per our discussion of reciprocity above, we should not be surprised to learn that the elements of communities of learning (e.g., shared goals) not only power professionalism but are, in turn, enriched by those values, orientations, and attitudes. *Community norms* concurrently define teacher teams and are the outcomes of the work of those groups. There is considerable evidence, for example, that as communities function, they create internal feedback loops that thicken the very norms that define professional community (e.g., shared accountability). We know, for example, that in the process of changing teacher culture and renorming the organization, collaborative work reinforces the vision and purpose of the school (Walker & Slear, 2011). Collective work also deepens and extends the threads of collaboration (Curry, 2008, Supovitz, 2002; Vescio et al., 2008), thus "sustaining and strengthening professional community" (Louis & Marks, 1998, p. 560) itself (Stoll et al., 2006; York-Barr & Duke, 2004). Similarly, community is defined by ownership and increases empowerment in the process of engagement (Ancess, 2003; Blase & Kirby, 2009; Drago-Severson, 2004), especially augmenting teacher buy in. Shared accountability is also reinforced and expanded by professional communities of practice (Kruse et al., 1995; Timperley, 2009). It is both an element of and a product of learning communities (Kruse et al., 1995; Printy, 2008). Finally, there is strong empirical support for the claim that trust and caring are enriched by enhanced professional capital (Louis, 2007; McLaughlin & Talbert, 2001).

In addition to influencing occupational and community norms, learning teams foster other *professional norms,* attitudes, and values. Scholarship on this dimension covers a good bit of territory, and a variety of taxonomies to capture this research have been crafted. We organize the literature on professional norms into three clusters: agency, work orientation, and identity. Collectively, concepts in these categories address teachers' professional citizenship behaviors and attitudes regarding the school as a place of work (Dirks & Ferrin, 2002), their "affective dispositions" (Leithwood, Day, et al., 2006, p. 89), and "personal and organizational behavior" (Goddard et al., 2000, p. 502).

The claim that communities of practice enhance individual and collective "agency" is one of the most visible themes in the storyline on professional norms and values (Katzenmeyer & Moller, 2001; Lieberman, 1992; Smylie et al., 2002), the belief that efficacy is perhaps the key pathway by which professional culture shapes student learning (Goddard et al., 2000; Sweetland & Hoy, 2000; Tschannen-Moran & Barr, 2004). Analysts define agency in similar ways. All definitions feature the essential idea of faculty "feel[ing] competent that they can teach in ways that enhance student success" (Printy, 2008, p. 200), the individual and collective sense that they can help ensure that the school achieves its goals and that they will have a positive impact on students (Goddard et al., 2000; Murphy, Weil, Hallinger, & Mitman, 1982; Olivier & Hipp, 2006). Raywid (1995, p. 70) refers to this as "a strong sense of their power over the life chances of students." Efficacy includes beliefs about competence (Dannetta, 2002; Gurr et al., 2005; Harris, 2004), the ability to employ that competence in the service of students, and the garnering of satisfaction linked to those efforts (Newmann et al., 1989, Roney et al., 2007; Wenger & Snyder, 2000).

Communities of learning also exercise a strong pull on the "work orientation" of teachers, both individually and collectively (Bryk et al., 2010; Riehl & Sipple, 1996). This orientation is visible in a number of values and behaviors, often in a reciprocal relationship with agency (Newmann et al., 1989). We know, for example, that professional communities of practice can create hope and a sense of possibility, a "more optimistic and encouraging culture" (Strahan, 2003, p. 130), frames often in short supply in schools serving students placed at risk (McLaughlin & Talbert, 2001). Professional community strengthens teachers' "willingness to struggle" (Ancess, 2003, p. 11). It adds to the "reservoir of resilience" (p. 11), providing new "sources of energy and renewal" (Strahan, 2003, p. 138) and reducing feelings of failure, cynicism, and burnout (Felner et al., 2007; Louis, 2007; Newmann et al., 1989). Community produces positive assessments from teachers about their work environments (Heck & Marcoulides, 1996). Professionalism also leads to additional effort (Newmann et al., 1989; Olivier & Hipp, 2006; Scheurich, 1998), what Useem and associates (1997, p. 58) refer to as the formation of a "norm of diligent work." Dedication is an important aspect of work orientation that grows in professional communities (Kruse et al.,

1995; Pounder, 1999; Riehl & Sipple, 1996). In general, teachers in communities of practice fuel commitment to the profession of teaching and to the school as a place of work (Ancess, 2003; Osterman, 2000; Somech & Bogler, 2002), an idea "typically conceptualized as a positive, affective attachment to one's work" (Dannetta, 2002, p. 145). More specifically, communities of professional practice strengthen commitment to student success (Dannetta, 2002; Darling-Hammond et al., 2002).

Motivation is also positively impacted by learning communities (Blase & Blase, 2000; Bryk et al., 2010; Felner et al., 2007), another condition that shares a relationship with agency (Goddard et al., 2000; Leithwood, 2008; Tschannen-Moran & Barr, 2004). So too is persistence in effort (Printy, 2008; Riester et al., 2002), with teacher professional communities coming to be defined by a "culture of teacher persistence" (Ancess, 2003, p. 77). Learning communities foster work orientations that privilege risk taking, proactiveness, and innovation (Blanc et al., 2010; Franke et al., 2001; Hoy et al., 1998), a "willingness to try new things" (Robinson, 2007, p. 20).

Researchers also affirm that communities of practice increase professional capital by strengthening personal and collective "identity" for teachers, identity that, in turn, powers better instructional practice (Bryk et al., 2010; Doyle, 2000; Stone, Horejs, & Lomas, 1997). Under conditions of community, sense of belonging and buy in are augmented (Battistich et al., 1997; Stoll et al., 2006). As we have noted above, the norm of ownership at the heart of professional community is enriched (Cosner, 2009; Etheridge, Valesky, Horgan, Nunnery, & Smith, 1992; Smylie, 1996). Teachers are "drawn in, involvement engagement, and affiliation" (Jackson, 2000, p. 72) expand. There is an enhanced feeling of fit (Au, 2002) and integration (Blase & Kirby, 2009; Newmann et al., 1989).

One way that learning communities build professional capital is by bolstering teacher morale (Blase & Kirby, 2009; Conley, 1991; Tschannen-Moran & Barr, 2004). Professional culture also adds to the storehouse of confidence and self-esteem (Blase & Kirby, 2009; Hattie, 2009; Roney et al., 2007). These identity changes occur because teachers feel more valued and more successful in socially and professionally dense cultures than they do working in isolation (Felner et al., 2007; Kruse et al., 1995; McLaughlin & Talbert, 2001). Finally, identity is nourished because teachers in learning communities experience greater job satisfaction than do their colleagues in nonprofessional anchored work environments (Cosner, 2009; Pounder, 1999), both in the short term and in their overall careers (McLaughlin & Talbert, 2001). They enjoy their work more (Battistich et al., 1997).

Teaching Practice and Student Learning

Well-developed PLCs have positive impact on both teaching practice and student achievement. (Vescio et al., 2008, p. 80)

We emphasize the importance of professional community largely because of the accumulating evidence that it is related both to improved instruction and to student achievement. (Louis et al., 2010, p. 319)

As we move to the far right-hand side of the model in Figure 5.1, we see that all the capital accumulated to date is linked to the improvement of instructional practice, which, in turn, powers important outcomes, especially student academic and social learning.

Teaching Practice

The improvement of professional practice is the most common rationale for the formation of teacher community. (Grossman et al., 2001, p. 15)

A major contribution of this research is the strong and significant impacts of teacher peer influence on instructional practice. (Supovitz et al., 2010, p. 45)

Knowledge capital and professional capital formation in communities impacts instructional practice (Curry, 2008; Horn, 2010; Supovitz, 2002). There is evidence that this linkage is real, positive, and reciprocal (Bryk et al., 2010; Leithwood, Jantzi, & McElheron-Hopkins, 2006; Louis et al., 2010; McDougall et al., 2007; Visscher & Witziers, 2004; Wahlstrom & Louis, 2008). Teacher practice is changed (Curry, 2008; Finnigan & Gross, 2007; Gray et al., 1999) and more productive learning opportunities are made available to students (Horn, 2005; McKeever, 2003; McLaughlin & Talbert, 2001).

While there is relative consistency and clarity to this point in the story (see Rowan and Miller, 2007 for some cautionary notes), deeper analyses provide less full-bodied descriptions. That is, while there are summative claims about improved instruction resulting from the work of teacher professional communities—stronger instructional norms, enhancements in teacher work, more effective teaching, better teachers, better pedagogy, and so forth, the specific nature of this improved teaching is not well explained. Here is what we do know. The more effective teaching linked to strong professional culture pivots on increasing academic press (Felner et al., 2007; Mulford & Silins, 2003; Sebastian & Allensworth, 2012). Stronger instruction in professional environments is nourished by deepening knowledge of students and their learning needs (Blanc et al., 2010; Hattie, 2009; Horn, 2005). It is also fostered by new approaches to addressing those needs, by a willingness to engage in new instructional designs in the face of problems (Wenger & Snyder, 2000). Finally, there is evidence that the more effective instruction in professional communities reflects the principles of authentic pedagogy and learning (Bidwell & Yasumoto, 1999; Levine & Marcus, 2010; Louis & Marks, 1998). Included here are practices such as student-focused work, constructivist activities, emphasis on higher level thinking, an achievement orientation, instruction more finely tuned to student needs, student exploration, inquiry-oriented work, and visible linkages between classroom work and the real world (Felner et al., 2007; Supovitz, 2002; Vescio et al., 2008).

Student Learning

Professional community has significant indirect effects on achievement. (Louis et al., 2010, p. 330)

The literature supports the assumption that student learning increases when teachers participate in PLCs. (Vescio et al., 2008, p. 87)

The most salient question confronting everyone associated with professional communities of practice—"assuming that the magnitude of the relationship with workplace outcomes is a criterion for judging the practical importance of a construct" (Dirks & Ferrin, 2002, p. 26) is, Does professional culture result in enhanced organizational outcomes (Goddard et al., 2009; Stoll et al., 2006)? More specifically, given the current climate of high standards and accountability, the viability of professional communities as a pathway to reform will be established by their ability to enhance student learning (Mitchell & Sackney, 2006; Spillane & Louis, 2002; Vescio et al., 2008).

In terms of organizational outcomes, researchers document positive linkages between teacher professional community and school improvement, school effectiveness, goal attainment, change, and organizational efficiency (Adams, 2010; Bryk et al., 2010; Eilers & Camacho, 2007; Goddard et al., 2000; Heck & Marcoulides, 1996; Leithwood, Day, et al., 2006; Newmann et al., 2001; Olivier & Hipp, 2006; Silins et al., 2002). Fine-grained analyses (Bryk et al., 2010; Goddard et al., 2009) and the most scholarly reviews (Hattie, 2009; Vescio et al., 2008) confirm positive linkages between professional culture and student achievement. Consistently, this work concludes that these impacts are significant and meaningful (Bryk et al., 2010; Leithwood & Mascall, 2008; Louis et al., 2010).

Investigators have also discovered positive relationships between teacher community and other valued outcomes. They confirm linkages between professional communities and lower numbers of student suspensions, reduced dropout rates, reduced teacher turnover, and stronger connections with parents (Bulkley & Hicks, 2005; Louis, 2007; O'Donnell & White, 2005).

We close here with two additional insights. First, there is increasing evidence that the impact of professional culture is particularly strong in schools with high concentrations of students placed at risk and schools in disadvantaged areas (Bryk et al., 2010; Stoll et al., 2006). Second, achievement effects are mediated by student motivation, persistence, and engagement (Stoll et al., 2006; Useem et al., 1997). That is, improved teacher practice works by enhancing participation and effort among students (Bruggencate et al., 2012; Horn, 2005; Silins & Mulford, 2004).

CONCLUSION

Chapters in this part of the book address the issue of professional culture, communities of professional practice. They are situated between the narratives on culture of support for students and communities of engagement for parents. This chapter was devoted to the task of providing a deep analysis of the concept of professional culture. Anchoring on Figure 5.1, we explored the elements of professional communities of practice and the impacts of professional culture in schools. We turn next to barriers and supports in the quest to develop more professional anchored schools.

6

Communities of Professionalism

Barriers and Supports

> To create a professional community, both structural conditions and social and human resources are essential. (Penuel et al., 2010, p. 58)

In the last chapter, we examined the concept of learning community. We examined each of the pieces of a community and explained how the idea actually works, building needed capacity to power stronger student performance. However, it is important to acknowledge that the construction of functional learning communities is not an easy task. As we will see, they run against the grain of extant school culture and climate. Additionally, they present all the difficulties associated with collaborative human exchanges. In this chapter, we turn our analytic torchlight on developing highly functional communities of practice. In the first half of the chapter, we examine barriers to the formation and development processes. Some are already in play, part of the organizational and cultural geography of the landscape (e.g., the isolation of teachers). Some emerge in the building process (e.g., unfounded assumptions.) We also present some cautions that should not be forgotten when it comes to forging teacher communities. In the second half of the chapter, we provide a rich description of the supports that will help productive communities of learning develop and flourish (e.g., carving out time for collaboration). All of these supports rely upon the commitment and constructions skills of school leaders.

CAUTIONS AND BARRIERS

> Recent research has shown that organizational restructuring alone does not increase the likelihood that groups will develop communities of instructional practice. (Supovitz & Poglinco, 2001, p. 17)

> Collective work is the vehicle for clarifying the expected and possible, as well as the prohibited and unthinkable. (Kruse, Seashore Louis, K., & Bryk, 1995, p. 40)

Cautions

> In contrast to the idealistic visions sketched in the advocacy literature on teacher community, bringing teachers together can hurt as well as help. (Grossman Wineburg, & Woolworth, 2001, p. 984)

> Collaborative cultures, which by definition have close relationships, are indeed powerful, but unless they are focusing on the right things they may end up being powerfully wrong. (Fullan & Ballew, 2002, p. 8)

The Empty Vessel Problem

One of the most critical concerns is a misguided faith in the ability of structure and policy to power change. Specifically, by ignoring the tendency for reforms to materialize sans engine and drive train, we often end up with a change in name only (McLaughlin & Talbert, 2001). In this case, that would be a group of teachers bound together by time but without the trust, vision, resources, and responsibility to transform into a community (Penuel et al., 2009; Stein & Coburn, 2008; Youngs, 2007).

While we often describe this in terms of the creation of an "empty shell," a second "in name only" problem needs to be surfaced. We refer to the formation of inauthentic, artificial, or pseudo community (Grossman et al., 2001; McLaughlin & Talbert, 2001; Vescio et al., 2008). Pseudo community may actually be more harmful than the empty structure because it has the potential to actively solidify nonproductive patterns of interactions among teachers (Hoy et al., 1998), for example, burying conflicts and problems and silencing joint exchange (Grossman et al., 2001).

A third issue here merits attention as well. There is an ongoing reminder in the literature that teaching communities are in the service of valued outcomes, not ends in themselves (Morrissey, 2000). Yet it is not difficult to find goal displacement, schools where the objective becomes to develop a professional community—a way station on the way to the real goal of student learning.

Acknowledgment of Hard Work

A particularly troubling problem in the teacher community literature is the undertreatment of the hard slog necessary to create communities of practice (Grossman et al., 2001; Levine & Marcus, 2010). While a few analysts have cautioned about romanticizing learning communities (Goldenberg, 2004; Wenger, 1998; Wilson & Berne, 1999), these warnings often go unheeded (Leithwood et al., 2010). As Borko (2004, p. 7) reminds us, "the development of teacher communities is difficult and time consuming work," never guaranteed (Horn, 2005; Supovitz & Poglinco, 2001) and hardly the walk in the park implied in many of the writings in this area. All of the barriers we discuss below are robust. They require concerted attention to dismantle, slay, or bypass. Successful change, generally a difficult proposition, demands even more thoughtful work when the task is creating learning communities.

One caution here is that too often assumptions trump the planning and learning required to ensure the success of a community of professionalism. For example, there is abundant evidence that teachers are not accustomed to working together. Neither, contrary to the extant assumption, do they bring a great deal of expertise to collaborative professional work (Wilson & Berne, 1999). The possibility of pooling bad ideas is quite real (Fullan & Ballew, 2002; Timperley, 2005, 2009). So too is the potential for current frames to choke out new ideas or to bend them to accommodate existing norms and practices (Wilson & Berne, 1999). The laws of resistance to change and regression to the known do not disappear when working on community building (Goldstein, 2004; Orr et al., 2008). It is often difficult for teachers (or anyone else) to see beyond the horizons they know. The tools to undertake work do not materialize simply because the idea of learning communities has gained legitimacy. These are not insurmountable problems, but they often go unaddressed under the patina of romanticism covering professional community in much of the literature.

Accounting for Context

School contexts are not blank slates where pure ideas are tried out. (Craig, 2009, p. 615)

As we have seen, teacher learning communities are defined by universal ideas (e.g., collective responsibility). But this does not mean that getting those principles and norms into play is the same in all situations (Supovitz, 2008; Vescio et al., 2008). As Craig (2009, p. 615) reminds us, community work "fuse[s] or collide[s] with the mixture of what is already going on." The cost of overlooking context in the area of learning communities is especially high (Walker & Slear, 2011). We know that subject matter is important in the community building process (Burch & Spillane, 2003;

McLaughlin & Talbert, 2001). That is, subject matter norms will mediate how teachers think about and respond to community building initiatives. The obvious corollary is that the department context matters for practice communities (Siskin, 1994; Stoll et al., 2006; Visscher & Witziers, 2004). History matters as well (Kochanek, 2005), as does the existing stock of relational trust (Bryk et al., 2010). Level of schooling is important (McLaughlin & Talbert, 2001; Moller & Eggen, 2005). District context and school size exert influence over community development (Dannetta, 2002; Louis, 2007; Mulford & Silins, 2003). Personal characteristics such as gender, race, and years of experience also shape the formation of professional communities (Grissom & Keiser, 2011; Printy, 2008; Visscher & Witziers, 2004).

A Trip Gone Awry

More nettlesome is the possibility that a practice community will misfire, producing negative results (Grossman et al., 2001; Wenger, 1998) in one or more of the phases in the model in Figure 5.1 (Curry, 2008; King, 2001). For example, researchers have documented how learning communities can operate: (1) "to perpetuate stereotypes, prejudice, and staid or destructive practices" (Printy, 2008, p. 181); (2) to reinforce exclusion, insularity, and marginalization; (3) to herald the status quo and staunch innovation (McLaughlin & Talbert, 2001; Smylie & Hart, 1999); (4) to nurture dysfunctional relationships (Stoll et al., 2006); and (5) to privilege management goals at the expense of professional objectives (Hayes et al., 2004).

One emerging concern is that communities will become vehicles to engage work unrelated to mission, in much the same way that guidance counselors were transformed into quasi-administrators. That is, teachers in communities will work on everything but instructional practice (Supovitz, 2002), a type of administrative usurpation and organizational goal development (Firestone & Martinez, 2007; Penuel et al., 2010). Another growing worry is that these professional communities will simply bury teachers under the weight of added responsibilities (Webb, 2005). More bothersome is some evidence that the downsides of open dialogue and constructive critical conversations can be unleashed in professional communities; that is, "community can have ambivalent as well as positive tendencies" (King, 2001, p. 247). Tensions and anxieties are often toxic byproducts of learning communities (Mullen & Hutinger, 2008).

It is also appropriate here to remind ourselves that once in place, communities are often fragile (Grossman et al., 2001; Palinscar et al., 1998; Printy, 2008). Regression to old patterns of behavior and norms is not unusual (Goldstein, 2004). Thus, cautions about stalling out merit scrutiny as well (Brooks et al., 2004; Greene & Lee, 2006; Levine & Marcus, 2007).

Unexamined Costs

There are substantial costs associated with creating professional communities (Drago-Severson, 2004). However, these are rarely addressed in the literature on birthing and molding collaborative work (Pounder, 1999). Although the potential of practice communities "to drain scarce resources and time" (Brooks et al., 2004, p. 260) from interactions with students is ever present, discussion of these "opportunity costs" are conspicuous by their absence. Not surprisingly, therefore, there is almost no discussion of cost benefit analysis in the theoretical or practical treatments of communities of professional practice.

Barriers

It would be naive to ignore the major structural, cultural and micropolitical barriers operating in schools. (Harris, 2004, p. 19)

Several barriers may impede the development of communities of instructional practice. (Supovitz & Poglinco, 2001, p. 7)

Many schools are structured in ways that are antithetical to teacher learning and in which collective norms of shared learning are not culturally embedded. (Jackson, 2000, p. 74)

An assortment of thoughtful reviewers reminds us that it is critical for us "to understand the mechanisms [and] conditions which undermine efforts of teacher communities to bring about instructional improvement" (Curry, 2008, p. 760). These obstacles are of two related varieties: the absence of conditions necessary to grow professional community (McLaughlin & Talbert, 2001) and the presence of barriers that get in the way of creating collaborative enterprise. Based on our analysis, we cluster all these impediments into two domains, cultural and organizational problems (see also Bulkley & Hicks, 2005; Murphy, 2005).

Cultural Barriers

The privatization of practice common in most schools makes teachers' commitment to their work a private and personal matter. (Ancess, 2003, p. 40)

Schools have built up all kinds of cultural barriers to sharing. (Fullan & Ballew, 2002, p. 11)

The cultural seedbed of schooling is toxic to the development of learning communities (Grossman et al., 2001; Saunders et al., 2009; Smylie, 1996).

More specifically, there are powerful norms, beliefs, and values that push and pull teachers in directions at odds with the concept of collaborative professional work (Lortie, 1975; Rosenholtz, 1989; Young, 2006). While scholars use different terms to describe these norms (e.g., autonomy, civility, conflict avoidance, privacy, noninterference, and so forth), there is consensus that they exert negative influence over the birth and development of teacher professional communities in schools (Levine & Marcus, 2010; McLaughlin & Talbert, 2001; Pounder, 1999). The result of these cultural norms is that teachers spend almost no time attending to the work of their colleagues (Curry, 2008) nor do they express any great desire to do so (Griffin, 1995; Visscher & Witziers, 2004). We explore these cultural norms below.

One value that is deeply entwined in the cultural tapestry of schools is what might best be labeled the *norm of legitimacy:* what counts as appropriate work for teachers. The literature confirms that authentic activity is what unfolds in classrooms (Goldstein, 2004; Little, 1982). For both the public and teachers themselves, teaching is determined almost completely by time inside classrooms working with students (Little, 1988; Saunders et al., 2009). Time spent away from the classroom is viewed as lacking legitimacy (Smylie & Brownlee-Conyers, 1992).

A related standard is the *norm of the divide between teaching and administration* (Murphy, 2005; Rallis, 1990). One aspect of this deeply embedded norm is the belief that the job of teachers is to teach and the task of administrators is to lead (Goldstein, 2004; MacBeath, 2009). A second part is that it is the teacher's assignment to implement designs developed by their higher ups in the bureaucracy (Boles & Troen, 1996; Teitel, 1996; Wasley, 1991). Teachers are to follow (Moller & Katzenmeyer, 1996). This role division is heavily buttressed by the structure of schooling that we explore in the next section, especially the tenets of hierarchy.

Related to the above belief is the *norm of the managerial imperative,* what Keedy (1999, p. 787) refers to as the "norm of the authority and power of administrators." This viewpoint has a deep root structure, one that routinely chokes out perspectives on professional communities of teachers (Bryk et al., 2010). At the heart of the prerogative standard is the belief that school action outside of classrooms is the rightful domain of school administrators. Given this culture, teachers are "reluctant to challenge traditional patterns of principals' authority" (Smylie, 1992, p. 55). Understandings have been forged over time between administrators and teachers (Murphy, Hallinger, Lotto, & Miller, 1987; Sizer, 1984). They often show considerable reluctance to overturn such negotiated arrangements, especially when doing so would undercut established patterns of power and autonomy (Harris, 2003; Smylie, 1992). Cast in less generous terms, the argument holds that teachers are powerless to influence activities beyond the classroom (Troen & Boles, 1994), that principals are resistant to actions that would alter this dynamic (Bishop, Tinley, & Berman, 1997;

Brown & Sheppard, 1999; Goldstein, 2004), and that efforts on the part of teachers to challenge the norm would produce unpleasant repercussions (Clift et al., & Veal, 1992), including micropolitical dynamics that threaten patterns of power and status (Chrispeels & Martin, 2002; Cochran-Smith & Lytle, 1999; Visscher & Witziers, 2004).

Researchers over the last 40 years have also thrown considerable illumination on the *norm of autonomy* at the heart of the teaching profession and the well-established patterns of teacher isolation (Grossman et al., 2001; Levine & Marcus, 2007; Smylie & Hart, 1999). Most teachers work alone, disconnected from their peers (Ancess, 2003; Stigler & Hiebert, 1999) and they prefer it that way (Griffin, 1995). They "value autonomy more than the chance to influence others' work" (Levine & Marcus, 2007, p. 128). They see this freedom from external review as a right of the job (Uline & Berkowitz, 2000). They equate autonomy with professionalism. And they practice the art of noninterference in the instructional affairs of their colleagues in the school (Teitel, 1996; Murphy, 2005; Wilson, 1993). This powerful norm hinders the development of productive relationships that form the core of communities of practice.

Tightly linked to professional and cultural values about autonomy is the *norm of privacy* (Feiman-Nemser & Floden, 1986; Grossman et al., 2001; Levine & Marcus, 2007)—what Griffin (1995) calls "the privacy of practice" (p. 40). As Uline and Berkowitz (2000) document, the interaction rules in a culture of privacy parallel those found in highly autonomous climates and "include never interfering in another teacher's classroom affairs, and always being self-reliant with one's own" (p. 418), holding the classroom inviolate (Feiman-Nemser & Floden, 1986; Moller & Eggen, 2005). The standard of professional privacy is construed "as freedom from scrutiny and the right of each teacher to make independent judgments about classroom practice" (Little, 1988, p. 94). While Little (1990) acknowledges that providing help to colleagues is acceptable within tight parameters, in a culture of noninterference and nonjudgmentalness teachers are primarily expected to address problems alone (Feiman-Nemser & Floden, 1986; Useem et al., 1997). As was the case with the previous norms, the norm of privacy undercuts collaboration, sharing, and responsibility for colleagues which help define communities of instructional practice (Siu, 2008).

Analysts have also shown that the culture of the profession writ large and the culture of schools are characterized by *egalitarian norms* (York-Barr & Duke, 2004). At its core, the egalitarian ethic of teaching—"the fact that all teachers hold equal position and rank separated by number of years of experience and college credit earned" (Wasley, 1991, p. 166) "rather than function, skill, advanced knowledge, role, or responsibility" (Lieberman et al., 1988, p. 151)—"suggests that all teachers should be equal" (Katzenmeyer & Moller, 2001, p. 4). Communities of inquiry on the other hand clash with this norm (Friedkin & Slater, 1994; Pounder, 1999). Teachers separate themselves from colleagues by the knowledge and skills they possess and by their degree of adherence to professional norms such as efficacy and belonging. Without some renorming of the profession, practice communities will regularly lose the fight with egalitarian norms.

A final standard that often impedes the development of a culture of professional collaboration is the *norm of civility.* As Griffin (1995) reminds us, "schools are nonconfrontative social organizations, at least in terms of how teachers interact with one another" (p. 44). There is strong pressure for cordiality and getting along with others (Conley, 1991; Hart, 1990; Levine & Marcus, 2007). Not fueling conflict and not hurting the feelings of others trumps productive exchanges (Chrispeels & Martin, 2002; Grossman et al., 2001). Peer critique is considered to be unprofessional and requests for assistance are seen as signs of incompetence (Dannetta, 2002). Coupled with this are accepted modes of interaction among teachers, such as contrived collegiality and "induced collaboration" (Little, 1990, p. 509) that promote the appearance of cooperation while maintaining deeply ingrained norms of autonomy, privacy, and egalitarianism. And coupled to all these other standards are *norms of conservatism* and *aversion to risk taking* (Lortie, 1975; Rosenholtz, 1989) that privilege the status quo in the face of learning and change that anchor professional communities.

Structure

> Teacher learning communities are constrained by the structures and mandates that make up the regulatory frameworks and policy contexts within which teachers teach. (McLaughlin & Talbert, 2001, p. 136)

> However, attempts to create and maintain such a professional community must overcome significant organizational obstacles. (Useem et al., 1997, p. 58)

Scholars who expose the workings of institutions have carefully documented how "the structure of the organization directs and defines the flow and pattern of human interactions in the organization" (Johnson, 1998, p. 13), how the values and actions of teachers are molded by the structures under which they work (Smylie & Brownlee-Conyers, 1992; Wenger, 2000). Structures reflect values and principles that thus exercise considerable pull on the possibility of communities of practice developing in schools. Indeed, there is considerable evidence that these structures are implicated in the effectiveness of learning communities (McLaughlin & Talbert, 2001; Stoll et al., 2006).

Unfortunately, as was the case with culture, the prevailing structure of schooling hinders the formation of teacher professional community (Bidwell & Yasumoto, 1999; Donaldson, 2001; Jackson, 2000). In particular, analysts conclude that the highly bureaucratic and institutional nature of schooling creates a framework that supports isolation, autonomy, and privatization while damping down cooperation and undercutting professional community norms (Harris, 2004; Scribner et al., 1999; Useem et al., 1997).

A number of dimensions of structure need to be surfaced. First, existing organizational arrangements benefit some members of the school, actors who are not simply willing to promote the creation of alternative structures that threaten their advantaged positions (Chrispeels & Martin, 2002; Crowther et al., 2002; Timperley, 2009). For example, McLaughlin and Talbert (2001, p. 127) do an excellent job of exploring this reality in the context of high school departments, exposing how "informal career systems and seniority structures leave communities of practice on the margins of secondary education."

Second, for most educators, the current organizational system is the only one they have known. It is difficult to move to the unknown even when one can glimpse its contours. In addition, even if the change process can be engaged, there are strong inclinations to regress to the familiar. As Lieberman and Miller (1999) remind us, "new behaviors are difficult to acquire, and in the end it is easier to return to old habits than to embrace new ones" (p. 126); needed changes are often "abandoned in favor of more familiar and more satisfying routines" (Little, 1987, p. 493). Or as Heller (1994) observes, "people become used to a hierarchical structure which can be comforting. Someone else is responsible. Someone else takes the blame, finds the money, obtains the permission, and has the headaches" (p. 289).

Third, the current arrangements are not especially malleable (Donaldson, 2001). The "forces of organizational persistence" (Smylie & Hart, 1999, p. 421) and "institutional precedent" (Smylie, 1992, p. 55) are quite robust (McLaughlin & Talbert, 2001). Hierarchy has an extensive and deep root structure and enjoys a good deal of legitimacy (Murphy et al., 2001, 2009). The system also displays considerable capacity to engage in the ritual of change (Meyer & Rowan, 1975) and to absorb new ideas and initiatives in ways that leave existing organizational structures largely unaffected (Cohen, 1988; Elmore, 1987; Weick, 1976). The reality in many schools of limited financial resources compounds structural obstacles standing in the way of teacher communities (Drago-Severson, 2004).

Fourth, structure sets time in schools and generally in ways that make collaboration a mere footnote in the teacher workday (Cosner, 2011; Desimone, 2002; Scribner et al., 1999). The traditional school "offers few opportunities for learning to interact with colleagues outside of abbreviated interchanges. Extended periods of adult-to-adult interaction in the workplace are irregular, episodic, and rare" (Grossman et al., 2001, p. 987; Newmann et al., 1989; Useem et al., 1997). The absence of time, in turn, acts to calcify the already inflexible institutional backbone of schooling (Firestone & Martinez, 2007; Foster & St. Hilaire, 2003). There is a general sense in the literature on communities of practice that time is the "biggest obstacle" (Doyle, 2000, p. 38), the most significant "barrier" (Blegen & Kennedy, 2000, p. 5; LeBlanc & Shelton, 1997, p. 44), and "the most pervasive problem" (Wasley, 1991, p. 137).

Finally, while some currents buoy concepts such as professionalism and collaborative norms, stronger currents support the movement to centralization and to the hardening of the hierarchical forms of schooling (Murphy, Hallinger, & Heck, 2013) that "are having a challenging effect on the teaching profession and on the inclination and ability of teachers to assume broad leadership within their schools" (Barth, 2001, p. 445). Especially problematic for the creation of community are the following ideas embedded in hierarchical structures, the idea of a single leader (Moller & Katzenmeyer, 1996); "traditional patterns of relationships" (Conley, 1989, p. 2) featuring a boss and subordinates; the idea that the leader is "synonymous with boss" (Moller & Katzenmeyer, 1996, p. 4); and the metaphor of leader as supervisor (Hallinger, Heck, & Murphy, 2014; Myers, 1970).

Hierarchical organizations also define power and authority in ways that dampen the viability of community (Clark & Meloy, 1989; Sergiovanni, 1991b; Sykes & Elmore, 1989). Specifically, by defining authority in centralized and solitary terms (Fay, 1992b; Barth, 1988), the traditional structure of school undermines teacher professionalism by providing very little space for teacher voices to be considered.

Bureaucracies also exert negative force on teacher professional community through the use of structures that reinforce the cultural norms we explored above. Two elements are featured in these structures: time schedules (Conley, 1991; Coyle, 1997) and systems for dividing up work responsibilities (Harris, 2003; Pellicer & Anderson, 1995; Printy, 2004; York-Barr & Duke, 2004). Both of these strands promote segmentation (Katzenmeyer & Moller, 2001). They slot teachers into self-contained classrooms (Buckner & McDowelle, 2000). All of this promotes the use of an "egg crate" (Boles & Troen, 1996, p. 59) structure that reinforces teaching as an autonomous affair that makes it very difficult for teachers to work collaboratively, making any type of real interdependence quite rare (Katzenmeyer & Moller, 2001; Little & McLaughlin, 1993).

Unions as a piece of the organizational mosaic require attention here because as Useem and colleagues remind us (1997, p. 70), "It is not only administrative policies but teachers' union work rules as well that fragment and separate school staffs." At the macro level, unions can act as a brake on the development of community throughout the profession (Pellicer & Anderson, 1995; Stone et al., 1997). This is most likely to occur when shared work is viewed as unsettling well-established patterns of collective bargaining (Wasley, 1991). At the micro level, union contracts can inhibit the creation of collaborative strategies and forms at schools (Blegen & Kennedy, 2000; Goldstein, 2004; Useem et al., 1997), directly through rules and indirectly by influencing negatively the climate between teachers and administrators (Killion, 1996).

SUPPORT FOR CREATING PROFESSIONAL LEARNING COMMUNITIES

> Supportive school policies are critical to the formation of professional community. (Wahlstrom & Louis, 2008, p. 463)

> If teacher inquiry is to succeed as a lasting mechanism for change in the current climate of short-lived reforms, it will require a sustained commitment to creating and protecting these conditions and building site-level capacity to maximize them. (Ermeling, 2010, pp. 387–388)

In the first half of the chapter, we investigated how efforts to forge collaborative communities of professional practice can founder, derail, or self-destruct. Practitioners, developers, and policy makers require a firm understanding of these dynamics. Equally important, however, they need an operational manual and a well-stocked toolbox to create conditions that nurture teacher communities. Leithwood and team (1999, p. 215) capture this as follows: "The principal challenge facing those designing schools as learning organizations is to determine the organizational conditions that foster individual and collective learning and to build these conditions into the school." Fullan (Fullan & Ballew, 2002, p. 14) outlines the assignment thus: "the obligation is to remove barriers to sharing, create mechanisms for sharing, and reward those who do share." Some of the pages in the manual and some of the tools are generic in nature. For example, we have proven designs and a well-stocked tool belt for addressing the assignments of building teamwork and implementing reforms. Knowledge directly addressing the creation of professional communities (as opposed to understanding its qualities) is less well developed (Blanc et al., 2010), as is knowledge about the tools to conduct the work (Blanc et al., 2010; Leithwood et al., 1999). Visscher and Witziers (2004, p. 786) frame up this reality for us:

> Although there seems to be agreement about the elements of practice that constitute a professional community, the concept seems to be rather "fuzzy" when it comes to questions like which structural arrangements and instruments are at the disposal of school management to promote the professional development and learning of teachers within the context of communities.

The Pivotal Role of the Principal

> While many factors affect whether or not professional community exists in a school, one of the most significant factors is strong principal leadership. (Louis, Dretzke, & Wahlstrom, 2010, p. 319)

> Learning communities are characterized by strong leadership from the school principal. (Mitchell & Sackney, 2006, p. 631)

> The responsibility for creating these opportunities for collaboration rests with school leaders. (Halverson, Grigg, Prichett, & Thomas, 2007, p. 170)

Although we possess less knowledge than we might desire, we have accumulated some understandings about principals and learning communities over the last 20 years. We know, for example, that there is a set of key domains in which preemptive prevention, removal of existing barriers, and/or the construction of an infrastructure to support professional communities occur. We also understand now that the principal has a hallmark position in this work, a conclusion found in nearly every study of teacher communities of practice (Cosner, 2011; Louis et al., 2010; Stoll et al., 2006). We are aware that there are important differences in the shape and texture of leadership in schools with robust communities and those with weak communities (Mangin, 2007; Leithwood et al., 1997; Youngs & King, 2002): "principals can construct their role to either support or inhibit the strength and quality of teacher community" (McLaughlin & Talbert, 2001, p. 101). More and more we are discovering that it is the principal who acts as the catalyst to bring other important supports to life (Bryk et al., 2010; Murphy, 2013a, 2013b). Without effective leadership, resources, time, and structures have almost no hope of emerging to support collaborative work (Cosner, 2009; Hayes et al., 2004; Murphy & Datnow, 2003b). We also know that principal leadership and professional community are interdependent, having an iterative relationship (McLaughlin & Talbert, 2001). Perhaps most important, there is a growing knowledge base which suggests that of all the ways that principals have at their disposal to influence student learning, developing and supporting collaborative communities of professional practice may be the most powerful (Supovitz et al., 2010).

It is important to acknowledge that for many principals, growing community necessitates a difficult transformation of their own understanding of leadership and their own leadership roles (Goldstein, 2004). "The implications for school principals are considerable" (Crowther et al., 2002, p. 64), and this repositioning presents a real challenge for principals (Brown & Sheppard, 1999). As we have illustrated throughout this chapter, communities of practice are in some essential ways "at odds with the dominant conceptions of the principalship that have been in place in most educational systems for decades" (Crowther et al., 2002, p. 6). Thus just as teachers are being asked to step outside traditional perspectives of their roles (Mayrowetz et al., 2009), so also must principals think in new ways about their roles (Harrison & Lembeck, 1996). Or, as Blegen and Kennedy (2000) conclude, "accepting and encouraging teacher leadership requires a [new] knowledge and skill base" (p. 4) and a new set of performances that are not often in the education of school administrators (Childs-Bowen et al., 2000; Klecker & Loadman, 1998). New metaphors for the principalship emerge as well (Beck & Murphy, 1993; Sergiovanni, 1991a, 1991b)—metaphors that reflect the role of the principal not in terms of one's fit in the organizational structure but in terms of membership in a community of leaders (Beck & Murphy, 1993; Murphy, 2005; Scribner et al., 1999).

The point to be underscored here is that for many principals, a personal transformation in leadership must accompany the quest to rebuild schooling to cultivate communities of practice. Absent this change, it is difficult to imagine that principals will develop the sense of security that is, as Barth (1988) reminds us, "a precondition upon which development of a community of leaders rests" (p. 142). Likewise, cultivating teacher community in a hierarchical and bureaucratic organizational seedbed is problematic at best. New conceptions of organizations provide the foundations for developing the skills to foster norms of community. This is challenging work, but principals who do not begin here are not likely to be effective in making teacher inquiry a reality in their schools.

Frameworks of Support

> For communities of instructional practice to develop, I posit that three conditions must be fulfilled. First, groups need structures that provide them with the leadership, time, resources, and incentives to engage in instructional work. Second, groups need to develop a culture of instructional practice, one that encourages them to continuously and safely identify, explore, and assess instructional strategies that show promise of success with their students. Third, they need a particular kind of professional development to enable them to engage in a continuous honing of their skills and strategies. (Supovitz, 2002, p. 1618)

Over the years, analysts have cobbled together various frameworks to capture the array of factors and conditions that support the development of teacher communities. Stoll and colleagues (2006, p. 23) employ four categories: focusing on learning processes; making the best of human and social resources; managing structural resources; and interacting with and drawing on external agents. Mullen and Hutinger (2008, p. 280) also describe four sets of actions: manage resources, provide support and direction, exert appropriate pressure to achieve goals, and mediate group dynamics. Printy (2008, p. 211) discusses three functions: communicate vision, support teachers, and buffer teachers from outside influences. Focusing in on the principal, McLaughlin and Talbert (2001, p. 98) offer this list of related actions:

For better or worse, principals set conditions for teacher community by the ways in which they manage school resources, relate to teachers and students, support or inhibit social interactions and leadership in the faculty, respond to the broader policy context, and bring resources into the school.

In their work, Supovitz and Poglinco (2001, p. 7) uncovered five strategies that leaders employ in their efforts to create professional communities of practice:

First, these instructional leaders carefully developed a safe environment within which their teachers could take the risks associated with change. Second, they emphasized open channels of communication and strong collaboration amongst their faculty for the purpose of expanding the networks of engagement around issues of instructional improvement. Third, they cultivated informal and formal leaders in their schools to both allow themselves time for instructional attention and to broaden the base for change in the school. Fourth, [they] employed powerful and symbolic actions and events to dramatize and reinforce their message. Finally, they developed strong systems for accountability even as they expanded teachers' flexibility to further develop their instructional practices.

A slightly different architecture is provided by Printy (2008, p. 199) who sees community building occurring through three roles:

As *agenda setters,* leaders select policy messages to communicate to teachers and establish specific expectations or goals for teachers' work. As *knowledge brokers,* leaders focus teachers' attention on instructional matters, create the conditions for productive teacher conversations, scaffold teachers' learning as appropriate, and facilitate the translation and alignment of meanings across communities. As *learning motivators,* leaders nurture positive relationships, establish urgency for new approaches and hold teachers accountable for results, in essence tightening the connections between policy and practice.

Saunders and team (2009, p. 1028) highlight the centrality of time, administrative support, and structures. This is consistent with our claim that the traditional "functions" of principals can be engaged to nurture collaborative work (e.g., coordinating, monitoring). More parsimonious lists have been provided by Kruse and associates (1995, p. 34): structural conditions and characteristics of human resources; by Hurd (cited in Morrissey, 2000, p. 6): structural conditions and collegial relationships; and McDougall and colleagues (2007, p. 54): settings and processes.

Taking a slightly different approach, Scribner and team (1999) describe administrative, moral, and political support from the principal employed in the service of creating communities of practice.

In the second half of the chapter, starting with the groundwork presented above, we explore what the research confirms about the specific acts that foster professional communities. Before we do so, however, we need to reinforce some core ideas. First, the goal of leadership is not the development of learning communities. The objective is the creation of human and social capital that enhances the quality of instruction in the service of student learning. The wager here is that such communities provide a robust pathway to reach these more distal ends. Second, the focus is not primarily on beefing up each of the six elements in our model individually. The best strategy is to deploy supports that forge an integrated scaffolding. For example, carving additional time for teachers to work collectively can deepen ownership, shared responsibility, and collaboration.

We also recognize that principal actions need to be consistent with the perspective on leadership we introduced in Chapter 2. More specifically, principals have two primary bases of influence, hierarchical position and community leadership (Friedkin & Slater, 1994). Creating community necessitates the use of both (Bryk et al., 2010; Young, 2006) but with greater reliance on the latter (Blumenfeld et al., 2000; Leithwood et al., 2010; Wenger & Snyder, 2000), especially the array of behaviors underscored in the transformational leadership literature.

Finally, there are two activities that receive very limited treatment in the educational literature but rise to the level of considerable importance in the research on organizations more broadly defined (Wenger & Snyder, 2000). To begin with, an essential responsibility is to identify people with the commitment, energy, and skills to do good work and bring them together, recognizing that these forged communities often do not follow existing organizational structures (e.g., grade level). Also important is the need to identify existing informal associations of people with shared interests (e.g., worries about a spike in homeless children in the school) and support them functioning as collaborative communities. A key insight from these two lessons is that community is not isomorphic with the organizational chart.

Activity Domains

Executives must be prepared to invest time and money in helping communities reach their full potential. (Wenger & Snyder, 2000, p. 144)

To bring people together in a school requires different mind-sets and different structures. (Mitchell & Sackney, 2006, p. 635)

Administrators provide the necessary organizational and structural supports for collaborative work among staff. (Morrissey, 2000, p. 5)

As is the case throughout the book, we carefully and deliberately build on the work of colleagues to arrive at our framework of principal supports for teacher communities. Concomitantly, we add new pillars to the structure and contextualize and add nuance to the collective body of evidence. We examine the following supports: creating structures and time, supporting learning, and managing the work.

Creating Structures and Time

The manner in which organizations structure the time and space of the work environment can provide useful clues regarding underlying organizational assumptions. (Scribner et al., 1999, p. 153)

Leaders cannot force or guarantee teacher learning. They can design the conditions that will be supportive of the kinds of interactions that will provide opportunities for meaningful teacher learning. (Stein & Coburn, 2008, p. 585)

For some schools, it is a matter of re-purposing settings that already exist and for others it is about carving out new settings. (Ermeling, 2010, p. 387)

We know a good deal about organizational structures in general and in the area of school improvement more specifically. As we reported in the first half of the chapter, structures shape what unfolds in schools partially determining what is and what is not possible. As the flip side of culture (Leithwood, Day, et al., 2006), structures allow norms to flourish, or wither (Brooks et al., 2004; Cochran-Smith & Lytle, 1999; Kruse et al., 1995). Our focus at this point in the analysis is on the positive side of the narrative, that is, how well-resourced and thoughtfully developed forums in schools can help collaborative communities grow. The door through which we enter the analysis is "collaboration," the element of shared work that provides a seedbed for the growth of relationships, shared trust, and mutual responsibility (Bryk et al., 2010). In short, we review what is known about creating supportive collaborative structures.

A recurring theme throughout this book is that structural change does not predict organizational performance, student learning in the case of schools. We are also cognizant that simply giving teachers a platform to talk will not ensure the development of valued professional norms and human and social capital (Levine & Marcus, 2007; Newmann et al., 2001). So while we acknowledge the essentiality of time and space to undertake collaborative work, we define structure in terms that underscore what is required to power the model in Figure 5.1. At the core then, structure is about "interactive settings" (Cosner, 2009, p. 255) and "interaction patterns" (p. 273). It is about opportunities for forging relationships, for creating patterns of networks, and for promoting professional exchange through new channels of communication (May & Supovitz, 2011; Spillane Diamond, et al., 2001; Stoll et al., 2006). In short, it is about fostering professional collaboration (Ancess, 2003; Cosner, 2009; Newmann et al., 1989).

Research helps us discern some ways to work "structurally" to create and nurture teacher communities. On the issue of *forums,* there is unanimous agreement that schools must take advantage of existing space and time configurations, to re-purpose them (Cosner, 2009; Rossmiller, 1992; Stein & Coburn, 2008). For example, community-building work is conspicuous by its absence from most faculty meetings. These meetings, and many others, can be redesigned to deepen collaboration. At the same time, as we detail below, there is general agreement that new forums will need to be created as well. Second, a *variety* of community-building structures are needed, not simply reliance on professional learning community meetings (Leithwood, Jantzi, & McElheron-Hopkins, 2006; McLaughlin & Talbert, 2001).

Analysts also advance the idea that both *formal and informal* opportunities for building community need to be captured, with an eye open for the informal opportunities that often lay fallow (Cosner, 2009; McLaughlin & Talbert, 2001). As we discussed above, joining together, teachers who in informal ways already demonstrate working connections, beliefs, and relationships can be an important piece of the community building plan (Penuel et al., 2009; Useem et al., 1997). Additionally, Raywid (1995) reminds us of the importance of nurturing the relationships among individual teachers in the service of community development.

Lastly, it appears that creating structures that promote both *horizontal and vertical networks* and exchanges is wise (Johnson & Asera, 1999). Here scholars point to collaborative structures that stimulate cross-grade and cross-departmental linkages, what Cosner (2009, pp. 268–269) calls "new interaction patterns." Also emphasized here are forums that allow teachers from different collective teams to collaborate (Kruse et al., 1995; Stein & Coburn, 2008), by "structuring communities with overlapping boundaries and multimembership" (Printy, 2008, p. 217).

The handmaiden to structure is time (Ancess, 2003; Harris, 2003; York-Barr & Duke, 2004). Without time, the development of collaborative forums becomes nearly impossible (Darling-Hammond & McLaughlin, 1995; Eilers & Camacho, 2007; Morrissey, 2000). Alternatively, teacher community researchers reveal that in schools where community flourishes, time is made available for collaborative work and professional learning (Huberman et al., 2011; Youngs, 2007). A similar conclusion is evident in studies of effective schools and effective principals (Blase & Blase, 2004; Drago-Severson, 2004; King, 2001).

Researchers have also teased out clues about how space and time can be well employed in the service of community development. One approach to enhance interactions is to bring members of current or proposed collaboratives into close physical proximity (Bulkley & Hicks, 2005;

Leithwood, Steinbach, & Ryan, 1997; Supovitz, 2008). According to these investigators, proximity can assist in overcoming the dysfunctional norms such as privatization that we examined above (Ancess, 2003; Gray et al., 1999; Kruse et al., 1995). A second suggestion is to take maximum advantage of formal teacher leadership positions in school (e.g., data coach), to have them organize and lead forums in which small groups of teachers can interact (Cosner, 2009; Murphy, 2005). Relatedly, collaboration can be nurtured by infusing distributed leadership throughout the school (Leithwood, Jantzi, & McElheron-Hopkins, 2006; Silins & Mulford, 2004). Finally, schools moving to deepen collaborative communities of professional practice can create what Saunders and team (2009, p. 1011) call "predictable, consistent settings"; what Blase and Blase (2004, p. 68) refer to as "teacher collaborative structures"; and what Ermeling (2010, p. 387) describes as "dedicated and protected times where teachers meet on a regular basis to get important work done." As posited above, these can be new arrangements or re-purposed existing settings. Whatever the designs, these predictable, patterned forums are the most efficacious method of enhancing community development among teachers (Pounder, 1999).

Our review also uncovers information on specific forums in play in schools working toward creating stronger collaboration (Penuel et al., 2009). Re-purposed staff and departmental meetings find a home here (Cosner, 2009; Mitchell & Castle, 2005; Spillane, Diamond, et al., 2001). So too do reconfigured school schedules to allow for late start or early dismissal on selected days (Cosner, 2009; King, 2001). Creating blocks of time for teachers to observe in the classrooms of peers is a special category of collaboration (Blase & Blase, 2004; Harris, 2003). Ad hoc groups such as book study teams, inquiry groups, and action research teams are found in some community anchored schools (Cosner, 2009; King, 2001; Newmann et al., 2001). So too are structures and time for teachers to collaborate around school governance and planning (Leithwood, Jantzi, & McElheron-Hopkins, 2006; McLaughlin & Talbert, 2001). Induction and mentoring programs can provide forums to stimulate collaboration and learning (Cosner, 2009; Kruse et al., 1995; Youngs, 2007). So also does the use of team teaching arrangements (Johnson & Asera, 1999). The most used strategy is the creation of a master schedule that establishes common planning time for groups of teachers, usually by grade level, subject area, or teaching team (Cosner, 2009).

Finally, a crosscutting analysis of the research on teacher communities exposes some of the essential touchstones of these collaborative forums. We learn that these gatherings for work and learning should: (1) occur frequently, for a reasonable block of time, and across the full year (Felner et al., 2007; Raywid, 1995); (2) be intensive; (3) focus on student learning and instructional matters (Johnson & Asera, 1999); (4) maximize interdependency (Cosner, 2009; Kruse et al., 1995); and (5) feature specific tasks that structure time usage (Center for Teaching Quality, 2007; Penuel et al., 2009). From our earlier discussion, we recall that resources such as protocols, leader participation, and external assistance are often associated with productive use of collaborative time.

Supporting Learning

Two features are essential to creating a climate of collaboration giving teachers: the time to talk and helping them learn how to talk with each other. (Drago-Severson, 2004, p. 49)

The leadership dimension that is most strongly associated with positive student outcomes is that of promoting and participating teacher learning and development. (Robinson, Lloyd, & Rowe, 2008, p. 667)

Time and working structures are important and necessary. But they are insufficient to power communities of practice (Ancess, 2003; Ermeling, 2010). As we have seen, teacher communities produce valued outcomes by fostering the development of professional norms and promoting teacher learning. Leaving this to happen by chance is not a wise idea. What is required is what we call "learning to learn," the development of the knowledge and the mastery of skills that make teacher growth a reality, what Supovitz (2002, p. 1618) refers to as "continuous capacity building." We examine the "learning" in the "learning to learn" paradigm for learning communities below.

For most teachers, working with students is a nearly all-consuming activity. Consequently, they have spent very little time working with other adults. Not surprisingly, therefore, developing "managerial skills in dealing with people" (Ainscow & Southworth, 1996, p. 234) is an essential component of professional development designed to help teachers work effectively in learning communities (Adams; 2010; Borko, 2004). Or, as Little (1987) reports it, "the specific skills and perspectives of working with a colleague are critical" (p. 512) for teacher communities to develop. The centrality of building relationships cannot be overstated in the work of practice communities (Cosner, 2009); neither can the development of relationship-building capabilities (Lynch & Strodl, 1991).

Scholars have isolated an assortment of interpersonal capacities that promote productive working relationships with colleagues (Brooks et al., 2004). They conclude that professional development should assist teachers in developing proficiencies around a number of interpersonal issues (Crow & Pounder, 2000). For example, Katzenmeyer and Moller (2001) conclude that the development should begin with personal knowledge. Professional development in this area builds from the assumption that focusing "on increasing their own self-awareness, identity formation, and interpretive capacity" (Zimpher, 1988, p. 57) is critical. It is this understanding that permits teachers to (1) recognize the values, behaviors, philosophies, and professional concerns that underlie their personal performance and

(2) understand their colleagues, especially those whose experiences and viewpoints do not mirror their own (Katzenmeyer & Moller, 2001).

A bushel of competencies that lubricate effective working relations are often mentioned as candidates for inclusion in professional development for teacher groups. For example, analysts assert that "skills that will make teachers sensitive to seeing others' points of view" (Katzenmeyer & Moller, 2001, p. 67) and "sensitive to others' needs" (LeBlanc & Shelton, 1997, p. 38) are important. Also, because teacher leaders often "report that they became more influential through using good listening techniques with peers" (Katzenmeyer & Moller, 2001, p. 93), gaining proficiency in the area of listening skills is important. In a similar view, because friction that sometimes surfaces in group interactions is greatly influenced by the form of those exchanges, teachers in communities are advantaged when they possess well-developed facilitation skills (Zimpher, 1988). In its broadest form, facilitation means "knowing how to help a group take primary responsibility for solving its problems and mitigat[ing] factors that hinder the group's ability to be effective" (Killion, 1996, p. 72). More specifically, it includes the ability to establish trust and rapport and to navigate through problems (Kilcher, 1992). Likewise, there is agreement that teachers develop consulting skills (Manthei, 1992) and proficiency in conferencing with colleagues (Zimpher, 1988) if they are to be effective in inquiry communities. The "principles and skills of advising" (Little, 1985, p. 34) are also key pieces in the portfolio of tools that help establish a productive context for collaborative work. So too are influencing skills (Hart, 1995; Katzenmeyer & Moller, 2001).

In addition to the social lubrication skills just outlined, analysts assert that professional development should address a variety of skills for attacking joint work endeavors and provide a set of group process skills (Kilcher, 1992) for understanding and managing the "group dynamics" that accompany collaborative work. Perhaps most important here is the broad array of communication skills needed to interact with colleagues (LeBlanc & Shelton, 1997). Indeed, it is almost an article of faith in the literature in this area that inquiry communities "benefit from ongoing learning and practice in effective communication" (Killion, 1996, p. 72). Problem-solving and decision-making skills are also seen as quite important. As Killion (1996) reports, "knowing various decision-making methods, selecting the most appropriate method for a particular situation, and having a repertoire of strategies for helping others reach a decision with the chosen methods are [also] critical skills" (p. 74). Finally, teachers generally benefit from professional development in conflict management (Hart, 1995) and conflict resolution (Fay, 1992b). "Teacher leaders who not only understand the factors that lead to conflict but also have a range of strategies for managing and resolving it will be more successful" (Killion, 1996, p. 73).

Although it is undertreated in the literature, to promote learning teachers also require deep knowledge in content or discipline areas (Eilers & Camacho, 2007; Leithwood, Louis, Anderson, & Wahlstrom, 2004;

McLaughlin & Talbert, 2001). Part of the content knowledge includes critical skills such as evidence-based teaching and establishing markers of success (Cosner, 2011; Levine & Marcus, 2007). That is, as Kruse and her associates (1995, p. 38) so nicely put it, "Professional community is based on an intellectual and practical grasp of the knowledge base and skills underlying the field." In addition, in order "to help teachers engage thorny issues of teaching and learning . . . and critique each other's practice" (Levine & Marcus, 2007, p. 135) deep grounding in one's subject discipline(s) is necessary (Timperley, 2005; York-Barr & Duke, 2004). Indeed, this may be the most critical learning needed for teacher communities to reach their potential (McLaughlin & Talbert, 2001).

Managing for Collaboration

Studies have revealed substantial differences in the nature of principal leadership between schools with strong and weak professional communities. (Youngs & King, 2002, p. 648)

Leadership for teaching learning communities builds around the core of teaching and learning and focuses on the quality of teachers' professional relationships. (McLaughlin & Talbert, 2001, p. 137)

The general message is that principals have two roles here. First, they need to get professional communities up and running. Second, they need to hold at bay the natural entropy associated with collaborative work. They must help keep communities viable and vibrant. They also need to master the craft of layering in multiple, integrated supports.

One of the conclusions that has emerged in this area over the last two decades is that it is difficult, if not impossible, to create learning communities from which the principal is detached (Louis et al., 2010; Murphy, 2005; Printy, 2008). The principal needs to be a part of communities, not simply a distant overseer (Barnett & McCormick, 2004; Halverson et al., 2007; Scribner et al., 1999). Principals should exemplify the norms of community (Gurr et al., 2006; Young, 2006). Meaningful participation allows principals to undertake a variety of supportive tasks, both symbolic and substantive, such as modeling appropriate behavior, being highly visible, monitoring progress, demonstrating consideration, and so forth (Drago-Severson, 2004; Louis, 2007; Mitchell & Sackney, 2006). Being part of the community tapestry in a school also increases the legitimacy of the principal and permits more effective use of the person-centered leadership practices that are much needed in collaborative work (Adams, 2010; Printy, 2008).

Principals need to be diligent in setting expectations for communities of practice. A clear vision for inquiry communities must be crafted along with a tangible set of expectations (Murphy, 2005). Also because prospects for community will be heavily influenced by school practices, values and expectations need to be bolstered by "enabling policies" (Lieberman & Miller, 1999, p. 28). Bishop and his colleagues (1997) outline the case as follows:

> Since policies usually guide the course of action of an organization, and their statements include objectives that guide the actions of a substantial portion of the total organization, teachers will believe that they are empowered when they feel that their actions are undergirded and protected by such formalized policy statements (p. 78)

Little (1987) concurs, arguing that "at its strongest—most durable, most rigorously connected to problems of student learning, most command-ing of teachers' energies, talents, and loyalties—cooperative work is a matter of school policy" (p. 512) and that "high levels of joint action are more likely to persist" (p. 508) when a supportive policy structure is in place.

Throughout the research on implementation, change, and school improvement, the importance of adequate resources is a recurring theme. Nowhere is this finding more accurate than in the area of teacher communi-ties (Grossman et al., 2001; Mitchell & Sackney, 2006; Mullen & Hutinger, 2008). Resources, in addition to time, in the professional community research include materials, such as "teachers' guides, activity sheets, and commercially prepared videos" (Burch & Spillane, 2003, p. 530). Protocols that direct collaborative work into productive channels is a type of material often underscored in studies of effective teacher communities (Cosner, 2011; Saunders et al., 2009). These designed activities help generate shared lan-guage, maintain focus, teach group process skills, and reinforce professional norms, while damping down dysfunctional behavior and project derailment so often observed in work teams (Cosner, 2011; Ermeling, 2010; Young, 2006).

The provision of access to expertise external to the school, usually bro-kered by the principal, to help teachers work more effectively together is also featured in the research (King, 2001; McLaughlin & Talbert, 2001; Saunders et al., 2009). Such expertise can assume the form of content experts, models of best practice (Curry, 2008; Levine & Marcus, 2007), appropriate research (Vescio et al., 2008), and the assistance of a facilitator (Borko, 2004; Saunders et al., 2009). Commitments such as these often require principals to secure new resources or reallocate existing ones to purchase materials, expertise, and time (Ancess, 2003; Cosner, 2009, 2011). In collaborative communities, all of these resources are employed to create human and social capacity and to deepen professional norms (Silins & Mulford, 2004).

For teacher communities to function effectively, principals need to become active and central figures in communication systems, using both formal and informal procedures (Brooks et al., 2004; Cosner, 2011; Walker & Slear, 2011). When this happens understanding is deepened and questions and misconceptions are addressed before they can become toxic (Cosner, 2011; Kochanek, 2005; Saunders et al., 2009).

Other "managing communities" responsibilities for principals can be teased out of the research as well. Not surprisingly given its importance in the general literature, the principal has a central role in ensuring that explicit understandings of the rationale for, workings of, and outcomes needed from teacher communities are established (Printy, 2008; Quint, 2006). Analysts also affirm that principals in schools with well-functioning teacher communities are adept at buffering teachers from external pressures that can hinder progress (King, 2001; Rossmiller, 1992). They filter demands that are not aligned with community work (Cosner, 2011; Robinson, 2007) and reshape others so that they do fit (Printy, 2008).

The necessity for ongoing monitoring of the activities and outcomes of collaborative work is routinely discussed in the research as well (Dinham et al., 1995; Quint, 2006; Stoll et al., 2006). Participation in community meetings, review of group documents, and comparative benchmarking are often featured in the monitoring portfolio (Heller & Firestone, 1995; MacBeath, 2005; Mullen & Hutinger, 2008). Monitoring that keeps "leaders in touch with teachers' ongoing thinking and development" (Levine & Marcus, 2007, p. 134) leads directly to another responsibility, that of providing feedback to collaborative work teams. A school culture that honors shared engagement (Harrison & Lembeck, 1996) is yet another indispensable element in the managing collaboration portfolio. So, too, is a system of incentives and rewards that motivates teachers to privilege mutually. Currently, the picture that emerges from the literature is one in which there are few external incentives for community work. In fact, there are numerous disincentives (Little, 1988) to change to collaborative work at the heart of teacher communities. In many schools, there is limited recognition for the work and there are few rewards for additional effort (Crowther et al., 2002). In too many places, "the only rewards for teacher leadership are added responsibilities" (Moller & Katzenmeyer, 1996, p. 14).

In schools, two types of recognition energize teacher leaders. First, the actions of persons of status and influence (Hart, 1994) carry considerable weight. Administrators, union leaders, and well-respected veteran teachers merit notice (Blase & Kirby, 2009; Hart, 1994; Silins & Mulford, 2004). Second, peer acceptance and recognition is important to teacher leaders, the absence of which can negatively affect the growth of teacher community in a school (LeBlanc & Shelton, 1997; Mulford & Silins, 2003).

While "rewarding teachers who are willing to move beyond their classrooms to lead is a complicated issue" (Moller & Katzenmeyer, 1996, p. 13), in the end schools "must provide incentives and rewards for teachers who take the lead in tackling tasks and solving problems" (Boles & Troen, 1996, p. 60): Principals, in turn, need to identify ways to acknowledge teachers in ways teachers value (Harrison & Lembeck, 1996). Moller and Katzenmeyer (1996) uncovered three ways in which principals were able to provide support and incentives for teacher work in communities of practice.

> First, the principals provided access to information and resources and gave their personal time. Second, they honored teacher leaders' requests for professional development and sometimes initiated opportunities for them to attend conferences or represent the school at important meetings. Finally, they gave them the gift of time, covering classes for them, providing substitute teachers, or assigning support personnel to assist them. (pp. 13–14)

Responsibility for showcasing and providing recognition for quality work rests squarely with the principal (Drago-Severson, 2004; Mulford & Silins, 2003).

CONCLUSION

In this chapter, we provided information to help schools bring communities of professional practice to life. We began with conditions that make those efforts problematic, especially barriers associated with the existing culture and structures that define schooling. In the second half of the chapter, we examined approaches that can be followed and strategies that can be employed to address barriers and promote productive teacher communities.

7

Communities of Engagement for Parents

It might seem tempting for a principal to close the door on the community surrounding his or her school and focus on what can be done to build culture within the school's walls. However, given that the majority of the variance in student achievement can be explained by factors beyond the school and that children spend about two thirds of each day outside of the school, this approach would be short sighted and detrimental to students. If no connection between the school and the community exists, some children will create separate identities to fit each environment (Hattie, 2009). Depending on the child's cultural capital, which is largely contingent on his or her socioeconomic status (SES) and race, school and nonschool identities can be very similar or widely divergent and aid or inhibit student achievement. For low-income, minority students, the latter outcome is more likely to be the case.

Because parents are a child's first teacher (Moles, 1996) and children spend significant amounts of time with their families, teachers depend on parents and families to get students to school, to make sure students are healthy, to help diffuse behavior problems, and to enforce good study habits (Bryk et al., 2010). Parents, on the other hand depend on teachers and school staff to provide them with information on their child's progress and strategies on how to best support their children academically (Eccles & Harold, 1996).

In the first part of this chapter, we provide an overview for considering home-school connections. In the second half, we craft an action framework to guide principals in creating a productive culture for parents.

THE LANDSCAPE OF PARENT INVOLVEMENT

Impact

Research has shown that when parents are involved with their children's education within the home, children tend to do better academically (Feldman & Matjasko, 2005; Goldenberg, 2004; Leithwood, Patten, & Jantzi, 2010). In fact, several researchers claim that improving the home educational environment, also called the "curriculum of the home," may yield the most leverage for increasing student achievement (Goldenberg, 2004; Mulford & Silins, 2003), and for older students, it can increase graduation rates (Ensminger & Slusarcick, 1992).

Epstein (1996) found positive outcomes for students who discussed academics with family members on a regular basis. In a study of high-achieving, black, low-income students, Finn and Rock (1997) found that parents were actively engaged in creating a supportive, encouraging home education environment. Parents who have higher expectations for their children also tend to be more involved with their child's education (Alexander et al., 1997; Griffith, 2001). Moreover, students internalize those high expectations and are likely to perform better in school (Hattie, 2009) and be more resilient (Finn & Rock, 1997). Indeed, the attitudes and expectations that parents have for their children regarding their schooling are more important than family structure in predicting student achievement (Hattie, 2009).

More broadly, aspects of the home environment not directly related to schooling influence student achievement (Bierman, 1996). Some research shows that sociopsychological components of the home, measured by indicators such as how parents use punishment, how responsive they are to children's needs, and the types of enrichment materials present at home, are closely linked to student learning (Hattie, 2009). Other research indicates additional nonacademic characteristics of the home environment that are related to student achievement, including parents establishing clear boundaries and acting as an authority, consistently enforcing rules, having numerous books, being nurturing and supportive, and respecting the intelligence of their children (Garmezy, 1991). Garmezy also finds that a home environment characterized by minimal conflict is positively associated with student learning.

Unfortunately, the home environment can also be "a toxic mix of harm and neglect with respect to enhancing learning" (Hattie, 2009, p. 33). Neglect and abuse, as well as less extreme behaviors such as using external rewards and negative controls to influence child behavior, are negatively correlated with achievement. Also, the number of hours of TV a student watches each day, which can be regulated by parents, is negatively related to student academic outcomes, and this relationship becomes stronger as students progress through school (Hattie, 2009).

Parent's sense of efficacy in relation to their children is linked with how involved they are with their children's academic life (Eccles & Harold, 1996). Parents with a strong sense of efficacy, defined as the belief that they have the "skills and knowledge to help their children, that they can teach or assist their children, and that they can find extra resources for their children," are more likely to be involved in their child's education in the home environment (Sheldon, 2002, p. 303).

Involving parents in schools has been shown consistently to increase the academic achievement of students at all grade levels (Feldman & Matjasko, 2005) and subjects (Bryk et al., 2010; Epstein, 1996). Parent involvement in the school and the community is also related to higher rates of high school graduation and college enrollment (Goddard, 2003). An increased proportion of involved parents in a school is related not only to individual student achievement, but also to the effectiveness of the school as a whole (Auerbach, 2007).

The academic outcomes of parent involvement depend on the type and nature of the connections. In a study of teacher practices to increase parent engagement in their child's academics, Epstein (1996) found that if parents increased their involvement in reading, reading scores improved, but there was no impact on math scores. Likewise, Hattie (2009) reports that when parents are more actively engaged with their children academically, for example by tutoring their children as opposed to listening to them read, there are stronger effects on student achievement.

Parent and community involvement is also associated with improved culture in the school (Bryk et al., 2010). For example, research shows that parent involvement can increase the sense of caring within a school (Sanders & Harvey, 2002). Moreover, strong relationships between parents and the school are related to increased safety and order within the school (Bryk et al., 2010). When there is alignment between the home and the school on the values and beliefs regarding the education of the child, parents are more likely to be involved, and students are more likely to have positive, trusting relationships with teachers (Adams, 2010). Students also report having more positive attitudes toward homework and being more engaged when their parents are involved in their education (Epstein, 1996).

Increased parent involvement also influences teacher perceptions (Esptein, 1996). Goldenberg (2004) relates that when he began reaching out to parents early in the year to seek their support in achieving mutually devised goals for the student, he was able to cultivate a more asset-based view of parents. As teachers increase their contact with families, they may also better understand the communities of the children they teach and thus be better able to support those children (Haynes & Ben-Avie, 1996).

Historically, schools have been tasked with inculcating students with democratic values and creating engaged citizens (Meier, 2003). Some research suggests that creating school-home-community connections can help schools attain this goal (Auerbach, 2009).

Most strategies to increase home-school connections do not directly impact student achievement (Goldenberg, 2004). We also know that many of the benefits from parent involvement are indirect. For example, research shows that partnership practices are related to an increase in student attendance (Epstein, 1996; Feldman & Matjasko, 2005), which is a clear prerequisite for student academic success. Likewise, if parents are volunteering at the school or participating in school governance, this might increase their buy-in to the vision of the school and the alignment of their home practices with those expected by the school, thus increasing student success (Bierman, 1996). Finally, while research indicates that involving parents in decision making may only have limited impact on student achievement (Murphy & Beck, 1995), including parents in school government may help keep the focus of school decision making on outcomes for students (Leithwood, Day, et al., 2006).

Involving parents in the school community can also have a positive impact on the health of the family, especially in the case when the school partners with health or social service providers (Auerbach, 2009). Bryk and colleagues (2010) document that instructional productivity depends on the supports for academic, social, and health needs available through the school and in the home. Schools that serve high numbers of students living in poverty will be better able to advance students' academic learning if they support both the students' academic and health related needs (Bryk et al., 2010).

Types of Involvement

The outcomes related to parental involvement are contingent on the specific ways that parents are involved with their child's education (Eccles & Harold, 1996). Researchers have found that parents can be involved in their child's education in a variety of ways and in different venues. The most well-known framework for understanding home-school connections is Joyce Esptein's explanation of six types of parental involvement (Epstein, 1996): basic parenting, learning in the home, communication with the school, volunteering, participating in school decision making, and making connections to the community. These activities occur in the home (types one through three), at the school (types four and five), and within the wider community (type six).

Others have elaborated on aspects of this basic framework. Leithwood and colleagues (2004, p. 47) delve into a more nuanced explanation of "family educational culture," which encompasses two of Epstein's involvement categories: basic parenting and learning in the home. This concept delineates the type of academic supports that parents provide in the home. These include (1) modeling and teaching positive work habits; (2) providing academic guidance and assistance, academic stimulation, adequate healthcare and nutrition; (3) holding high aspirations and expectations; and (4) creating a home setting conducive to academic work. Other research has highlighted additional activities that parents undertake to create a positive "family educational culture" including tutoring their children, reading with them, taking them to cultural events, helping their children with homework, supervising the child within the home, and engaging in academic discussions (Bierman, 1996; Eccles & Harold, 1996; Sui-Chu & Willms, 1996).

Several researchers have expanded Epstein's idea of "volunteering" to include multiple forms of participation within the school (Eccles & Harold, 1996; Haynes & Ben-Avie, 1996). This more general conceptualization includes volunteering time to help in the school or classroom and participating in or supporting school events. Eccles and Harold (1996) also expand on how parents communicate with the school, distinguishing between contacting the school about their child's progress and contacting the school for suggestions for how to help their child.

Reasons for Limited Involvement

The literature on building partnerships with parents is usually premised on the notion that parents are not sufficiently involved, but it typically does not detail ideal levels of involvement. What is common is research that contrasts the relative level of involvement demonstrated by parents of different races, ethnicities, and/or socioeconomic classes. This literature typically demonstrates that minority and low-income parents participate less frequently than middle- and upper-class white parents. It also details parent/family and school-related barriers that explain differences in the level and types of involvement.

Chavis and colleagues (1997) succinctly outline the parent-related obstacles as insufficient resources, abilities or skills, and cultural capital. Alexander and his collaborators (1997) make the important addition of the barrier imposed by parent attitudes and values. On the issue of resources, parents' time for involvement with the school or with helping their children at home may be limited by work schedules and family obligations (Chavis et al., 1997; Eccles & Harold, 1996). Limited financial resources might keep parents from providing additional educational experiences at home or in the community (Chin & Phillips, 2004; Goldenberg, 2004). Obstacles engendered by poverty are exacerbated when poverty is concentrated in the community in which the school is embedded (Bryk et al., 2010; Murphy, 2010a).

Limited parental skills and abilities can be manifested in several ways. Less-educated parents may be less able to help their students with course work, especially as students advance to middle and high school. Parents with higher levels of education are more likely than those with lower levels of education to read to their children, as well as tutor their children at home in a manner consistent with the teaching style typical in school, making this tutoring time more advantageous (Murphy, 2010a).

Cultural barriers often arise between minority and low-income parents and middle-class, predominantly white school staff. Some parents feel uncomfortable or unfamiliar with the language or methods for learning used at school and thus may be at a disadvantage when attempting to help their children at home or unwilling to participate actively at the school (Delgado-Gaitan, 1992; Hattie, 2009). For example, Goldenberg (2004) highlights how the distinct experiences of immigrant parents, who are educated in different schooling systems, present an obstacle for building home-school connections.

Parent attitudes and values toward school are shaped by their own schooling experiences (Alexander et al., 1997; Murphy, 2012). Those parents who had positive schooling experiences are more likely than those who had negative experiences to form connections with the school (Eckert, 1989). We also know that attitudes and experiences toward schooling tend to align with class status, whereby middle-class parents have often had more positive experiences in schooling than their working-class counterparts (Eccles & Harold, 1996).

School-related obstacles can be summarized as a lack of understanding on the part of school staff of the various types of parental involvement, negative and unwelcoming attitudes on the part of teachers or administrators, and limited physical and human resources within the school (Auerbach, 2009; Chavis et al., 1997).

The first two school-based obstacles are related. School staff sometimes develop negative attitudes toward parents because they do not understand or do not value how parents are involved in their child's education outside of the school setting. For example, there is a widespread belief held by teachers that parents are not sufficiently involved (Weis, 1990) either because they do not care about their children's education or are incapable, due to personal deficiencies, of helping their children succeed academically. Epstein (1996) concluded that teachers perceive parents very differently than parents perceive themselves and are often unaware of the goals parents have for their children. Teachers may attribute a lack of school-based parent involvement to a "culture of poverty," a theory that ascribes present time orientation and a sense of resignation to poor and marginalized individuals (Goldenberg, 2004). Teachers rooted in a belief in the culture of poverty often hold that parents are "apathetic, indifferent, or hostile about schooling" (Goldenberg, 2004, p. 111).

Assumptions such as these, which reflect the belief that parents are a major part of the problem of low student achievement, can result in a school not pursuing parent involvement, either because staff expect a lack of response, or, in more extreme cases, because they believe that poor, minority parents will "mess [the kids] up" (Auerbach, 2007, p. 711; Eccles & Harold, 1996). These attitudes may lead to neglect of or palpable hostility toward parents, which in turn makes parents feel unwelcome in the school (Eccles & Harold, 1996).

School staff may not trust parents sufficiently to yield power, or find that involving parents directly may decrease their autonomy (Powell, 1991). Dornbusch and Glasgow (1996, p.40) reach the conclusion that "school officials and teachers gain from the ignorance of students and their parents" in terms of the power and autonomy that they can wield. While school staff may be adamant in their desire for parents to contribute to the home learning of their children, they may be less interested in parents being actively involved in making decisions at the classroom or school level because they find this type of engagement "risk . . . and conflict ridden" (Haynes & Ben-Avie, 1996, p. 46; Auerbach, 2007). Many principals thus act not as a bridge between parents and the school, but rather as a buffer between school staff and what staff regard as overzealous parents (Auerbach, 2009).

School-related obstacles to parent involvement also arise due to lack of resources, which include time, financial capital, trained staff, and space. Work that demands time from principals and teachers impedes their ability to focus their energy on parents (Auerbach, 2007). In other cases, principals may wish to advance policies and practices to involve parents and the community but are constrained by district, state, or federal mandates (Auerbach, 2009).

Training for schools' staff on how to effectively involve parents may also be a resource that is in short supply (Chavis et al., 1997). Greenwood and Hickman (1991) suggest that teachers need training on the importance of parent involvement, the types of parent involvement, and strategies for engaging parents. Other researchers add that teachers need additional training in understanding and engaging parents who are culturally and linguistically diverse (Gandara, Maxwell-Jolly, & Driscoll, 2005).

Lack of physical space can also be an impediment to developing strong ties between the home and the school. Ideally, there would be a space for parents within the school to meet with teachers, work on school projects, connect with members of community service organizations, or meet with other parents. However many schools, already overcrowded, cannot provide this amenity (Auerbach, 2009).

Parent/family and school-related obstacles can interact to create mistrust and misperceptions among the various actors. Many times parents, the school, and community members have diverging role expectations for each other. Unaligned expectations can in turn lead to misunderstanding and frustration. When frustration on the part of teachers or parents is unresolved, it can lead to withdrawal and disengagement. Many of these problems stem from what psychologists label the fundamental attribution error, or the propensity for people to attribute behavior to personal characteristics instead of situational influences (Kennedy, 2010).

The way that parents conceive of their role within the school varies by socioeconomic status. Middle-class parents typically see their role as being active participants in their child's education, while lower class parents tend to regard educational staff as experts and thus defer the responsibility of educating their children to the school (Alexander & Entwisle, 1996; Bierman, 1996; Lareau, 1996). This difference in role construction is important because if parents conceive of their role as more active, they are more likely to be involved in their child's schooling (Auerbach, 2007). Lower-SES parents might disengage from school partnership if they perceive that the school is not doing enough to support their child's academic achievement (Weis, 1990) and/or are confronted with school staff that do not recognize or value their contributions. Thus, to conclude, "each (parents and school personnel), in a sense, blames the other for not taking responsibility for the children of the working class" (Weis, 1990, p. 174).

In addition to unaligned expectations, there can be a misalignment in what each set of actors believes is in the best interest for students. For example, lower-SES and working-class parents tend to value perceived safety above academic rigor when selecting schools (DeLuca & Rosenblatt, 2010). Moreover, these same parents tend to take a more hands-off approach to schooling and place the onus for learning on the child, instead of on the teachers or school staff (Lareau, 1989; DeLuca & Rosenblatt, 2010). DeLuca and Rosenblatt (2010) found that these differences led to lower-SES and middle-class parents engaging with school staff less frequently and focusing more attention on nonacademic issues.

Differences in how parents and school staff think about what constitutes good behavior and appropriate enforcement of rules also exist, and these often follow class and color lines. One example is differences between how lower-SES and working-class parents and middle-class parents view the role of physical force in resolving problems (Lareau, 1996). Lareau (1996) notes that where lower and working-class parents will often use physical force in disciplining their children, and encourage their children to use physical force to resolve issues with other children, middle-class parents are more likely to use and encourage "verbal negotiation" to resolve problems (p. 61). Middle-class conflict resolution strategies are better aligned with the expectations of the school, leading to teachers' more positive perceptions of these students and families, thus fostering deeper connections between school and home.

FOSTERING COMMUNITIES OF ENGAGEMENT FOR PARENTS

In this section, we discuss the following strategies for forming strong linkages between the home and school: setting goals to increase parent involvement, increasing trust through effective communication, and building collaboration. Before we do so, we offer a few insights about the importance of context in forming these connections.

Understanding Context

As we have noted throughout this volume, context matters. Here we add that principals of schools that are effective at engaging with parents recognize the contextual challenges and assets and attend to them in crafting a vision for building home-school connections (Auerbach, 2009). Context is defined by the characteristics of the family, school, and community (Bierman, 1996).

Principals should be aware of the circumstances of families within their schools, acknowledging the variability in family situations and providing options for all families to participate. The ways that parents are involved in the school can be partially predicted by their personal characteristics. For example, low-income parents and minority parents are more likely to be involved in types of engagement that occur in the home (Auerbach, 2007), whereas white and higher-income parents are also likely to be involved in types of engagement that occur in the school (Eccles & Harold, 1996). Other salient family characteristics are the family's structure (e.g., single-parent household, household with stepparents, multigenerational household), cultural background, language proficiency, education level, employment status, and home educational culture.

A principal highlighted in a study by Kochanek (2005) illustrates how a leader can build a culture of engagement while attending to contextual factors. To engage with her low-income parents with limited English proficiency, she began by providing English language instruction to parents after school. Then she employed those very parents who had benefited from the program as aides in the school. She then created multiple opportunities for parents to participate within the school. Finally, she changed the timing of programming to be more flexible so that working parents could participate. What is key to this story is not *what* the principal did, but the fact that she shaped her program for parent involvement according to the needs of the families in her schools. No single practice was expected to solve the problem of low parent engagement; instead, the policies and practices she utilized in her school were multiple, flexible, and adaptable.

Important school contextual factors include level (elementary, middle, high school), size, mobility rate, and existing teacher capacity. To begin with, we know that parent involvement looks different as students age, and schools should be responsive to how parents can and will be involved at each level of student development. Research indicates that parents are most involved in their child's education in the home in elementary school, and even through middle school, but that in later years this type of participation begins to ebb (Eccles & Harold, 1996). Eccles and Harold (1996) posit that this change may be due to school structure, a decreased sense of parent efficacy as content becomes more difficult, a desire on the part of parents to give children more independence as they age, and/or a decreased sense of attachment to a school that is not located as close to the home.

Teachers and school staff are also less likely to reach out to parents as students age (Auerbach, 2007; Eccles & Harold, 1996). This is due in part to the structure of middle and high schools, in which teachers instruct many more students in departmentalized programs than elementary teachers do in self-contained classrooms. In addition, high school teachers tend to regard themselves as subject area experts, and as such, not responsible for engaging with parents beyond managing specific classroom problems (Levine & Marcus, 2007).

For principals of middle and high schools, there is less research on building connections with parents from which to learn; however, there is evidence of effective strategies for parental involvement at these levels. For instance, middle schools that coordinate transition efforts that bridge the jump from elementary school tend to have more parent engagement (Epstein, 1996). Additionally, effective secondary schools create structures that enable closer collaboration among teachers around a smaller group of students, such as a student house or cohort system, in order to mitigate obstacles to parental engagement (Eccles & Harold, 1996).

School size and family mobility rate can also impact the relationship between parents and teachers within a school (Bryk et al., 2010). Some research shows that smaller schools are better able to attend to students and develop a culture of caring (Cotton, 1996; Stewart, 2008). School staff in smaller schools are likely to teach fewer students and thus may be better able to develop connections with parents (Gardner, Ritblatt, & Beatty, 1999). Mobile parents are less likely to reach out to school staff (Kohl, Lengua, & McMahon, 2000), and teachers may be less able to develop deep connections with students who are not a consistent part of the school community. Schools with a high level of student mobility often demonstrate higher levels of teacher and principal mobility as well that can have adverse effects on school culture and parental support systems (Murphy, 2010a).

Knowledge of how to effectively involve parents also varies across schools (Chavis et al., 1997). Leaders need to assess their own capacity and the capacity among their staff for how to engage with parents (Auerbach, 2007, 2009). One dimension of this is investing teachers in the vision for parent involvement. Their dedication to increasing parent engagement is the lynchpin of effective implementation. It is important that teachers, not outside consultants or program staff, lead the charge in building relationships with parents as ultimately it is the teachers who must learn from and engage with parents about their children (Auerbach, 2009).

Principals must also heed community characteristics that are relevant to the task of building community for parents. Community characteristics describe the resources, conditions, and physical space in the neighborhood where the school's students live, what we describe as "community capital." Specifically, community characteristics include the resources available to community members, the safety of the community, and the strength of social networks (both within the community and extending outside of the community) (Bryk et al., 2010). Bryk and his team found that when these community characteristics were more positive, school change was more likely to be successful.

The quality of available community resources is related to a family's ability to nurture their children. Effective principals seek out and use the resources within the community to support their visions, whereas ineffective principals at best ignore these resources and, at worst, eschew them (Leithwood & Montgomery, 1982). We take up the issue of community beyond parents in the following chapter.

Developing a Vision for a Culture of Engagement

Principals who lead schools effective at engaging with parents tend to be mission driven. That is, the principals are strongly motivated by the will to change and make choices that support parent engagement goals. These principals understand that parent involvement is key to student success and inspire parents and school staff to buy in to this belief. Their hopes for students and parents stem from a connection with the families in the schools powered by their compassion and dedication. Auerbach (2009, p. 24) relates the sense of possibility expressed by one principal:

> [She] insisted that leadership for family engagement begins with a belief, what she called "a natural feeling" for the role of parents in education and a sense of collective responsibility for children. The administrator has to believe that family engagement can happen in what she termed a "ghetto school" like hers and understand that low-income, immigrant parents are "devoted parents, hard working, trusting, compassionate, and very open. Very open to change."

Research tells us that most parents *want* to be involved, regardless of socioeconomic status, race, or ethnicity (Hoover-Dempsey et al., 2005; Eccles & Harold, 1996). Principals must have faith in this truth and demonstrate a concerted will to involve parents in the schooling of their children. The vision for parent involvement is driven by the leader's dedication to making parents an integral part of the school community. This means that the principal must be deeply involved in planning and implementing the vision for parent engagement.

Principals with the will to involve parents know that they need to develop a comprehensive program for parent involvement that addresses the specific requirements of the parents and children in their school.

These programs should be multifaceted, involve parents at all levels of the school's operation, acknowledge the multiple ways that parents can be involved in their child's education, and underscore program elements described in research studies (Goldenberg, 2004).

Principals show their commitment to parent involvement by offering a diverse array of programs and policies to attract all parents and overcome practical constraints (Auerbach, 2007; Johnson & Asera, 1999). While any individual policy or program might not be sufficient to reshape parent involvement, a comprehensive vision will feature multiple avenues for parents to become more deeply involved. Just as teachers should incorporate student interests when differentiating their lessons, schools should incorporate parent interests in differentiating their programs for parental involvement. A powerful vision will underscore multiple opportunities for parents to be involved both at the school site and in the home (Cotton, 2000; Goldenberg, 2004).

Being committed also entails that principals be personally involved in efforts to involve parents (Auerbach, 2009). Principals of effective schools spend considerably more time building relationships with the parents and the community (Cotton, 2003). The involvement of the principal also reinforces the symbolic aspects of the vision, signaling to school staff and parents that they are committed to increasing parent participation and ownership (Auerbach, 2007).

Commitment also means resourcing the work. Principals of effective schools do not simply rely on existing capital but seek out additional resources from the district and the community. These can be in the form of additional human resources, physical resources, or time (Desimone, 2002). A principal in Auerbach's (2007, p. 719) study captured this type of commitment as follows:

> At the school level, I think only the principal can set the stage for parent engagement to occur because the principal's got to include it on the calendar . . . the principal has got to deploy resources to make it happen when they're planning the budget, when they're making assignments of staff, when they make their own time available to work with parents.

Change takes time and setbacks can be frustrating to school staff (Bryk et al., 2010). However, in schools that are successful at creating community for parents, there is a norm of continuous improvement. Setbacks in implementation are met with different strategies or with patience and the commitment to see the effort through. Policies and practices implemented in an effort to increase parent engagement must become an integral part of the school program, so that in times of financial strain or other external shocks they remain central to the vision (Powell, 1991).

Finally, a culture of parental engagement includes collective responsibility shared by the school, family, and community to educate children (Auerbach, 2009; Cotton, 2003) because these three entities make up overlapping spheres of influence that together shape the education of a child (Epstein, 1996).

Bringing a vision of community for parents to life necessitates the principal and school staff setting goals and creating expectations. Goals and expectations must be context specific, strategic, and integrated. A plan that is context specific begins with data collection. In order to create a strategic plan for reaching goals related to parental involvement, leaders should collect and use data on related parent and teacher needs. This data can serve several purposes: (1) to assess the types of existing parent engagement efforts; (2) gauge the level of teacher capacity for parent outreach; and (3) evaluate the quality and effectiveness of current efforts to build a culture of meaningful parental involvement.

The literature to date does not speak much to this issue, but as accountability structures continue to become ingrained in schools, it only makes sense that data on parent involvement would be collected and analyzed. Documents, artifacts, surveys, interviews, and focus groups can be used to assess effectiveness. These data can then be used to refine goals and strategies to address deficiencies and build on existing assets (Leithwood et al., 1999; Hayes et al., 2004). There are some accounts of informal data collection guiding principal actions regarding parent engagement (Dinham et al., 1995), but nothing as structured as the sort of data mechanisms commonly used to assess student achievement or teacher effectiveness.

Building Trust

When working to build buy-in from parents for a vision of community of engagement, it is imperative that principals build trust and strong lines of communication. As discussed above, mistrust between school actors and parents is a major obstacle to the development of a participatory culture. Principals who effectively engage with parents overcome mistrust and misperceptions by both actively reaching out to parents and communicating their vision and expectations.

Policies and practices that bring parents, students, and teachers together can help build trust among the three parties. Activities can be located in the school (Auerbach, 2009; Johnson & Asera, 1999), in the home (Lloyd, 1996), or in community spaces. Schools that effectively involve parents welcome parents into the school by allowing for observations of classes (Johnson & Asera, 1999) or by creating spaces for parents within the school building (Leithwood, 2008; Leithwood et al., 2010; Epstein, 1996). Leithwood and Montgomery (1982) highlight other strategies used by principals to nurture participatory community including holding community meetings, facilitating parent-teacher groups, and being visible within the school and community themselves. By welcoming parents into the school, school staff reaffirm respect and appreciation for parents, characteristics imperative to building trusting relationships (Scheurich, 1998).

Simply reaching out to parents can promote a culture of engagement. Eccles and Harold (1996) found a positive association between how often teachers reached out to parents and how involved those parents were in the school community. This is true at the elementary, middle, and high school levels (Epstein, 1996) and especially so for low-income or minority parents (Auerbach, 2007). Schools see the most success engaging with parents when they (1) include parents in crafting the vision to make sure that parents are a voice in the process from the beginning and (2) ensure that expectations of all parties are clear (Cotton, 2003; Scanlan & Lopez, 2012). Principals can enhance trust by reaching out to parents before enacting reforms (Cooper, 1996; Leithwood et al., 1999).

Many schools use parent coordinators to ensure that parents are being contacted regularly by someone other than the classroom teacher. Parent coordinators can be especially effective for fostering trust among parents who are culturally and linguistically diverse (Epstein, 1996). Parent coordinators can be used to reach out to parents, build social networks among the parents, and represent parent interests at the school (Kochanek, 2005). Having parent voices be heard and represented by the coordinator can help leaders craft strategies of engagement that are tailored to the interests of the parent community (Haynes & Ben-Avie, 1996).

Principals also build trust by practicing asset-based thinking. Researchers have defined some of the assets existing within families as "rituals, traditional values, family dreams and aspirations, cultural norms for student behavior, racial identity development, practices that involve families in their children's education and schools, and formal and informal community organizations that support families" (Epstein, 1996, pp. 231–232).

Asset-based thinking about parents is present in the manner in which school staff communicates with parents. When school staff see parents as important members of the school community, they treat them with respect and find ways to meet their needs (Auerbach, 2007). Principals in effective schools focus on points of commonality shared by school staff and parents rather than on differences (Goldenberg, 2004).

Extant social networks that often overlap with kinship networks that parents already look to for support represent an important asset that can be utilized by schools building cultures of parental engagement (Bierman, 1996). This work can include actively seeking the support of grandparents who are more likely to be an integral part of the family unit in low-income and minority neighborhoods (Bryk et al., 2010). As we discuss more fully in the next chapter, principals of community-anchored schools use the resources that exist outside of the school to bolster engagement in the service of students learning (Sanders & Harvey, 2002).

Leaders of schools with a strong culture of engagement recognize and honor parents' desire to be involved as an asset. These principals do not leave the formation of this culture to the parents themselves but know that the onus of involving parents, especially in schools serving low-income and minority parents, lies with the school (Auerbach, 2009). In these schools, principals act as boundary spanners, trying to bridge the divide between the home and the school, instead of as a buffer against parental involvement (Hallinger & Heck, 1998). They lead parents through a process of socialization in which they engage with parents to build buy-in and trust and help them see that their engagement is a prerequisite not only for the achievement of their own student but for the success of the school (Haynes & Ben-Avie, 1996).

Building Collaboration

To create a culture of engagement, leaders implement policies and practices that accommodate varied family structures and needs. This includes extending available times for conferences to allow working parents to participate, hiring interpreters to aid with communication with non-English-speaking parents, implementing culturally responsive family nights, and/or providing transportation to school events (Powell, 1991).

Activities for parent involvement can be academic or nonacademic. Their purpose is to nurture collaboration between parents and students, parents and teachers, and students and teachers. Academic activities can include content-related nights where students are able to share the work they do at school with parents and teachers and to explain the content being taught in the classroom. Nonacademic activities could include recreational activities such as participation in sports, games, or movies. Both types of activities open the lines of communication between parents and school staff and help bolster mutual understanding.

To increase involvement within the school, leaders must collaborate with parents to devise coherent ways for parents to volunteer. Collaboration is essential for matching parent assets to the needs of the school. Volunteer opportunities within the school should be managed by school staff and parents to maximize the impact of the parent's time and effort. Ideally, volunteers would help where their particular skills were most beneficial, would have clear guidelines for what they should be doing, and would become an integral part of the classroom (Haynes & Ben-Avie, 1996).

Principals may also work collaboratively to help parents strengthen the educational environment in the home. Policies and practices that may influence change in the home environment, which include parenting classes, are aimed at helping parents help their children academically in the home. These classes might cover academic topics such as how to support children in specific content areas (Auerbach, 2007). They may also be aimed at building the skills of the parents themselves by providing GED, computer literacy, job search, or literacy classes (Auerbach, 2007; Bryk et al., 2010). Classes may also be used to provide information on nonacademic topics such as health, community issues, laws, and political issues (Auerbach, 2009). Some schools direct programs toward helping parents change their sense of efficacy in regard to helping their children. Other programs help parents understand their role in the school (Griffith, 2001). Programs and policies meant to educate parents or change the home learning environment should focus on making sure that parents hold high expectations for their students and then give parents the information and training they need to turn those expectations into reality (Hattie, 2009). Effective educational programs for parents are concrete. They provide parents with specific strategies to target adult or student needs in particular areas. Ostensibly, better-educated and better-informed parents will be better able to support their students (Dauber & Epstein, 1993).

Teacher requests for parents to help students at home with homework or school projects, sending home newsletters informing parents of what content is being covered, and explaining strategies for helping students in those areas are common ways that school staff work collaboratively to influence home educational culture (Bryk et al., 2010; Cotton, 2000; Eccles & Harold, 1996). Homework can be an effective means for teachers to encourage parents to help their children academically at home (Goldenberg, 2004). Teachers can request parents to sign student assignments on a regular basis (Kochanek, 2005) or call parents when students do not complete their homework (Goldenberg, 2004). In addition to teachers reaching out to parents with generalized information about how to help their children, teachers should also provide individualized information to parents to help parents monitor the specific learning needs of their child (Bierman, 1996). School staff should guide parents in understanding the information they provide so that it is meaningful and results in building trusting relationships and collaborative efforts instead of being a source of frustration that ultimately fosters mistrust (Bierman, 1996).

CONCLUSION

We began this chapter by outlining the positive outcomes associated with parental communities of engagement, the different ways that parents are commonly involved in schools, and the common barriers limiting the formation of these communities. In the second part of the chapter, we discussed the critical importance of context when developing a vision of communities of parental engagement. We then laid out an action plan for how principals can begin to enact change in this area.

8

Communities of Engagement for Stakeholders

Progress will require coordinated, integrated actions involving a wide spectrum of people. (Williams, 2003, p. 7)

In previous chapters, we have focused on how schools can build positive cultures of engagement for students, teachers, and parents. Principals are likely to engender the most change in culture within the school and between the school and the home, given that these are the spheres of influence they directly confront on a regular basis. However, schools and families exist within extended communities, defined as both the geographically bounded neighborhoods within which they are located as well as the social networks to which they have access (Sanders, 2001). Principals seeking to create a culture of engagement within their school must, therefore, also seek to involve the larger community. In this chapter, we explore how leaders and schools can partner with the community, a sphere of influence related to student academic and social success (Epstein, 1996; Rouse & Fantuzzo, 2009).

LANDSCAPE

Generally, partnerships between the school and the community can be defined by the strength of the relationship (Franklin & Streeter, 1995), the intended outcomes, and the organizations with which a school partners (Bryk et al., 2010; Darling-Hammond et al., 2002; Drago-Severson, 2004; Sanders & Harvey, 2002).

Partnerships' Designs

Franklin and Streeter (1995) provide a useful starting point for understanding types of partnerships by describing a continuum of contact between schools and community organizations characterized by five levels: informal relations, coordination, partnerships, collaboration, and integration (see also Tierney, Gupton, & Hallett, 2008). Informal relations are characterized by two-way, casual acknowledgments. This is the least involved level and takes little effort on the part of the school or community organizations. At the next level, coordination, school staff actively refer students and families to the available community organizations and services; however, the community organizations do not work or plan directly with school staff. In a partnership, the school and organization are working together on a regular basis in order to provide necessary services to the children and families; however, the partnering organization and the school remain autonomous. Collaboration is similar, but at this level, schools and organizations pool resources to address mutual needs. The final level, integration, is exemplified by the community school model in which schools and community organizations work together to merge two (or more) public support systems into a unified "service delivery system" (Franklin & Streeter, 1995, p. 777). As schools and community organizations move along this spectrum toward integration, they relinquish more of their individual organizational autonomy. Most school-community connections documented in the literature can be categorized as coordination, partnership, or collaboration. Integration, exemplified by community schools, is less frequent as it necessitates a considerable amount of planning and shared work (Sprick & Rich, 2010).

Previous scholarship describes the multiple purposes for school-community partnerships. Schools link with community entities in order to support students and families, school improvement, and/or community development (Sanders & Harvey, 2002). These three categories bleed into one another but can be differentiated by who is receiving benefits and where the locus of action exists.

Finally, depending on the intention of the partnership and the available community capital, schools can choose to engage with myriad organizations or individuals: advocates for children and their families maintain that a collaborative network should "include a wide variety of service providers" (James, Smith, & Mann, 1991, p. 306), both public and private. Key service providers highlighted in the literature include those in the educational, social, and health fields, including the following: medical personnel, mental health agencies, disaster relief organizations, housing providers, universities, public parks and recreation departments, police departments, child welfare agencies, transportation departments, elected officials, social service departments, and food and nutrition programs (Duffield, 2000; Eddowes & Butcher, 2000; Julianelle, 2007; Nunez & Collignon, 2000; Vostanis, Grattan, Cumelia, & Winchester, 1997; Woronoff, Estrada, & Sommer, 2006). In addition, it is often proposed that community groups, such as local foundations, businesses, faith-based organizations, and civic groups, be woven into the collaborative tapestry (Masten et al., 1997; Nunez & Collignon, 2000; Quint, 1994; Stronge & Hudson, 1999).

Community Schools: A Special Case

As mentioned above, the community school exemplifies an integrated school-partner relationship. While the least pervasive form of partnership, community schools are gaining considerable traction as a reform strategy. In 2010, the U.S. Department of Education awarded grants to twenty-one "Promise Neighborhoods" designed to build community-anchored schools able to support the academic and developmental needs of students living in high poverty areas (Gallagher, Zhang, & Comey, 2013). Principals of community schools envision schools as the pillar of the community and as a member of the extended family (Powell, 1991). These schools work to move beyond simply working to increase parent participation in school activities or bolster financial and other resources through partnerships of convenience, practices that arguably reify existing separations between the home, school, and community (Baron, 2003; Dworsky, 2008; Moore, 2005a). Instead, the purpose of community schools is to diminish the separation between the various spheres of influence (home, school, and community) in order to create a "community of commitment" (Tyack & Hansot, in Scheurich, 1998) or "human resource development centers" (Haynes & Ben-Avie, 1996).

Policies to support this vision require buy-in and support from the community and typically include offering health and social services, adult education, or career counseling through the school. Advocates for community school reforms see the school as the optimum distribution point for social services as they are interspersed across the country (Cibulka & Kritek, 1996; Franklin & Streeter, 1995; Murphy & Tobin, 2011; Powell, 1991). These schools aim to serve not only the students who are enrolled but also their families and the community at large. Community schools can help to generate social networks within fractured neighborhoods and revive depressed communities (Bryk et al., 2010; Haynes & Ben-Avie, 1996; Leithwood et al., 1999; Powell, 1991). At their best, community schools can help empower parents and community leaders as they become more deeply involved in planning, implementing, or participating in a host of programs housed within the school walls (Bryk et al., 2010).

Community schools require that leaders move "beyond a focus on the components of the problem (families, teachers, texts) to a focus on the functional requirements of a healthy, curious, and productive child" (Powell, 1991, p. 309). These schools are especially effective in serving students and families in low-income neighborhoods or in communities with a high concentration of disadvantaged families where there is limited access to social and health resources (Leithwood et al., 1999). For students living in neighborhoods characterized by extreme poverty and violence, community schools provide "an island of safety and order, established social routine, and new norms for academic effort [that can] counter the external forces pushing students in very different directions" (Bryk et al., 2010, p. 211).

Community-based schools provide a safety net for families and children. Schools step in to provide what families are unable to acquire from their communities and what students are not receiving in the home (Bierman, 1996). Powell (1991, p. 309) suggests that supporters of community schools "propose a new role for schools that involves serving as a broker of the multiple services that can be used to achieve the functions previously filled by families or families and schools acting together." Building community schools requires that services provided by outside partners, such as health care centers and other social services, be integrated into the functioning, vision, planning, and everyday operations of the school (Franklin & Streeter, 1995). This sort of planning requires buy-in and active participation from the community and should begin with a needs assessment that helps shape the services provided according to a specific context. As important, leaders must keep the needs of the community in mind. Services should be brought in that are not already easily available and that meet the particular needs of school community members (Franklin & Streeter, 1995).

BARRIERS AND SUPPORTS

In the following section, we discuss the ever-important role of context in making decisions for a school and building community. We then describe the barriers and supports that enable or hinder the development of strong linkages between schools and community organizations.

The Role of Context

As described extensively in the previous chapter on creating communities of engagement for parents, local context moderates the success of partnerships (Auerbach, 2009; Bryk et al., 2010; Connolly & James, 2006).

For example, available community and school resources, the level of community efficacy, the shared history of previous collaborations between particular institutions, and individual personalities and capacities shape the nature of school-community connections (Bryk et al., 2010; Sprick & Rich, 2010).

Before putting forth efforts toward engaging with community members, principals should assess the capacity, will, and need that exists among potential partners. This step is essential in order to form connections that have collective support and the greatest likelihood of positive impact. In conducting a needs assessment, principals should seek input from parents, teachers, students, and community members (Sprick & Rich, 2010). For example, parents might indicate a desire for before or after-school care for their children to accommodate work schedules (Johnson & Asera, 1999). Students may request resources to start or support extracurricular activities. Teachers may express the need for professional development or additional resources for their classrooms. Community members may see a need to provide health or social services through the school in order to improve the outcomes for their particular organizations.

Another aspect of local context principals should investigate is the attitude teachers and parents have toward the community and vice versa. Schools might be reticent to use resources to build relationships with community partners they do not know well or see as credible, and vice versa. Buy-in from teachers is especially important for creating partnerships, as teachers are often the point of contact between the school and the home as well as responsible for implementing new programs and policies (Sprick & Rich, 2010). Leaders of schools that cultivate effective relationships with the community spend the time to inform the school community of the potential benefits of community partnerships in order to build buy-in (Franklin & Streeter, 1995).

Principals should also be aware of resources, including the social networks to which school staff and parents belong, that exist within the school and the neighborhood (Sprick & Rich, 2010). Access to resources is highly variable, and as described above, securing additional capital is often the motivation for establishing partnerships. Principals who take stock of what is available can be more strategic in seeking out partners. They will avoid redundancies in the resources they obtain, and they will be better able to build from their school's assets.

Obstacles

Wepner and her colleagues (2012) provide a framework for understanding obstacles between schools and university partners, and by extension other community partners. They highlight four major obstacles: problems communicating, institutional culture clashes, conflicting expectations, and a one-way flow of activities from a partner to the school.

Problems in communication are a frequently cited source of conflict between partners. Initially, communication is essential so that schools and partners are aware of each other's needs and assets (Sanders & Harvey, 2002). Subsequently, sustained communications is important for avoiding confusion when the needs of either the school or a partner evolve (Sanders & Harvey, 2002). When leadership in either camp changes, communication between new and remaining members becomes even more imperative in maintaining a healthy relationship (Sanders & Harvey, 2002).

Institutional culture clashes refer to conflicts that emerge as a result of differing operating norms, including how participants communicate and are evaluated, and the structure and expectations of management (Wepner et al., 2012). Lack of understanding and appreciation for the work of other partners can also cause friction (Moore, 2005a; Penuel & Davey, 1998), especially if partners fail to "take the time to become familiar with the roles and requirements of other agencies" (Stronge & Hudson, 1999, p. 12). Institutional clashes can either be the source or result of conflicting expectations between partners and schools. Clashes are likely to become more problematic as partnerships become deeper and individual organizations become less autonomous if possible misunderstandings are not anticipated.

To avoid these problems, school leaders and the leaders of community organizations need to become copartners and make expectations and roles explicit by creating formalized contracts (Joselowsky, 2007; Moore, 2005a; Sanders & Harvey, 2002). These contracts may delineate the mission grounding the partnership, how often, when, and where partners will meet, how decisions will be made, and how disagreements will be resolved (Memphis Latino Student Success Collaborative, n.d.).

Finally, Wepner and colleagues (2012) explain that partnerships may not be successful when activity flows in only one direction. In the context of a partnership with a university, they write:

> A major concern from K–12 partners is a one way flow of activities from the university to classrooms with little reason for teachers to take ownership of a project or to consider using the activities that have been developed by others not directly involved with the curriculum (Tomanek, 2005). Little regard seems to be given to what the teachers in the classroom want and need. As a result, the services offered by a university do not last longer than the time that university faculty and students are in a school. (p. 123)

Effective collaboration is also hindered by the inflexible bureaucratic structure at the heart of the various agencies (Moore, 2005a; Stronge & Hudson, 1999): "Bureaucracies are often slow enough without having to coordinate with other equally slow bureaucracies" (Helm, 1992, p. 40). Absence of genuine commitment and a dearth of leadership have been singled out as a problem in the literature as well (Penuel & Davey, 1998). Advocating for a specific agency rather than the common mission can also impede collaborative work, as can failing to develop avenues to effectively share information (Moore, 2005a, 2005b).

Helping Collaborations Work

Research has uncovered some important lessons for promoting effective collaboration. We highlight the most important of these below:

- Take the time to learn about and understand the other partners in the collaborative: "It is vital to know the other collaborative agencies and their staff members" (Moore, 2005a, p. 30).
- Develop buy-in: "Establish the expectation that everyone will contribute" (Moore, 2005a, p. 30).
- Develop clear goals and a "collective vision" (Stronge & Hudson, 1999, p. 13) and "clear expectations for the relationships" (Moore, 2005a, p. 30).
- Maintain focus on the vision and goals: "Begin with client issues and problems" (Moore, 2005a, p. 31) instead of prepackaged solutions, agency agendas, or procedures and remember, "collaborating is not the goal but the means to accomplish the goal" (Moore, 2005a, p. 5).
- Establish rules and expectations to guide action (Penuel & Davey, 1998; Stronge & Hudson, 1999).
- Make sure that "the right people are at the table" (Moore, 2005a, p. 8) and "empower decision making authority within the collaborative instead of requiring each member to clear decisions through their agency channels" (Moore, 2005a, p. 31).
- Begin with "a small manageable project [that] will build confidence to maintain momentum and undertake larger tasks" (Moore, 2005a, p. 31).
- Create a productive and trusting climate for mutual work: "Successful collaborators should plan to spend as much time nurturing relationships as planning and implementing projects" (Moore, 2005a, p. 8).
- "Establish honest and frank communication patterns" (Moore, 2005a, p. 31): "Communication unites efforts of model programs to make them successful" (Nunez & Collignon, 2000, pp. 58–59).

NORMS OF EXTENDED COMMUNITY

In the previous chapter, we described a model for developing a culture of engagement for parents within schools. Most of the norms and attitudes we uncovered are necessary for building strong school-community relationships as well. For instance, we explained that strong relationships with parents are predicated on trust, respect, and open communication, and the same holds true for school-community relationships. Similarly, to engage deeply with community partners, schools and partners will have to share a vision and create collaborative working conditions (Moore, 2005a).

Several authors have suggested models for understanding the norms of successful partnerships between schools and community organizations (Woods, Bennett, Harvey, & Wise, 2004; Connolly & James, 2006; Sanders, 2001; Sanders & Harvey, 2002; Wepner et al., 2012). In this section, we provide a synthesis of these discreet but related models. Productive school-community relationships are grounded in the norms of commitment, collaboration, and trust. Partnerships predicated on these norms can be utilized to increase resources, effectiveness, efficiency, and accountability, which better enables schools to support students and families.

Commitment

Schools that are successful in creating long-term partnerships have the capacity and motivation to cultivate relationships (Connolly & James, 2006). Leaders in these schools are outward looking and seek to involve their schools in programs for positive change (Dinham, 2005; Johnson & Asera, 1999). Finally, these leaders have an in-depth understanding of the local community and a positive attitude toward community engagement.

Building and maintaining partnerships is hard work, and as noted above, commitment to a shared vision is necessary in order to coordinate the efforts of the school and myriad outside partners (Bosma, Sieving, Ericson, Russ, Cavender, & Bonine, 2010; Bryk et al., 2010). Principals and partners show their mutual commitment by taking time to plan, collaborate, and educate their staffs (Franklin & Streeter, 1995).

Part of the school's commitment to engaging with the community is using the resources of time, money, and influence to seek out and establish cooperative endeavors. Principals must be ready to manage the partnerships they help create, "otherwise commitment ebbs, people lose interest, resources dwindle, or other problems crop up" (Bryk et al., 2010, p. 59). Leaders with limited time may hire or enlist staff to serve as coordinators or grant writers within the school in order to facilitate the process of recruiting partners (Bosma et al., 2010; Connolly & James, 2006; Johnson & Asera, 1999; Wepner et al., 2012). Grant writers with knowledge of where to find resources and how to apply for grants can be especially useful in fostering professional relationships (Johnson & Asera, 1999).

Leaders may also use their social networks, both professional, personal, and community-based, to nurture commitment. Principals often are involved in district governing boards or committees and may use their influence in these positions to enlist commitment (Gurr et al., 2005).

Collaboration

Successful connections between schools and community organizations that move beyond informal relations and coordination toward partnerships and integration (Franklin & Streeter, 1995) "thrive when a shared culture is developed that establishes a new entity that is not merely a collection of the individual partnership organizations" (Goldring & Sims, 2005, p. 238). Both the school and community partners must commit to a vision for the partnership that is either mutually constructed or mutually agreed upon (Moore, 2005a). Commitment to this vision must be voluntary and mutually beneficial and can be established by co-planning, distributing leadership, and sharing accountability (Connolly & James, 2006).

Planning a vision that will ground a long-term relationship must be done conscientiously. Both schools and community organizations need to be aware of each other's mutual and divergent priorities and be willing to compromise in order to meet an agreed upon outcome (Bosma et al., 2010). Leaders from the school and partner organization should create norms for communication, establish roles for each organization, and set benchmarks for evaluation (Goldring & Sims, 2005; Sprick & Rich, 2010; Wepner et al., 2012).

Part of ensuring productive connections grounded in a shared vision is selectivity in creating partnerships. The resources that partners bring must benefit the school program, not detract or distort the mission (Newmann et al., 2001). If the vision of the school and the partnering organization are unaligned, frustration is likely to lead to disunion. The resources—human, physical, financial, and social—that partners may bring to a school are limited and should be used strategically. For instance, studies of schools with a culture of extended community engagement describe how principals and teachers often identify the students most in need to participate in supplemental programs or to receive additional resources (Johnson & Asera, 1999; Kochanek, 2005; Murphy, 2010).

Successful partnerships are beneficial for both schools and the partner organizations. They are borne out of the needs of each, and thus the needs of both parties must be at the forefront of collaborative work. For example, a school that partnered with local businesses to provide internship opportunities restricted the school schedule to make sure that participating students were able to complete their course work and the employers would always have available students (Leithwood et al., 1999).

Collaboration frequently means pooling and sharing resources (Bosma et al., 2010). These resources, as described above, can include knowledge and expertise, social networks, or financial assets. Each partner also brings a reputation they can share with other partners for mutual benefit (Bosma et al., 2010).

Trust

The success of a school-community partnership is contingent on the level of trust that exists between organizations (Goddard et al., 2009): "Trust is necessary because both parties must compromise their practices and even possibly some of the assumptions on which those practices are based to come to mutually agreeable implementation that links with system goals and exigencies" (Blumenfeld et al., 2000, p. 160).

Partnerships must be crafted intentionally and require open communication between institutions (Dinham, 2005; Sanders & Harvey, 2002). Each partner must know its role within the school and be able to communicate when their needs and capacities change (Sanders & Harvey, 2002). Open dialogue requires that communication be ongoing and occur in both directions (Bosma et al., 2010; Goldring & Sims, 2005). Regular face-to-face meetings as well as ongoing e-mail or phone communication can be used to resolve implementation problems (Bosma et al., 2010). Moreover, as in the case with school-family communication, regular respectful exchange is key in building trusting collaborative relationships in extended school communities (Goldring & Sims, 2005). Communication between partners should be documented, preferably in writing, and should be accessible to all concerned parties (Sprick & Rich, 2010; Wepner et al., 2012). Partnership facilitators can also help build trust and increase transparency between organizations by working as boundary spanners (Goldring & Sims, 2005).

IMPACT

The evidence is clear. School districts alone cannot maintain the momentum and resources needed for systemic change. Some type of broader school-community alliance is needed. (Joselowsky, 2007, p. 259)

As suggested by the preceding quotation, partnerships often prove essential for enacting systemic change within a school. Unfortunately, many schools, especially those located in low-income areas, do not have the requisite funds to resource important work. Lack of funding affects a school's ability to provide needed services and programs (Drago-Severson, 2004). Given the need for a massive infusion of capital in schools, nourishing partnerships is an indispensible part of managing schools well. For many underresourced schools in particular, the additional assets provided through partnerships are not a luxury but essential for the effective functioning of the school. Extended communities enable schools to more effectively address the needs of children and their families (Drago-Severson, 2004).

Schools partners engage in these collaborative arrangements to supplement existing capital (including financial capital, physical capital, human capital, and social capital) (Bryk et al., 2010; Johnson & Asera, 1999; Leithwood et al., 1999; Sanders & Harvey, 2002; Stoll et al., 2006). Financial capital, which comes in the form of monetary assistance such as grants or donations, as well as social capital, which comes in the form of social and professional networks, can be used to create other forms of capital.

Financial and physical capital includes curricular materials, facilities, personnel, and so forth. Johnson and Asera (1999) profile a school that used its connection with a local hotel to secure a space for special events and awards ceremonies, and a partnership with a local church resulted in a space for the school's graduation. Moreover, this same school partnered with a local business that provided the labor and supplies to refurbish the building.

Financial capital can also support professional development, a key resource in developing the human capital of school staff. Consultants, university personnel, and community members can work with the school to help teachers build content and pedagogical knowledge (Anderson et al., 2009; Cotton, 2000; Darling-Hammond et al., 2002; Spillane et al., 2009); manage classroom activities or school events; catalogue, analyze, and interpret student and school level data (Kerr et al., 2006); and develop and implement programs (Johnson & Asera, 1999; Newmann et al., 2001; Quint, 2006). These partners can also help teachers plan effectively or form study groups focused on incorporating research-based practices into their teaching repertoires (Burch & Spillane, 2003; Phillips, 2003).

Partnerships between schools and community organizations increase the social capital available to school staff (Morrissey, 2000; Shear et al., 2008; Spillane, Diamond, et al., 2001). Social capital is another important tool for developing human capital and increasing financial capital (Spillane, Diamond, et al., 2001). The social networks that teachers create can aid them in developing professional skills as well as securing resources for their classroom. Spillane, Diamond, and their team (2001) describe a school that formed multiple partnerships with universities and consultants in order to access training and resources to improve its science curriculum. Over the course of the study, the school was able to implement systemic change in how it approached science with the aid of their partners. The authors explain: "Especially in resource-hungry and marginalized subject areas, such as urban elementary science education, networks of relations create the capacity for change and reflection" (2001, p. 936). In this case, there was a clear link between the development of social capital, by helping teachers create networks with community partners, and the development of human capital, in the form of teacher knowledge and skill (Spillane, Diamond, et al., 2001). Another study described how a group of teachers at one school used its ties with a university to supplement the curriculum and make it more culturally relevant for African-American students (Cooper, 1996). These teachers were able to use partnerships to increase financial and social capital for themselves and their school, as well as cultural capital for their students.

While partnerships for school improvement are typically formed to provide human and material resources, they can also be used to reenergize and support the individual and collaborative work of teachers (Drago-Severson, 2004). Outsiders may be able to provide new ideas or fresh perspectives on persistent challenges, insights that increase and sustain the momentum for systemic change (Joselowsky, 2007).

Community involvement in school, whether through formal partnerships or informal contacts, creates what some authors term environmental press, defined as a "strong press from the parents and community to change school policy and influence the functioning of the school" (Hoy et al., 1998, p. 342). Environmental press, often perceived as negative interference by teachers, is correlated with improved academic outcomes for students (Hoy et al., 1998). Similarly, combining community and school-based interventions has been shown to strengthen the effects of school reform (Cuijpers, 2002).

In addition to strengthening schools, students, and families, school-community partnerships can increase the capacity of the neighborhood. Strong schools become a source of social capital for the entire community (Auerbach, 2009; Bryk et al., 2010). Communities with strong social capital enable stronger parent-school relationships, more productive climates for children, increased likelihood of school improvement, and increased investment in the school (Bryk et al., 2010; Franklin & Streeter, 1995; Gold et al., 2005).

Analysts often point to gains that accrue to the agencies themselves from the collaborative work, including deeper understanding of issues related to children and families as well as better communication with colleagues with similar interests (Eddowes & Hranitz, 1989). They also maintain that more collaborative work leads to a better system of service that permits some partners to cover potential service gaps. In addition, in partnership collaborators often find "that working together makes each person's job easier" (Moore, 2005a, p. 15). Duffield (2000), in turn, adds that collaboration is valuable because "there is strength in numbers, and resources can be quickly deployed by working with other groups" (p. 211). The take away message is that "collaborative efforts can increase efficiency and reduce duplication of services, which can translate into an expansion of services . . . they enable agencies to work together to craft more comprehensive strategies" (Julianelle, 2007, p. 5) to help students and their families.

CONCLUSION

In this chapter, we have reviewed what the literature suggests is important for cultivating partnerships between the school and community organizations and examined the norms that are essential for building and maintaining these partnerships. In schools that have created successful linkages with the extended community, there is a community and family focus in the school (Mulford & Silins, 2003) and a reciprocal family and school focus in the community (Epstein, 1996). In community-focused schools, teachers and administrators have positive perceptions and working relationships with community organizations and agencies (Mulford & Silins, 2003). Building a functional extended community of shared norms and experiences between school members and partners is a result of collaboration, trust, and commitment.

References

Ackerman, R. H., & Maslin-Ostrowski, P. (2002). *The wounded leader: How real leadership emerges in times of crisis.* San Francisco, CA: Jossey-Bass.

Adams, C. (2010). Social determinants of student trust in high poverty elementary schools. In W. K. Hoy & M. DiPaola (Eds.), *Analyzing school contexts: Influences of principals and teachers in the service of students* (pp. 255–280). Charlotte, NC: Information Age.

Adams, C., & Forsyth, P. (2009). Conceptualizing and validating a measure of student trust. In W. K. Hoy & M. DiPaola (Eds.), *Studies in school improvement* (pp. 263–277). Charlotte, NC: Information Age.

Ainscow, M., & Southworth, G. (1996). School improvement: A study of the roles of leaders and external consultants. *School Effectiveness and School Improvement, 7*(3), 229–251.

Alexander, K., & Entwisle, D. (1996). Schools and children at risk. In A. Booth & J. Dunn (Eds.), *Family-school links: How do they affect educational outcomes?* (pp. 67–88). Mahwah, NJ: Erlbaum.

Alexander, K., Entwisle, D., & Horsey, C. (1997). From first grade forward: Early foundations of high school dropout. *Sociology of Education, 70*(2), 87–107.

Allensworth, E. M., & Easton, J. Q. (2005). *The on-track indicator as a predictor of high school graduation.* Chicago, IL: Consortium on Chicago School Research at the University of Chicago.

Ancess, J. (2000). The reciprocal influence of teacher learning, teaching practice, school restructuring, and student learning outcomes. *The Teachers College Record, 102*(3), 590–619.

Ancess, J. (2003). *Beating the odds: High schools as communities of commitment.* New York, NY: Teachers College Press.

Anderson, R. E., & Dexter, S. (2005). School technology leadership: An empirical investigation of prevalence and effect. *Educational Administration Quarterly, 41*(1), 49–82.

Anderson, S., Moore, S., & Sun, J. (2009). Positioning the principals in patterns of school leadership distribution. In K. Leithwood, B. Mascall, & T. Strauss (Eds.), *Distributed leadership according to the evidence* (pp. 111–136). London, UK: Routledge.

Antrop-Gonzalez, R. (2006). Toward the school as sanctuary concept in multicultural urban education: Implications for small high school reform. *Curriculum Inquiry, 36*(3), 273–301.

Antrop-Gonzalez, R., & De Jesus, A. (2006). Toward a theory of critical care in urban small school reform: Examining structures and pedagogies of caring in two Latino community-based schools. *International Journal of Qualitative Studies in Education, 19*(4), 409–433.

Au, K. H. (2002). Communities of practice: Engagement, imagination, and alignment in research on teacher education. *Journal of Teacher Education, 53*(3), 222–227.

Auerbach, S. (2007). Visioning parent engagement in urban schools. *Journal of School Leadership, 17*(6), 699–734.

Auerbach, S. (2009). Walking the walk: Portraits in leadership for family engagement in urban schools. *School Community Journal, 19*(1), 9–32.

Baenen, N., Dulaney, C., Yamen, K., & Banks, K. (2002). *Gaps in academic achievement: WCPSS status, 2001–02.* Raleigh, NC: Wake County Public Schools, Department of Evaluation and Research.

Baker, J. A., Terry, T., Bridger, R., & Winsor, A. (1997). Schools as caring communities: A relational approach to school reform. *The School Psychology Review, 26*(4), 586–602.

Balfanz, R., & Byrnes, V. (2006). Closing the mathematics achievement gap in high-poverty middle schools: Enablers and constraints. *Journal of Education for Students Placed at Risk, 11*(2), 143–159.

Balfanz, R., Herzog, L., & MacIver, D. (2007). Preventing student disengagement and keeping students on the graduation path in urban middle-grades schools: Early identification and effective interventions. *Educational Psychologist, 42*(4), 223–235.

Barber, B. R. (1984). *Strong democracy: Participatory politics for a new age.* Berkeley, CA: University of California Press.

Barker, B. (2001). Do leaders matter? *Educational Review, 53*(1), 65–76.

Barnes, C. A., Camburn, E., Sanders, B. R., & Sebastian, J. (2010). Developing instructional leaders: Using mixed methods to explore the black box of planned change in principals' professional practice. *Educational Administration Quarterly, 46*(2), 241–279.

Barnett, K., & McCormick, J. (2004). Leadership and individual principal-teacher relationships in schools. *Educational Administration Quarterly, 40*(3), 406–434.

Barnett, K., McCormick, J., & Conners, R. (2001). Transformational leadership in schools: Panacea, placebo, or problem? *Journal of Educational Administration, 39*(1), 24–46.

Baron, S. (2003). Street youth violence and victimization. *Trauma, Violence, and Abuse, 4*(1), 22–44.

Barth, R. S. (1988). School: A community of leaders. In A. Lieberman (Ed.), *Building a professional culture in schools* (pp. 129–147). New York, NY: Teachers College Press.

Barth, R. S. (2001). Teacher leader. *Phi Delta Kappan, 82*(6), 443–449.

Barton, P. E. (2003). *Parsing the achievement gap.* Policy Information Report. Princeton, NJ: Educational Testing Service.

Bass, B. M. (1990). *Bass & Stogdills's handbook of leadership: Theory, research & managerial applications* (3rd ed.). New York, NY: The Free Press.

Battistich, V., Solomon, D., Kim, D., Watson, M., & Schaps, E. (1995). Schools as communities, poverty levels of student populations, and students' attitudes, motives, and performance: A multilevel analysis. *American Educational Research Journal, 32*(3), 627–658.

Battistich, V., Solomon, D., Watson, M., & Schaps, E. (1997). Caring school communities. *Educational Psychologist, 32*(3), 137–151.

Beachum, F., & Dentith, A. M. (2004). Teacher leaders creating cultures of school renewal and transformation. *Educational Forum 68*(3), 276–286.

Beck, L. G., & Foster, W. (1999). Administration and community: Considering challenges, exploring possibilities. In J. Murphy & K. S. Louis (Eds.), *Handbook of research on educational administration* (pp. 337–358). San Francisco, CA: Jossey-Bass.

Beck, L. G., & Murphy, J. (1993). *Understanding the principalship: Metaphorical themes,* 1920's–1990's. New York: Teachers College Press.

Beck, L. G., & Murphy, J. (1996). *The four imperatives of a successful school.* Newbury Park, CA: Corwin.

Becker, B. E., & Luthar, S. S. (2002). Social-emotional factors affecting achievement outcomes among disadvantaged students: Closing the achievement gap. *Educational Psychologist, 37*(4), 197–214.

Beers, D., & Ellig, J. (1994). An economic view of the effectiveness of public and private schools. In S. Hakim, P. Seidenstat, & G. W. Bowman (Eds.), *Privatizing education and educational choice: Concepts, plans, and experiences* (pp. 19–38). Westport, CT: Praeger.

Bell, L., Bolam, R., Cubillo, L. (2003). *A systematic review of the impact of school leadership and management on student outcome*s. London, UK: EPPI Centre, Social Science Research Unit, Institute of Education.

Berends, M., Bodilly, S., & Kirby, S. N. (2002). District and school leadership for whole-school reform. In J. Murphy & A. Datnow (Eds.), *Leadership for school reform: Lesson from comprehensive school reforms* (pp. 109–131). Thousand Oaks, CA: Corwin.

Berends, M., Lucas, S. R., Sullivan, T., & Briggs, R. J. (2005). *Examining gaps in mathematics achievement among racial-ethnic groups, 1972–1992.* Santa Monica, CA: Rand Corporation.

Berry, B., & Ginsberg, R. (1990, April). Creating lead teachers: From policy to implementation. *Phi Delta Kappan, 71*(8), 616–621.

Betts, J., & Shkolnik, J. (1999). The behavioral effects of variations in class size: The case of math teachers. *Educational Evaluation and Policy Analysis, 21*(2), 192–213.

Betts, J., Zau, A., & Koedel, C. (2010). *Lessons in reading reform: Finding what works.* San Francisco, CA: Public Policy Institute of California.

Bidwell, C. E., & Yasumoto, J. Y. (1999). The collegial focus: Teaching fields, collegial relationships, and instructional practice in American high schools. *Sociology of Education, 72*(4), 234–256.

Bierman, K. L. (1996). In A. Booth & J. F. Dunn (Eds.), *Family-school links: How do they affect educational outcomes?* (pp. 276–287). Mahwah, NJ: Erlbaum.

Birch, S., & Ladd, G. (1997). The teacher-child relationship and children's early school adjustment. *Journal of School Psychology, 35*(1), 61–79.

Bishop. H. L., Tinley, A., & Berman, B. T. (1997). A contemporary leadership model to promote teacher leadership. *Action in Teacher Education, 19*(3), 77–81.

Blair, M. (2002). Effective school leadership: The multi-ethnic context. *British Journal of Sociology of Education, 23*(2), 179–191.

Blanc, S., Christman, J. B., Liu, R., Mitchell, C., Travers, E., & Bulkley, K. E. (2010). Learning to learn from data: Benchmarks and instructional communities. *Peabody Journal of Education, 85*(2), 205–225.

Blase, J., & Blase, J. (1999). Principals' instructional leadership and teacher development: Teachers' perspectives. *Educational Administration Quarterly, 35*(3), 349–378.

Blase, J., & Blase, J. (2000). Effective instructional leadership: Teachers' perspectives on how principals promote teaching and learning in schools. *Journal of Educational Administration, 38*(2), 130–141.

Blase, J., & Blase, J. (2004). *Handbook of instructional leadership: How really good principals promote teaching and learning.* Thousand Oaks, CA: Corwin.

Blase, J., & Kirby, P. (2009). *Bringing out the best in teachers: What effective principals do.* Thousand Oaks, CA: Corwin.

Blegen, M. B., & Kennedy, C. (2000). Principals and teachers, leading together. *NASSP Bulletin, 84*(616), 1–6.

Bloomberg, L., Ganey, A., Alba, V., Quintero, G., & Alvarez-Alcantara, L. (2003). Chicano-Latino youth leadership institute: An asset-based program for youth. *American Journal of Health Behavior, 27*(1), 45–54.

Blumenfeld, P., Fishman, B. J., Krajcik, J., Marx, R. W., & Soloway, E. (2000). Creating usable innovations in systemic reform: Scaling up technology embedded project based science in urban schools. *Educational Psychologist, 35*(3), 149–164.

Boles, K., & Troen, V. (1996). Teacher leaders and power: Achieving school reform from the classroom. In G. Moller & M. Katzenmeyer (Eds.), *Every teacher as a leader: Realizing the potential of teacher leadership* (pp. 41–62). San Francisco, CA: Jossey-Bass.

Bolman, L., & Deal, T. (2008). *Reframing organizations: Artistry, Choice and Leadership.* San Francisco, CA: Jossey-Bass.

Borko, H. (2004). Professional development and teacher learning: Mapping the terrain. *Educational Researcher, 33*(8), 3–15.

Borman, G. D. (2005). National efforts to bring reform to scale in high-poverty schools: Outcomes and implications. *Review of Research in Education, 29*(1), 1–27.

Borman, G. D., Hewes, G. M., Overman, L. T., & Brown, S. (2003). Comprehensive school reform and achievement: A meta-analysis. *Review of Educational Research, 73*(2), 125–230.

Bosma, L. M., Sieving, R. E., Ericson, A., Russ, P., Cavender, L., & Bonine, M. (2010). Elements for successful collaboration between K–8 school, community agency, and university partners: The lead peace partnership. *Journal of School Health, 80*(10), 501–507.

Bossert, S., Dwyer, D., Rowan, B., & Lee, G. (1982). The instructional management role of the principal. *Educational Administration Quarterly, 18*(3), 34–64.

Boyan, N. J. (1988). Describing and explaining administrator behavior. In N. J. Boyan (Ed.), *The handbook of research on educational administration* (pp. 77–98). New York, NY: Longman.

Boyer, E. L. (1983). *High school: A report on secondary education in America.* New York, NY: Harper and Row.

Branch, G., Rivkin, S., & Hanushek, E. (2003). School leaders matter: Measuring the impact of effective principals. *Education Next, 13*(1), 1–8.

Braxton, J. M., Hirschy, A. S., & McClendon, S. A. (2011). *Understanding and reducing college student departure: ASHE-ERIC higher education report* (Vol. 16). San Francisco, CA: Jossey-Bass.

Brewer, D. J. (1993). Principals and student outcomes: Evidence from US high schools. *Economics of Education Review, 12*(4), 281–292.

Brookover, W., Beady, C., Flood, P., Schweitzer, J., & Wisenbaker, J. (1979). *School social systems and student achievement: Schools can make a difference.* New York, NY: Praeger.

Brookover, W. B., & Lezotte, L. W. (1977). *Changes in school characteristics coincident with changes in student achievement.* East Lansing: College of Urban Development, Michigan State University.

Brookover, W. B., Schweitzer, J. J., Schneider, J. M., Beady, C. H., Flood, P. K., & Wisenbaker, J. M. (1978). Elementary school social climate and school achievement. *American Educational Research Journal, 15*(2), 301–318.

Brooks, J. S., Scribner, J. P., & Eferakorho, J. (2004). Teacher leadership in the context of whole school reform. *Journal of School Leadership, 14*(3), 242–265.

Brown, J., & Sheppard, B. (1999). *Leadership, organizational learning, and classroom change.* Paper presented at the annual meeting of the American Educational Research Association, Montreal, Quebec.

Broyles, I. L. (1991, April). *Transforming teacher leadership through action research.* Paper presented at the annual meeting of the New England Educational Research Association, Portsmouth, NH.

Bruggencate, G., Luyten, H., Scheerens, J., & Sleegers, P. (2012). Modeling the influence of school leaders on student achievement: How can school leaders make a difference? *Educational Administration Quarterly, 48*(4), 699–732.

Brunner, C., Fasca, C., Heinze, J., Honey, M., Light, D., Mandinach, E., & Wexler, D. (n.d.). *Linking data and learning: The grow network study.* New York, NY: Education Development Center.

Bryk, A. S., Lee, V., & Holland, P. B. (1993). *Catholic schools and the common good.* Cambridge, MA: Harvard University Press.

Bryk, A. S., & Schneider, B. L. (2002). *Trust in schools: A core resource for school improvement.* New York, NY: Russel Sage Foundation.

Bryk, A. S., Sebring, P. B., Allensworth, E., Luppescu, S., & Easton, J. (2010). *Organizing schools for improvement: Lessons from Chicago.* Chicago, IL: University of Chicago Press.

Bryman, A. (2004). Qualitative research on leadership: A critical but appreciative review. *The Leadership Quarterly, 15*(6), 729–769.

Bryman, A., Stephens, M., & Campo, C. A. (1996). The importance of context: Qualitative research and the study of leadership. *The Leadership Quarterly, 7*(3), 353–370.

Buckner, K. G., & McDowelle, J. O. (2000). Developing teacher leaders: Providing encouragement, opportunities, and support. *NASSP Bulletin, 84*(616), 35–41.

Bulkley, K. E., & Hicks, J. (2005). Managing community: Professional community in charter schools operated by educational management organizations. *Educational Administration Quarterly, 41*(2), 306–348.

Burch, P., & Spillane, J. P. (2003). Elementary school leadership strategies and subject matter: Reforming mathematics and literacy instruction. *The Elementary School Journal*, 519–535.

Burke, C. (1992). Devolution of responsibility to Queensland schools: Clarifying the rhetoric critiquing the reality. *Journal of Educational Administration, 30*(4), 33–52.

Burns, J. M. (1978). *Leadership.* New York, NY: Harper & Row.

Caldwell, B. J. (1998). Strategic leadership, resource management and effective school reform. *Journal of Educational Administration, 36*(5), 445–461.

Callahan, R. E. (1962). *Education and the cult of efficiency.* Chicago, IL: University of Chicago Press.

Camburn, E., Rowan, B., & Taylor, J. E. (2003). Distributed leadership in schools: The case of elementary schools adopting comprehensive school reform models. *Educational Evaluation and Policy Analysis, 25*(4), 347–373.

Carbonaro, W., & Gamoran, A. (2002). The production of achievement inequality in high school English. *American Educational Research Journal, 39*(4), 801–827.

Carnegie Forum on Education and the Economy. (1986). A nation prepared: Teachers for the 21st Century. Washington, DC: Carnegie Forum on Education and the Economy.

Carter, T. P., & Maestas, L. C. (1982). *Bilingual education that works: Effective schools for Spanish speaking children.* Report submitted to the California State Department of Education.

Catalano, R. F., Loeber, R., & McKinney, K. C. (1999). School and community interventions to prevent serious and violent offending. *Juvenile Justice Bulletin, 1*–12.

Center for Teaching Quality. (2007). *Teaching and learning conditions improve high school reform efforts.* Chapel Hill, NC: Author.

Chatterji, M. (2005). Achievement gaps and correlates of early mathematics achievement: Evidence from the ECLS K-First grade sample. *Education Policy Analysis Archives, 13*(46), 1–35.

Chavis, G., Ward, L., Elwell, T., & Barret, C. (1997). *Improving student performance in high poverty schools.* (Report Number: 96–86). Tallahassee, FL: Office of Program Policy Analysis and Government Accountability.

Cheney, D., Blum, C., & Walker, B. (2004). An analysis of leadership teams' perceptions of positive behavior support and the outcomes of typically developing and at-risk students in their schools. *Assessment for Effective Intervention, 30*(1), 7–24.

Childs-Bowen, D., Moller, G., & Scrivner, J. (2000, May). Principals: Leaders of leaders. *NASSP Bulletin, 84*(616), 27–34.

Chin, T., & Phillips, M. (2004). Social reproduction and child-rearing practices: Social class, children's agency, and the summer activity gap. *Sociology of Education, 77*(3), 185–210.

Chrispeels, J. H., & Martin, K. J. (2002). Four school leadership teams define their roles within organizational and political structures to improve student learning. *School Effectiveness and School Improvement, 13*(3), 327–365.

Christensen, J. C. (1987). Roles of teachers and administrators. In P. R. Burden (Ed.), *Establishing career ladders in teaching: A guide for policy makers* (pp. 88–110). Springfield, IL: Charles C Thomas.

Christle, C. A., Jolivette, K., & Nelson, C. M. (2005). Breaking the school to prison pipeline: Identifying school risk and protective factors for youth delinquency. *Exceptionality, 13*(2), 69–88.

Cibulka, J. G. (1999). Ideological lenses for interpreting political and economic changes affecting schooling. In J. Murphy & K. S. Louis (Eds.), *Handbook of research on educational administration* (2nd ed., pp. 163–182). San Francisco, CA: Jossey-Bass.

Cibulka, J. G., & Kritek, W. J. (Eds.). (1996). *Coordination among schools, families, and communities: Prospects for educational reform.* Albany, NY: SUNY Press.

Clark, C., Dyson, A., Millward, A., & Robson, S. (1999). Theories of inclusion, theories of schools: Deconstructing and reconstructing the "inclusive school." *British Educational Research Journal, 25*(2), 157–177.

Clark, D. L., Lotto, L. S., & McCarthy, M. M. (1980). *Why do some urban schools succeed?* Bloomington, IN: Phi Delta Kappa.

Clark, D. L., & Meloy, J. M. (1989). Renouncing bureaucracy: A democratic structure for leadership in schools. In T. J. Sergiovanni & M. A. Moore (Eds.), *Schooling for tomorrow: Directing reform to issues that count* (pp. 272–294). Boston, MA: Allyn & Bacon.

Clift, R., Johnson, M., Holland, P., & Veal, M. L. (1992). Developing the potential for collaborative school leadership. *American Educational Research Journal, 29*(4), 877–908.

Cochran-Smith, M., & Lytle, S. (1999). Relationship of knowledge and practice: Teacher learning in communities. In A. Iran-Nejad & C. D. Pearson (Eds.), *Review of research in education.* (Vol. 24, pp. 249–306). Washington, DC: American Educational Research Association.

Cohen, D. K. (1988). *Teaching practice: Plus ça change.* (Issue paper 88–3). East Lansing, MI: The National Center for Research on Teacher Education.

Cohen, M. D., March, J. G., & Olsen, J. P. (1972, March). A garbage can model of organizational choice. *Administrative Science Quarterly, 17*(1), 1–26.

Coldren, A. F., & Spillane, J. P. (2007). Making connections to teaching practice: The role of boundary practices in instructional leadership. *Educational Policy, 21*(2), 369–396.

Collins & Valentine J. (2010). Testing the impact of student engagement on standardized achievement: An empirical study of the influence of classroom engagement on test scores across school types. Paper presented at the Annual Meeting of the University Council for Education Administration, New Orleans, LA. Retrieved from ERIC database.

Committee for Economic Development. (1994). *Putting learning first: Governing and managing the schools for high achievement.* New York, NY: Author.

Conchas, G. (2001). Structuring failure and success: Understanding the variability in Latino school engagement. *Harvard Educational Review, 71*(3), 475–505.

Conley, D. T. (1997). *Roadmap to restructuring: Charting the course of change in American Education.* Eugene, OR: ERIC Clearinghouse on Educational Management.

Conley, S. (1991). Review of research on teacher participation in school decision making. *Review of Research in Education, 17*, 225–266.

Conley, S. C. (1989). "Who's on first?": School reform, teacher participation, and the decision-making process. *Education and Urban Society, 21*(4), 366–379.

Connolly, M., & James, C. (2006). Collaboration for school improvement: A resource dependency and institutional framework of analysis. *Educational Management, Administration & Leadership, 34*(1), 69–87.

Consortium on Productivity in the Schools. (1995). *Using what we have to get the schools we need.* New York, NY: Columbia University, Teachers College, The Institute on Education and the Economy.

Cooper, J., Ponder, G., Merritt, S., & Matthews, C. (2005). High-performing high schools: Patterns of success. *NASSP Bulletin, 89*(645), 2–23.

Cooper, R. (1996). Detracking reform in an urban California high school: Improving the schooling experiences of African American students. *Journal of Negro Education, 65*(2), 190–208.

Cooper, R. (1999). Urban school reform: Student responses to detracking in a racially mixed high school. *Journal of Education for Students Placed At Risk, 4*(3), 259–275.

Correnti, R., & Rowan, B. (2007). Opening up the black box: Literacy instruction in schools participating in three comprehensive school reform programs. *American Educational Research Journal, 44*(2), 248–291.

Cosner, S. (2009). Building organizational capacity through trust. *Educational Administration Quarterly, 45*(2), 248–291.

Cosner, S. (2011). Supporting the initiation and early development of evidence-based grade-level collaboration in urban elementary schools: Key roles and strategies of principals and literacy coordinators. *Urban Education, 46*(4), 786–827.

Cotton, K. (1996). *School size, school climate, and student performance.* Portland, OR: Northwest Regional Educational Laboratory.

Cotton, K. (2000). *The schooling practices that matter most.* Alexandria, VA: Association for Supervision and Curriculum Development.

Cotton, K. (2003). *Principals and student achievement: What the research says.* Alexandria, VA: Association for Supervision and Curriculum Development.

Coyle, M. (1997). Teacher leadership vs. school management: Flatten the hierarchies. *Teacher Leadership, 70*(5), 236–239.

Craig, C. (2009). Research in the midst of organized school reform: Versions of teacher community in tension. *American Educational Research Journal, 46*(2), 598–619.

Creemers, B. P. M., & Reezigt, G. J. (1996). School level conditions affecting the effectiveness of instruction. *School Effectiveness and School Improvement, 7*(3), 197–228.

Cremin, L. A. (1955). The revolution in American secondary education, 1893–1918. *Teachers College Record, 56*(6), 295–308.

Cremin, L. A. (1961). *The transformation of the school: Progressivism in American education 1876–1957.* New York, NY: Vintage.

Cronin, T. E. (1989). *Direct democracy: The politics of initiative, referendum, and recall.* Cambridge, MA: Harvard University Press.

Croninger, R., & Lee, V. (2001). Social capital and dropping out of high school: Benefits to at-risk students of teachers' support and guidance. *Teachers College Record, 103*(4), 548–581.

Crosnoe, R. (2011). *Fitting in, standing out: Navigating the social challenges of high school to get an education.* Cambridge, MA: Cambridge University Press.

Crow, G. M., Hausman, C. S., & Scribner, J. P. (2002). Reshaping the role of the school principal. In J. Murphy (Ed.), *The educational leadership challenge: Redefining leadership for the 21st century* (pp. 189–210). Chicago, IL: University of Chicago Press.

Crow, G. M., & Pounder, D. G. (2000, April). Interdisciplinary teacher teams: Context, design, and process. *Educational Administration Quarterly, 36*(2), 216–254.

Crowther, E. (1997). The William Walker oration, 1996: Unsung heroes: The leaders in our classrooms. *Journal of Educational Administration, 35*(1), 5–17.

Crowther, F., Kaagan, S. S., Ferguson, M., & Hann, L. (2002). *Developing teacher leaders: How teacher leadership enhances school success.* Thousand Oaks, CA: Corwin.

Crowther, F., & Olsen, P. (1997). Teachers as leaders—an explanatory framework. *International Journal of Educational Management, 11*(1), 6–13.

Crum, K. S., & Sherman, W. H. (2008). Facilitating high achievement: High school principals' reflections on their successful leadership practices. *Journal of Educational Administration, 46*(5), 562–580.

Csikszentmihalyi, M., & Larson, R. (1984). *Being adolescent: Conflict and growth in the teenage years.* New York, NY: Basic Books.

Cuban, L. (1984a). *How teachers taught: Consistency and change in America's classrooms.* New York, NY: Longman.

Cuban, L. (1984b). School reform by remote control: SB 813 in California. *Phi Delta Kappan, 66*(3), 213–215.

Cuban, L. (1988). *The managerial imperative and the practice of leadership in schools.* Albany, NY: State University of New York Press.

Cuijpers, P. (2002). Effective ingredients of school-based drug prevention programs: A systematic review. *Addictive Behaviors, 27*(6), 1009–1023.

Curry, M. (2008). Critical friends groups: The possibilities and limitations embedded in teacher professional communities aimed at instructional improvement and school reform. *The Teachers College Record, 110*(4), 733–774.

Cusick, P. A. (1983). *The egalitarian ideal and the American high school: Studies of three schools.* New York, NY: Longman.

Dahrendorf, R. (1995). A precarious balance: Economic opportunity, civil society and political liberty. *The Responsive Community,* 13–19.

Dannetta, V. (2002). What factors influence a teacher's commitment to student learning? *Leadership and Policy in Schools, 1*(2), 144–171.

Darling-Hammond, L., Ancess, J., & Ort, S. (2002). Reinventing high school: Outcomes of the coalition campus schools project. *American Educational Research Journal, 39*(3), 639–673.

Darling-Hammond, L., Bullmaster, M. L., & Cobb, V. L. (1995). Rethinking teacher leadership through professional development schools. *The Elementary School Journal, 96*(1), 87–107.

Darling-Hammond, L., & McLaughlin, M. W. (1995). Policies that support professional development in an era of reform. *Phi Delta Kappan, 76*(8), 597–604.

Datnow, A., & Castellano, M. E. (2001). Managing and guiding school reform: Leadership in Success for All schools. *Educational Administration Quarterly, 37*(2), 219–249.

Datnow, A., & Castellano, M. (2002). Leadership and success for all. Draft copy of a manuscript (pp. 1–32) that later appeared in J. Murphy & A. Datnow (Eds.), *Leadership for school reform: Lessons from comprehensive school reforms* (pp. 187–208). Thousand Oaks, CA: Corwin.

Datnow, A., Park, V., & Kennedy, B. (2008). *Acting on data: How urban high schools use data to improve instruction.* Los Angeles, CA: Center on Educational Governance.

Dauber, S. L., & Epstein, J. L. (1993). Parents' attitudes and practices of involvement in inner-city elementary and middle schools. *Families and Schools in a Pluralistic Society,* 53–71.

Davison, M. L., Young, S. S., Davenport, E. C., Butterbaugh, D., & Davison, L. J. (2004). When do children fall behind? What can be done? *Phi Delta Kappan, 85*(10), 752–761.

Day, C. (2005). Sustaining success in challenging contexts: Leadership in English schools. *Journal of Educational Administration, 43*(6), 573–583.

Dede, C., & Honana, J. (2005). Scaling up success: A synthesis of themes and insights. In D. C. Dede, J. P. Honana, & L. C. Peters (Eds.), *Scaling up success: Lessons learned from technology-based educational improvement* (pp. 227–239). San Francisco, CA: Jossey-Bass.

Delgado-Gaitan, C. (1992). School matters in the Mexican-American home: Socializing children to education. *American Educational Research Journal, 29*(3), 495–513.

DeLuca, S., & Rosenblatt, P. (2010). Does moving to better neighborhoods lead to better schooling opportunities? Parental school choice in an experimental housing voucher program. *The Teachers College Record, 112*(5), 1443–1491.

Demaray, M. K., & Malecki, C. K. (2002a). The relationship between perceived social support and maladjustment for students at risk. *Psychology in the Schools, 39*(3), 305–316.

Demaray, M. K., & Malecki, C. K. (2002b). Critical levels of perceived social support associated with student adjustment. *School Psychology Quarterly, 17*(3), 213–214.

DeRidder, L. M. (1991). How suspension and expulsion contribute to dropping out. *Education Digest, 56*(6), 44–47.

Desimone, L. (2002). How can comprehensive school reform models be successfully implemented? *Review of Educational Research, 72*(3), 433–479.

Dinham, S. (2005). Principal leadership for outstanding educational outcomes. *Journal of Educational Administration, 43*(4), 338–356.

Dinham, S., Cairney, T., Craigie, D., & Wilson, S. (1995). School climate and leadership: Research into three secondary schools. *Journal of Educational Administration, 33*(4), 36–58.

Dirks, K., & Ferrin, D. (2002). Trust in leadership: Meta-analytic findings and implications for research and practice. *Journal of Applied Psychology, 87*(4), 611–628.

Dishion, T. J., Poulin, F., & Barraston, B. (2001). Peer group dynamics associated with iatrogenic effects in group interventions with high-risk adolescents. *New Directions for Child and Adolescent Development, 2001*(91), 79–92.

Donaldson, G. A. (2001). *Cultivating leadership in schools: Connecting people, purpose, and practice.* New York, NY: Teachers College Press.

Dornbusch, S. M., & Glasgow, K. L. (1996). The structural context of family-school relations. In A. Booth & J. Dunn (Eds.), *Family-school links: How do they affect educational outcomes?* (pp. 35–44). Mahwah, NJ: Erlbaum.

Downey, D. B., von Hippel, P. T., & Broh, B. A. (2004). Are schools the great equalizer? Cognitive inequality during the summer months and the school year. *American Sociological Review, 69*(5), 613–635.

Doyle, M. (2000). *Making meaning of teacher leadership in the implementation of a standards-based mathematics curriculum.* Paper presented at the annual meeting of the American Educational Research Association, New Orleans, LA.

Drago-Severson, E. (2004). *Helping teachers learn: Principal leadership for adult growth and development.* Thousand Oaks, CA: Corwin.

DuBrin, A. (2004). *Leadership: Research findings, practice, and skills.* New York, NY: Houghton Mifflin.

Duffield, B. (2000). Advocating for homeless students. In J. H. Stronge & E. Reed-Victor (Eds.), *Educating homeless students: Promising practices* (pp. 203–224). Larchmont, NY: Eye on Education, Inc.

DuFour, R., & Eaker, R. (1992). *Creating the new American school: A principal's guide to school improvement.* Bloomington, IN: National Education Service.

DuFour, R., & Eaker, R. (1998). *Professional learning communities at work: Best practices for enhancing student achievement.* Bloomington, IN: Association for Supervision and Curriculum Development.

Dumay, X. (2009). Origins and consequences of schools' organizational culture for student achievement. *Educational Administration Quarterly, 45*(4), 523–555.

Dworsky, A. (2008). *Educating homeless children in Chicago: A case study of children in the family regeneration program.* Chapin Hall at the University of Chicago.

Eccles, J. S., & Harold, R. D. (1996). Family involvement in children's and adolescents' schooling. In A. Booth & J. Dunn (Eds.), *Family-school links: How do they affect educational outcomes?* (pp. 3–34). Mahwah, NJ: Erlbaum.

Eckert, P. (1989). *Jocks and burnouts: Social categories and identity in the high school.* New York, NY: Teachers College Press.

Eddowes, E. A., & Butcher, T. (2000). Meeting the developmental and educational needs of homeless infants and young children. In J. H. Stronge & E. Reed-Victor (Eds.), *Educating homeless students: Promising practices* (pp. 21–43). Larchmont, NY: Eye on Education, Inc.

Eddowes, E., & Hranitz, J. (1989). Educating children of the homeless. *Childhood Education, 65*(4), 197–200.

Edmonds, R. (1979). Effective schools for the urban poor. *Educational Leadership, 37*(1), 15–24.

Edmonds, R., & Frederiksen, J. R. (1978). *Search for effective schools: The identification and analysis of city schools that are instructionally effective for poor children.* Cambridge, MA: Center for Urban Studies, Harvard University.

Eggert, L. L., Thompson, E. A., Herting, J. R., & Nicholas, L. J. (1995). Reducing suicide potential among high-risk youth: Tests of a school-based prevention program. *Suicide and Life-Threatening Behavior, 25*(2), 276–296.

Eilers, A. M., & Camacho, A. (2007). School culture change in the making: Leadership factors that matter. *Urban Education, 42*(6), 616–637.

Elbaum, B., Vaughn, S., Tejero Hughes, M., & Watson Moody, S. (2000). How effective are one-to-one tutoring programs in reading for elementary students at risk for reading failure? A meta-analysis of the intervention research. *Journal of Educational Psychology, 92*(4), 605–619.

Elmore, R. F. (1987). Reform and the culture of authority in schools. *Educational Administration Quarterly, 23*(4), 60–78.

Elmore, R. F. (1993). School decentralization: Who gains? Who loses? In J. Hannaway & M. Carnoy (Eds.), *Decentralization and school improvement* (pp. 33–54). San Francisco, CA: Jossey-Bass.

Elmore, R. F. (1995). Structural reform and educational practice. *Educational Researcher, 24*(9), 23–26.

Elmore, R. F., Peterson, P. L., & McCarthy, S. J. (1996). *Restructuring in the classroom: Teaching, learning, and school organization.* San Francisco, CA: Jossey-Bass.

Elshtain, J. B. (1995). *Democracy on trial.* New York, NY: Basic Books.

Ensminger, M., & Slusarcick, A. (1992). Paths to high school graduation or dropout: A longitudinal study of a first-grade cohort. *Sociology of Education, 65*(2), 95–113.

Entwisle, D. R., Alexander, K. L., & Olson, L. S. (2000). Summer learning and home environment. In R. D. Kahlenberg (Ed.), *A notion at risk: Preserving public education as an engine for social mobility* (pp. 9–30). New York: The Century Foundation Press.

Epstein, J. (1996). Perspectives and previews on research and policy for school, family, and community partnerships. In A. Booth & J. Dunn (Eds.), *Family-school links: How do they affect educational outcomes?* (pp. 209–246). Mahwah, NJ: Erlbaum.

Epstein, J., & McPartland, J. (1976). The concept and measurement of the quality of school life. *American Educational Research Journal, 13*(1), 15–30.

Ermeling, B. A. (2010). Tracing the effects of teacher inquiry on classroom practice. *Teaching and Teacher Education, 26*(3), 377–388.

Etheridge, C. P., Valesky, T. C., Horgan, D. D., Nunnery, J., & Smith, D. (1992). *School-based decision making: An investigation into effective and ineffective decision making processes and the impact on school climate variables.* Paper presented at the annual meeting of the American Educational Research Association, San Francisco, CA.

Farrell, E. (1990). *Hanging in and dropping out: Voices of at-risk high school students.* New York, NY: Teachers College Press.

Fay, C. (1992a, April). *The case for teacher leadership: Toward definition and development.* Paper presented at the annual meeting of the American Educational Research Association, San Francisco, CA.

Fay, C. (1992b). Empowerment through leadership: In the teachers' voice. In C. Livingston (Ed.), *Teachers as leaders: Evolving roles* (pp. 57–90). Washington, DC: National Education Association.

Feiman-Nemser, S., & Floden, R. F. (1986). The cultures of teaching. In C. W. Wittrock (Ed.), *Handbook of research on teaching* (3rd ed., pp. 505–526). New York, NY: Macmillan.

Feldman, A., & Matjasko, J. (2005). The role of school-based extracurricular activities in adolescent development: A comprehensive review and future directions. *Review of Educational Research, 75*(2), 159–210.

Felner, R., Seitsinger, A., Brand, S., Burns, A., & Bolton, N. (2007). Creating small learning communities: Lessons from the project on high-performing learning communities about "what works" in creating productive, developmentally enhancing, learning contexts. *Educational Psychologist, 42*(4), 209–221.

Fessler, R., & Ungaretti, A. (1994). Expanding opportunities for teacher leadership. In D. R. Walling (Ed.), *Teachers as leaders: Perspectives on the professional development of teachers* (pp. 211–222). Bloomington, IN: Phi Delta Kappa.

Finn, J. D., & Rock, D. (1997). Academic success among students at risk for school failure. *Journal of Applied Psychology, 82*(2), 221–234.

Finnigan, K. S., & Gross, B. (2007). Do accountability policy sanctions influence teacher motivation? Lessons from Chicago's low-performing schools. *American Educational Research Journal, 44*(3), 594–630.

Firestone, W., & Herriott, R. (1982). Prescriptions for effective elementary schools don't fit secondary schools. *Educational Leadership, 40*(3), 51–53.

Firestone, W. A., & Martinez, M. C. (2007). Districts, teacher leaders, and distributed leadership: Changing instructional practice. *Leadership and Policy in Schools, 6*(1), 3–35.

Firestone, W. A., & Martinez, M. C. (2009). Districts, teacher leaders, and distributed leadership: Changing instructional practice. In K. Leithwood, B. Mascall, &

T. Strauss (Eds.), *Distributed leadership according to the evidence* (pp. 61–86). London, UK: Routledge.

Forster, E. M. (1997, Fall). Teacher leadership: Professional right and responsibility. *Action in Teacher Education, 19*(3), 82–94.

Foster, R., & St. Hilaire, B. (2003). Leadership for school improvement: Principals' and teachers perspectives. *International Electronic Journal for Leadership in Learning, 7*(3), 1–18.

Franke, M. L., Carpenter, T. P., Levi, L., & Fennema, E. (2001). Capturing teachers' generative change: A follow-up study of professional development in mathematics. *American Educational Research Journal, 38*(3), 653–689.

Franklin, C., & Streeter, C. (1995). School reform: Linking public schools with human services. *Social Work, 40*(6), 773–782.

Fredricks, J. A., Blumenfeld, P. C., & Paris, A. H. (2004). School engagement: Potential of the concept, state of the evidence. *Review of Educational Research, 74*(1), 59–109.

Freiberg, H. J., Huzinec, C. A., & Templeton, S. M. (2009). Classroom management—a pathway to student achievement: A study of fourteen inner-city elementary schools. *The Elementary School Journal, 110*(1), 63–80.

Friedkin, N. E., & Slater, M. R. (1994). School leadership and performance: A social network approach. *Sociology of Education, 67*(2), 139–157.

Frost, D., & Durant, J. (2003, May). Teacher leadership: Rationale, strategy, and impact. *School Leadership & Management, 23*(2), 173–186.

Fullan, M. (1982). *The meaning of educational change.* New York, NY: Teachers College Press.

Fullan, M. (1993). *Change forces: Probing the depths of educational reform.* London, UK: Falmer.

Fullan, M. (1994). Teacher leadership: A failure to conceptualize. In D. R. Walling (Ed.), *Teachers as leaders: Perspectives on the professional development of teachers* (pp. 241–254). Bloomington, IN: Phi Delta Kappa.

Fullan, M. (2002). Leadership and sustainability. *Principal Leadership, 3*(4), 13–17.

Fullan, M., & Ballew, A. C. (2002). *Leading in a culture of change.* San Francisco, CA: Jossey-Bass.

Gall, M., Fielding, G., Schalock, D., Charters, W. W., & Wilczynski, J. M. (1985). *Involving the principal in teachers' staff development: Effects on the quality of mathematics instruction in elementary schools.* Eugene: Center for Educational Policy and Management, University of Oregon.

Gallagher, M., Zhang, S., & Comey, J. (2013). Moving to educational opportunity: A housing demonstration to improve school outcomes. Retrieved from http://www.urban.org/publications/412972.html

Galletta, A., & Ayala, J. (2008). Erasure and survival: Creating a future and managing a past in a restructuring high school. *Teachers College Record, 110*(9), 1959–1985.

Gamoran, A. (1996). Effects of schooling on children and families. In A. Booth & J. Dunn (Eds.), *Family-school links: How do they affect educational outcomes?* (pp. 107–114). Mahwah, NJ: Erlbaum.

Gandara, P., Maxwell-Jolly, J., & Driscoll, A. (2005). Listening to teachers of English language learners: A survey of California teachers' challenges, experiences, and professional development needs. UC Berkeley: University of California Linguistic Minority Research Institute. Retrieved from http://escholarship.org/uc/item/6430628z

Gardner, P. W., Ritblatt, S. N., & Beatty, J. R. (1999). Academic achievement and parental school involvement as a function of high school size. *The High School Journal, 83*(2), 21–27.

Garmezy, N. (1991). Resiliency and vulnerability to adverse developmental outcomes associated with poverty. *American Behavioral Scientist, 34*(4), 416–430.

Geijsel, F., Sleegers, P., Leithwood, K., & Jantzi, D. (2003). Transformational leadership effects on teachers' commitment and effort toward school reform. *Journal of Educational Administration, 41*(3), 228–256.

Goddard, H., & Goff, B. (1999). Terminal core values associated with adolescent problem behaviors. *Adolescence, 34*(133), 47–54.

Goddard, R. D. (2003). Relational networks, social trust, and norms: A social capital perspective on students' chances of academic success. *Educational Evaluation and Policy Analysis, 25*(1), 59–74.

Goddard, R. D., Hoy, W. K., & Hoy, A. W. (2000). Collective teacher efficacy: Its meaning, measure, and impact on student achievement. *American Educational Research Journal, 37*(2), 479–507.

Goddard, R. D., Salloum, S. J., & Berebitsky, D. (2009). Trust as a mediator of the relationships between poverty, racial composition, and academic achievement: Evidence from Michigan's public elementary schools. *Educational Administration Quarterly, 45*(2), 292–311.

Gold, E., Cucchiara, M., Simon, E., & Riffer, M. (2005). *Time to engage? Civic participation in Philadelphia's school reform.* Philadelphia, PA: Research for Action.

Goldenberg, C. N. (1996). Schools, children at risk, and successful interventions. In A. Booth & J. Dunn (Eds.), *Family-school links: How do they affect educational outcomes?* (pp. 115–124). Mahwah, NJ: Erlbaum.

Goldenberg, C. N. (2004). *Successful school change: Creating settings to improve teaching and learning.* New York, NY: Teachers College Press.

Goldring, E. B., & Pasternack, R. (1994). Principals' coordinating strategies and school effectiveness. *School Effectiveness and School Improvement, 5*(3), 239–253.

Goldring, E., & Sims, P. (2005). Modeling creative and courageous school leadership through district-community-university partnerships. *Educational Policy, 19*(1), 223–249.

Goldstein, J. (2004). Making sense of distributed leadership: The case of peer assistance and review. *Educational Evaluation and Policy Analysis, 26*(2), 173–197.

Gonzalez, R., & Padilla, A. (1997). The academic resilience of Mexican American high school students. *Hispanic Journal of Behavioral Sciences, 19*(3), 301–317.

Goodenow, C. (1993). Classroom belonging among early adolescent students: Relationships to motivation and achievement. *Journal of Early Adolescence, 13*(1), 21–43.

Goodlad, J. I. (1984). *A place called school: Prospects for the future.* New York, NY: McGraw-Hill.

Gray, J., Hopkins, D., Reynolds, D., Wilcox, B., Farrell, S., & Jesson, D. (1999). *Improving schools: Performance and potential.* Philadelphia, PA: Open University Press.

Greene, J. C., & Lee, J. H. (2006). Quieting educational reform . . . with educational reform. *American Journal of Evaluation, 27*(3), 337–352.

Greenwood, G. E., & Hickman, C. W. (1991). Research and practice in parent involvement: Implications for teacher education. *The Elementary School Journal,* 279–288.

Griffin, G. A. (1995). Influences of shared decision making on school and classroom activity: Conversations with five teachers. *The Elementary School Journal, 96*(1), 29–45.

Griffith, J. (2001). Principal leadership of parent involvement. *Journal of Educational Administration, 39*(2), 162–186.

Grissom, J., & Keiser, L. (2011). A supervisor like me: Race, representation, and the satisfaction and turnover decisions of public sector employees. *Journal of Policy Analysis and Management, 30*(3), 557–580.

Grissom, J., & Loeb, S. (2011). Triangulating principal effectiveness: How perspectives of parents, teachers, and assistant principals identify the central importance of managerial skills. *American Educational Research Journal, 48*(5), 1091–1123.

Gronn, P. (2009). Hybrid leadership. In K. Leithwood, B. Mascall, & T. Strauss (Eds.), *Distributed leadership according to the evidence* (pp. 17–39). London, UK: Routledge.

Grossman, P., Wineburg, S., & Woolworth, S. (2001). Toward a theory of teacher community. *Teachers College Record, 103*(6), 942–1012.

Grubb, W. N., & Flessa, J. J. (2006, Oct). "A job too big for one": Multiple principals and other nontraditional approaches to school leadership. *Educational Administration Quarterly, 42*(4), 518–550.

Guest, A., & Schneider, B. (2003). Adolescents' extracurricular participation in context: The mediating effects of schools. *Sociology of Education, 76*(2), 89–109.

Gurr, D., Drysdale, L., & Mulford, N. (2005). Successful principal leadership: Australian case studies. *Journal of Educational Administration, 43*(6), 539–551.

Gurr, D., Drysdale, L., & Mulford, B. (2006). Models of successful principal leadership. *School Leadership and Management, 26*(4), 371–395.

Guskey, T. R. (2003). Analyzing lists of the characteristics of effective professional development to promote visionary leadership. *NASSP Bulletin, 87*(637), 4–20.

Hallinan, M. T. (2001). Sociological perspectives on black-white inequalities in American schooling. *Sociology of Education, 74,* 50–70.

Hallinan, M. T., & Kubitschek, W. N. (1999). Curriculum differentiation and high school achievement. *Social Psychology of Education, 3*(1), 41–62.

Hallinger, P. (2013a). *Reviewing reviews of research in educational leadership: A proposed conceptual framework and empirical assessment.* Unpublished manuscript.

Hallinger, P. (2013b). *A proposed conceptual framework for conducting systematic reviews of research in educational leadership.* Unpublished manuscript.

Hallinger, P., Bickman, L., & Davis, K. (1996). School context, principal leadership, and student reading achievement. *The Elementary School Journal, 96*(5), 527–549.

Hallinger, P., & Heck, R. (1996). Reassessing the principal's role in school effectiveness: A review of empirical research, 1980–1995. *Educational Administration Quarterly, 32*(1), 5–44.

Hallinger, P., & Heck, R. (1998). Exploring the principal's contribution to school effectiveness: 1980–1995, *School Effectiveness and School Improvement, 9*(2), 157–191.

Hallinger, P., Heck, R. H., & Murphy, J. (2014). Teacher evaluation and school improvement: An analysis of the evidence. *Educational Assessment, Evaluation and Accountability,* 1–24.

Hallinger, P., & Murphy, J. (1985). Assessing the instructional management behavior of principals. *Elementary School Journal, 86*(2), 217–247.

Hallinger, P., & Murphy, J. (1986). The social context of effective schools. *American Journal of Education, 94*(3), 328–355.

Hallinger, P., & Murphy, J. (1987a). Assessing and developing principal instructional leadership. *Educational Leadership, 45*(1), 54–61.

Hallinger, P., & Murphy, J. (1987b). Instructional leadership in the school context. In William Greenfield (Ed.), *Instructional leadership: Problems, issues, and controversies.* Boston, MA: Allyn and Bacon.

Hallinger, P., & Murphy, J. (2013). Running on empty: Finding the time and capacity to lead learning. *NASSP Bulletin, 97*(1), 5–21.

Halverson, R., Grigg, J., Prichett, R., & Thomas, C. (2007). The new instructional leadership: Creating data-driven instructional systems in school. *Journal of School Leadership, 17*(2), 159–194.

Hamilton, L. S., McCaffrey, D. F., Stecher, B. M., Klein, S. P., Abby, R., & Bugliari, D. (2003). Studying large-scale reforms of instructional practice: An example from mathematics and science. *Educational Evaluation and Policy Analysis, 25*(1), 1–29.

Hamilton, L. S., Stecher, B. M., Russell, J. L., Marsh, J. A., & Miles, J. (2008). Accountability and teaching practices: School-level actions and teacher responses. In B. Fuller, M. K. Henne, & E. Hannum (Eds.), *Strong states, weak schools: The benefits and dilemmas of centralized accountability (Research in the Sociology of Education, 16,* pp. 31–66). St. Louis, MO: Emerald Group Publishing.

Harris, A. (2003). Teacher leadership as distributed leadership: Heresy, fantasy or possibility? *School Leadership & Management, 23*(3), 313–324.

Harris, A. (2004). Distributed leadership and school improvement. *Educational Management Administration & Leadership, 32*(1), 11–24.

Harris, A. (2009). Distributed leadership and knowledge creation. In K. Leithwood, B. Mascall, & T. Strauss (Eds.), *Distributed leadership according to the evidence.* London, UK: Routledge.

Harrison, J. W., & Lembeck, E. (1996). Emergent teacher leaders. In G. Moller & M. Katzenmeyer (Eds.), *Every teacher as a leader: Realizing the potential of teacher leadership* (pp. 101–116). San Francisco, CA: Jossey-Bass.

Hart, A. W. (1990). Impacts of the school social unit on teacher authority during work redesign. *American Educational Research Journal, 27*(3), 503–532.

Hart, A. W. (1994, November). Creating teacher leadership roles. *Educational Administration Quarterly, 30*(4), 472–497.

Hart, A. W. (1995, September). Reconceiving school leadership roles: Emergent view. *The Elementary School Journal, 96*(1), 9–28.

Hart, R., & Baptist, B. (1996). Developing teacher leaders: A state initiative. In G. Moller & M. Katzenmeyer (Eds.), *Every teacher as a leader: Realizing the potential of teacher leadership* (pp. 85–100). San Francisco, CA: Jossey-Bass.

Hatfield, R. C., Blackman, C. A., & Claypool, C. (1986). Exploring leadership roles performed by teaching in K–12 schools. Paper presented at the annual conference of the American Association of Colleges of Teacher Education, Chicago, IL.

Hattie, J. (2009). *Visible learning: A synthesis of over 800 meta-analyses relating to achievement.* New York, NY: Routledge.

Hawley, W. D. (1995, Summer). The false premises and false promises of the movement to private public education. *Teachers College Record, 96*(4), 735–742.

Hayes, D., Christie, P., Mills, M., & Lingard, B. (2004). Productive leaders and productive leadership: Schools as learning organisations. *Journal of Educational Administration, 42*(5), 520–538.

Haynes, N. M., & Ben-Avie, M. (1996). Parents as full partners in education. In A. Booth & J. Dunn (Eds.), *Family-school links: How do they affect educational outcomes?* (pp. 45–55). Mahwah, NJ: Erlbaum.

Heck, R. H. (2000). Examining the impact of school quality on school outcomes and improvement: A value-added approach. *Educational Administration Quarterly, 36*(4), 513–552.

Heck, R. H., & Hallinger, P. (2009). Assessing the contribution of distributed leadership to school improvement and growth in math achievement. *American Educational Research Journal, 46*(3), 659–689.

Heck, R. H., & Hallinger, P. (2010). Leadership: School improvement. In P. L. Peterson, E. L. Baker, & B. McGaw (Eds.), *International Encyclopedia of Education* (3rd ed., pp. 135–142). Oxford, UK: Elsevier.

Heck, R. H., & Hallinger, P. (n.d.). *Assessing the contribution of principal and collaborative leadership.* Unpublished manuscript.

Heck, R. H., & Marcoulides, G. A. (1996). School culture and performance: Testing the invariance of an organizational model. *School Effectiveness and School Improvement, 7*(1), 76–95.

Heckman, J. J. (1995). Review: Lessons from the Bell curve. *The Journal of Political Economy, 103*(5), 1091–1120.

Heller, D. A. (1994). The problem with power. In D. R. Walling (Ed.), *Teachers as leaders: Perspectives on the professional development of teachers* (pp. 287–297). Bloomington, IN: Phi Delta Kappa.

Heller, M. F., & Firestone, W. A. (1995). Who's in charge here? Sources of leadership for change in eight schools. *The Elementary School Journal, 96*(1), 65–86.

Helm, V. (1992). The legal context: From access to success in education for homeless children and youth. In J. H. Stronge (Ed.), *Educating homeless children and adolescents: Evaluating policy and practice* (pp. 26–41). Newbury Park, CA: Sage.

Henry, G., Fortner, C., & Thompson, C. (2012). *Targeted funding for disadvantaged school districts can boost student achievement growth: A regression discontinuity design study with slopes of student growth trajectories as outcomes.* Unpublished Manuscript.

Herbst, J. (1996). *The once and future school: Three hundred and fifty years of American secondary education.* New York, NY: Routledge.

Hill, H. C., Rowan, B., & Ball, D. L. (2005). Effects of teachers' mathematical knowledge for teaching on student achievement. *American Educational Research Journal, 42*(2), 371–406.

Hill, P., Pierce, L. C., & Guthrie, J. W. (1997). *Private provision in the public interest.* Chicago, IL: University of Chicago.

Hill, P. T., Foster, G. E., & Gendler, T. (1990). *High schools with character.* Santa Monica, CA: RAND.

Himmelstein, J. L. (1983). The new right. In R. C. Liebman and R. Wuthnow (Eds.), *The new Christian right: Mobilization and legitimization* (pp. 13–30). New York, NY: Aldine.

The Holmes Group. (1986). *Tomorrow's teachers: A report of the Holmes Group.* East Lansing, MI: Author.

Hoover-Dempsey, K. V., Walker, J. M., Sandler, H. M., Whetsel, D., Green, C. L., Wilkins, A. S., & Closson, K. (2005). Why do parents become involved? Research findings and implications. *The Elementary School Journal, 106*(2), 105–130.

Hord, S. M. (1997). *Professional learning communities: Communities of continuous inquiry and improvement.* Austin, TX: Southwest Educational Development Laboratory.

Horn, I. S. (2005). Learning on the job: A situated account of teacher learning in high school mathematics departments. *Cognition and Instruction, 23*(2), 207–236.

Horn, I. S. (2010). Teaching replays, teaching rehearsals, and re-visions of practice: Learning from colleagues in a mathematics teacher community. *Teachers College Record, 112*(1), 225–259.

Howell, J., & Costley, D. (2006). *Understanding behaviors for effective leadership.* Upper Saddle River, NJ: Prentice Hall.

Hoy, W., Hannum, J., & Tschannen-Moran, M. (1998). Organizational climate and student achievement: A parsimonious and longitudinal view. *Journal of School Leadership, 8*(4), 336–359.

Huberman, M., Parrish, T., Hannan, S., Arellanes, M., & Shambaugh, L. (2011). *Turnaround schools in California: Who are they and what strategies do they use?* San Francisco, CA: WestEd.

Hughes, S. (2003). An early gap in black-white mathematics achievement: Holding school and home accountable in an affluent city school district. *The Urban Review, 35*(4), 297–322.

Hulpia, H., Devos, G., & Rosseel, Y. (2009). Development and validation of scores on the distributed leadership inventory. *Educational and Psychological Measurement, 69*(6), 1013–1034.

Iatarola, P., Schwartz, A., Stiefel, L., & Chellman, C. (2008). Small schools, large districts: Small-school reform and New York City's students. *Teachers College Record, 110*(9), 1837–1878.

Ikemoto, G., Taliaferro, L., & Adams, E. (2012). *Playmakers: How great principals build and lead great teams of teachers.* New York, NY: New Leaders.

Ingram, D., Seashore Louis, K., & Schroeder, R. (2004). Accountability policies and teacher decision making: Barriers to the use of data to improve practice. *Teachers College Record, 106*(6), 1258–1287.

Jackson, D. S. (2000). The school improvement journey: Perspectives on leadership. *School Leadership and Management, 20*(1), 61–78.

Jackson, Y., & Warren, J. S. (2000). Appraisal, social support, and life events: Predicting outcome behavior in school-age children. *Child Development, 71*(5), 1441–1457.

James, W., Smith, A., & Mann, R. (1991). Educating homeless children. *Childhood Education, 67*(5), 305-308.

Jimerson, S. R., Anderson, G. E., & Whipple, A. D. (2002). Winning the battle and losing the war: Examining the relation between grade retention and dropping out of high school. *Psychology in the Schools, 39*(4), 441–457.

Johnson, B. L. (1998). Organizing for collaboration: A reconsideration of some basic organizing principles. In D. G. Pounder (Ed.), *Restructuring schools for collaboration: Promises and pitfalls* (pp. 9–25). Albany: State University of New York Press.

Johnson, J., & Hynes, M. C. (1997, Fall). Teaching/learning/leading: Synonyms for change. *Action in Teacher Research, 19*(3), 107–119.

Johnson Jr., J. F., & Asera, R. (1999). *Hope for urban education: A study of nine high-performing, high-poverty, urban elementary schools.* Washington, DC: U.S. Department of Education, Planning and Evaluation Services.

Johnson, S. M. (1989). Schoolwork and its reform. In J. Hannaway & R. Crowson (Eds.), The policy of reforming school administration. *1989 Yearbook of the Politics of Education Association* (pp. 95–112). New York, NY: Falmer Press.

Jordan, W., & Cooper, R. (2003). High school reform and black male students: Limits and possibilities of policy and practice. *Urban Education, 38*(2), 196–216.

Joselowsky, F. (2007). Youth engagement, high school reform, and improved learning outcomes: Building systemic approaches for youth engagement. *NASSP Bulletin, 91*(3), 253–276.

Judge, T. A., Bono, J. E., Ilies, R., & Gerhardt, M. W. (2002). Personality and leadership: A qualitative and quantitative review. *Journal of Applied Psychology, 87*(4), 765–780.

Julianelle, P. F. (2007). *The educational successes of homeless youth in California: Challenges and solutions.* California Research Bureau. Retrieved from http://www.library.ca.gov/crb/CRBSearch.aspx

Katz, M. B. (1971). From volunteerism to bureaucracy in American education. *Sociology of Education, 44*(3), 297–332.

Katzenmeyer, M., & Moller, G. (2001). *Awakening the sleeping giant: Helping teachers develop as leaders.* Newbury Park, CA: Corwin.

Keedy, J. L. (1999). Examining teacher instructional leadership within the small group dynamics of collegial groups. *Teaching and Teacher Education, 15*(7), 785–799.

Kelley, J. A. (1994). The National Board for Professional Teaching Standards: Toward a community of teacher leaders. In D. R. Walling (Ed.), *Teachers as leaders: Evolving roles* (pp. 91–113). Washington, DC: National Education Association.

Kennedy, M. M. (2010). Attribution error and the quest for teacher quality. *Educational Researcher, 39*(8), 591–598.

Kerr, K., Marsh, J., Ikemoto, G., Darilek, H., & Barney, H. (2006). Strategies to promote data use for instructional improvement actions, outcomes, and lessons from three urban districts. *American Journal of Education, 112*(4), 496–520.

Kilcher, A. (1992). Becoming a change facilitator: The first-year experience of five teacher leaders. In C. Livingston (Ed.) *Teachers as leaders: Evolving roles* (pp. 91–113). Washington, DC: National Educational Association.

Killion, J. P. (1996). Moving beyond the school: Teacher leaders in the district office. In G. Moller & M. Katzenmeyer (Eds.), *Every teacher as a leader: Realizing the potential of teacher leadership* (pp. 63–84). San Francisco, CA: Jossey-Bass.

King, M. (2001). Professional development to promote schoolwide inquiry. *Teaching and Teacher Education, 18*(3), 243–257.

Klecker, B. J., & Loadman, W. E. (1998, Spring). Defining and measuring the dimensions of teacher empowerment in reconstructing public schools. *Education, 118*(3), 358–371.

Kliebard, H. M. (1995). *The struggle for the American curriculum 1893–1958* (2nd ed.). New York, NY: Routledge.

Kober, N. (2001, April). *It takes more than testing: Closing the achievement gap.* A report of the Center on Education Policy. Washington, DC: Center on Education Policy.

Kochanek, J. R. (2005). *Building trust for better schools: Research-based practices.* Thousand Oaks, CA: Corwin.

Kohl, G. O., Lengua, L. J., & McMahon, R. J. (2000). Parent involvement in school conceptualizing multiple dimensions and their relations with family and demographic risk factors. *Journal of School Psychology, 38*(6), 501–523.

Koos, L. (1927). *The American secondary school.* Boston, MA: Ginn.

Kowalski, T. J. (1995). Preparing teachers to be leaders: Barriers in the workplace. In M. J. O'Hair & S. J. Odell (Eds.), *Educating teachers for leadership and change* (pp. 245–256). Thousand Oaks, CA: Corwin.

Krug, E. A. (1964). *The shaping of the American high school.* New York, NY: Harper & Row.

Krug, E. A. (1972). *The shaping of the American high school, 1920–1941.* Madison, WI: University of Wisconsin Press.

Kruse, S., Seashore Louis, K., & Bryk, A. (1995). An emerging framework for analyzing school-based professional community. In K. Seashore Louis & S. Kruse (Eds.), *Professionalism and community: Perspectives on reforming urban schools* (pp. 23–44). Thousand Oaks, CA: Corwin.

Lachat, M. A., & Smith, S. (2005). Practices that support data use in urban high schools. *Journal of Education for Students Placed at Risk, 10*(3), 333–349.

Laffey, J. (1982). The assessment of involvement with school work among urban high school students. *Journal of Educational Psychology, 74*(1), 62–71.

Lareau, A. (1996). Assessing parent involvement in education. In A. Booth & J. Dunn (Eds.), *Family-school links: How do they affect educational outcomes?* (pp. 57–63). Mahwah, NJ: Erlbaum.

Lasley, T. J., & Wayson, W. W. (1982). Characteristics of schools with good discipline. *Educational Leadership, 40*(3), 28–31.

Latimer, J. F. (1958). *What's happened to our high schools?* Washington, DC: Public Affairs Press.

LeBlanc, P. R., & Shelton, M. M. (1997, Fall). Teacher leadership: The needs of teachers. *Action in Teacher Education, 19*(3), 32–48.

Lee, V. E., & Burkam, D. T. (2002). *Inequality at the starting gate. Social background differences in achievement as children begin school.* Washington, DC: Economic Policy Institute.

Lee, V. E., & Burkam, D. T. (2003). Dropping out of high school: The role of school organization and structure. *American Educational Research Journal, 40*(2), 353–393.

Leithwood, K. (2005). Understanding successful principal leadership: Progress on a broken front. *Journal of Educational Administration, 43*(6), 619–629.

Leithwood, K. (2008). *School leadership, evidence-based decision making and large-scale student assessment.* Paper presented at International Perspectives on Student Assessment Lecture Series. University of Calgary.

Leithwood, K., Day, C., Sammons, P., Harris, A., & Hopkins, D. (2006). *Successful school leadership. What it is and how it influences pupil learning.* London, UK: Department of Education and Skills.

Leithwood, K., & Duke, D. L. (1999). A century's quest to understand school leadership in J. Murphy & Seashore Louis, K. (Eds.), *Handbook of research on educational administration* (2nd ed., pp. 45–72). San Francisco, CA: Jossey-Bass.

Leithwood, K., & Jantzi, D. (2000a). Principal and teacher leadership effects: A replication. *School Leadership & Management, 20*(4), 415–434.

Leithwood, K., & Jantzi, D. (2000b). The effects of transformational leadership on organizational conditions and student engagement with school. *Journal of Educational Administration, 38*(2), 112–129.

Leithwood, K., & Jantzi, D. (2005). A review of transformational school leadership research 1996–2005. *Leadership and Policy in Schools, 4*(3), 177–199.

Leithwood, K., & Jantzi, D. (2006). Transformational school leadership for large-scale reform: Effects on students, teachers, and their classroom practices. *School Effectiveness and School Improvement, 17*(2), 201–227.

Leithwood, K., Jantzi, D., & McElheron-Hopkins, C. (2006). The development and testing of a school improvement model. *School Effectiveness and School Improvement, 17*(4), 441–464.

Leithwood, K., Jantzi, D., & Steinbach, R. (1999). *Changing leadership for changing times.* Philadelphia, PA: Open University Press.

Leithwood, K., Louis, K. S., Anderson, S., & Wahlstrom, K. (2004). *How leadership influences student learning.* New York, NY: The Wallace Foundation.

Leithwood, K., & Mascall, B. (2008). Collective leadership effects on student achievement. *Educational Administration Quarterly, 44*(4), 529–561.

Leithwood, K., Mascall, B., Strauss, T., Sacks, R., & Yashkina, A. (2009). Distributing leadership to make schools smarter. In K. Leithwood, & T. Strauss (Eds.) *Distributed leadership according to the evidence.* London: Routledge.

Leithwood, K., & Montgomery, D. J. (1982). The role of the elementary school principal in program improvement. *Review of Educational Research, 52*(3), 309–339.

Leithwood, K., Patten, S., & Jantzi, D. (2010). Testing a conception of how school leadership influences student learning. *Educational Administration Quarterly, 46*(5), 671–706.

Leithwood, K., Steinbach, R., & Jantzi, D. (2002). School leadership and teachers' motivation to implement accountability policies. *Educational Administration Quarterly, 38*(1), 94–119.

Leithwood, K., Steinbach, R., & Ryan, S. (1997). Leadership and team learning in secondary schools. *School Leadership & Management, 17*(3), 303–325.

Leitner, D. (1994). Do principals affect student outcomes: An organizational perspective. *School Effectiveness and School Improvement, 5*(3), 219–238.

Levin, H., Belfield, C., Muenning, P., & Rouse, C. (2007). *The costs and benefits of excellent education for all of America's children.* New York, NY: Teachers College, Columbia University.

Levin, J. A., & Datnow, A. (2012). The principal role in data-driven decision making: Using case-study data to develop multi-mediator models of educational reform. *School Effectiveness and School Improvement, 23*(2), 179–201.

Levine, T. H., & Marcus, A. S. (2007). Closing the achievement gap through teacher collaboration: Facilitating multiple trajectories of teacher learning. *Journal of Advanced Academics, 19*(1), 116–138.

Levine, T. H., & Marcus, A. S. (2010). How the structure and focus of teachers' collaborative activities facilitate and constrain teacher learning. *Teaching and Teacher Education, 26*(3), 389–398.

Lezotte, L., Hathaway, D. V., Miller, S. K., Passalacque, J., & Brookover, W. B. (1980). *School learning climate and student achievement: A social system approach to increased student learning.* Tallahassee: The Site Specific Technical Assistance Center, Florida State University Foundation.

Lieberman, A. (1987). Teacher leadership. *The Teachers College Record, 88*(3), 400–405.

Lieberman, A. (1992). Teacher leadership: What are we learning? In C. Livingston (Ed.), *Teachers as leaders: Evolving roles* (pp. 159–165). Washington, DC: National Education Association.

Lieberman, A., & Miller, L. (1999). *Teachers—transforming their world and their work.* New York, NY: Teachers College Press.

Lieberman, A., Saxl, E. R., & Miles, M. B. (1988). Teacher leadership: Ideology and practice. In A. Lieberman (Ed.), *Building a professional culture in schools* (pp. 148–166). New York, NY: Teachers College Press.

Little, J. W. (1982). Norms of collegiality and experimentation: Workplace conditions of school success. *American Educational Research Journal, 19*(3), 325–340.

Little, J. W. (1985). Teachers as teacher advisors: The delicacy of collegial leadership. *Educational Leadership, 43*(3), 34–36.

Little, J. W. (1987). Teachers as colleagues. In V. Richardson-Koehler (Ed.), *Educators' handbook: A research perspective* (pp. 491–518). White Plains, NY: Longman.

Little, J. W. (1988). Assessing the prospects for teacher leadership. In A. Lieberman (Ed.), *Building a professional culture in schools* (pp. 78–105). New York, NY: Teachers College Press.

Little, J. W. (1990). The perspective of privacy: Autonomy and initiative in teachers' professional relations. *Teachers College Record, 91*(4), 509–536.

Little, J. W. (1995, September). Contested ground: The basis of teacher leadership in two restructuring high schools. *The Elementary School Journal, 96*(1), 47–63.

Little, J. W., & McLaughlin, M. W. (1993). Introduction: Perspectives on cultures and contexts of teaching. In J. W. Little & M. W. McLaughlin (Eds.), *Teachers' work: Individuals, colleagues, and contexts* (pp. 1–8). New York, NY: Teachers College Press.

Livingston, C. (1992). Teacher leadership for restructured schools. In C. Livingston (Ed.), *Teachers as leaders: Evolving roles* (pp. 9–17). Washington, DC: National Education Association.

Lloyd, G. (1996). Research and practical application for school, family, and community partnerships. In A. Booth & J. F. Dunn (Eds.), *Family-school links: How do they affect educational outcomes?* (pp. 276–287). Mahwah, NJ: Erlbaum.

Lomotey, K. (1989). *African-American principals: School leadership and success.* New York, NY: Greenwood Press.

Lortie, D. C. (1975). *Schoolteacher: A sociological study.* Chicago, IL: University of Chicago Press.

Louis, K. (2007). Trust and improvement in schools. *Journal of Educational Change, 8*(1), 1–24.

Louis, K. S., Dretzke, B., & Wahlstrom, K. (2010, Sept). How does leadership affect student achievement? Results from a national US survey. *School Effectiveness and School Improvement, 21*(3), 315–336.

Louis, K. S., & Marks, H. M. (1998). Does professional community affect the classroom? Teachers work and student experiences in restructuring schools. *American Journal of Education, 106*(4), 532–575.

Louis, K. S., Marks, H. M., & Kruse, S. (1996). Teachers' professional community in restructuring schools. *American Educational Research Journal, 33*(4), 757–798.

Louis, K. S., & Miles, M. B. (1990). *Improving the urban high school: What works and why.* New York, NY: Teachers College Press.

Louis, K. S., & Miles, M. B. (1991). Managing reform: Lessons from urban high schools. *School Effectiveness and School Improvement, 2*(2), 75–96.

Lynch, M., & Strodl, P. (1991). *Teacher leadership: Preliminary development of a questionnaire.* Paper presented at the annual conference of the Eastern Educational Research Association, Boston.

Ma, X. (2003). Sense of belonging to school: Can schools make a difference? *The Journal of Educational Research, 96*(6), 340–349.

Ma, X., & Klinger, D. (2000). Hierarchical linear modelling of student and school effects on academic achievement. *Canadian Journal of Education, 25*(1), 41–55.

MacBeath, J. (2005). Leadership as distributed: A matter of practice. *School Leadership and Management, 25*(4), 349–366.

MacBeath, J. (2009). Distributed leadership: Paradigms, policy, and paradox. In K. Leithwood, B. Mascall, & T. Strauss (Eds.), *Distributed leadership according to the evidence* (pp. 41–57). London, UK: Routledge.

Magnuson, K. A., & Duncan, G. J. (2006). The role of family socioeconomic resources in the black-white test score gap among young children. *Developmental Review, 26*(4), 365–399.

Maguin, E., & Loeber, R. (1996). Academic performance and delinquency. In M. Tonry (Ed.), *Crime and justice* (Vol. 20, pp. 145–264). Chicago, IL: University of Chicago Press.

Malen, B., & Rice, J. K. (2004). A framework for assessing the impact of education reforms on school capacity: Insights from studies of high-stakes accountability initiatives. *Educational Policy, 18*(5), 631–660.

Mangin, M. M. (2007). Facilitating elementary principals' support for instructional teacher leadership. *Educational Administration Quarterly, 43*(3), 319–357.

Manthei, J. (1992). *The mentor teacher as leader: The motives, characteristics and needs of seventy-three experienced teachers who seek a new leadership role.* Paper presented at the annual meeting of the American Educational Research Association, San Francisco, CA. (ERIC Document Reproduction Service No. ED 346042).

Marks, H. M. (2000). Student engagement in instructional activity: Patterns in the elementary, middle, and high school years. *American Educational Research Journal, 37*(1), 153–184.

Marks, H. M., & Printy, S. M. (2003). Principal leadership and school performance: An integration of transformational and instructional leadership. *Educational Administration Quarterly, 39*(3), 370–397.

Marsh, H. W., & Kleitman, S. (1992). Extracurricular activities: Beneficial extension of the traditional curriculum or subversion of academic goals? *Journal of Educational Psychology, 84*(4), 553–562.

Marsh, H. W., & Kleitman, S. (2002). Extracurricular school activities: The good, the bad, and the nonlinear. *Harvard Educational Review, 72*(4), 464–515.

Marshall, R., & Tucker, M. (1992). *Thinking for a living: Work, skills, and the future of the American economy.* New York, NY: Basic Books.

Martin, B., & Crossland, B. J. (2000). *The relationships between teacher empowerment, teachers' sense of responsibility for student outcomes and student achievement.* Paper presented at the annual meeting of the Mid-Western Education Research Association, Chicago.

Masten, A., Sesma, A., Si-Asar, R., Lawrence, C., Miliotis, D., & Dionne, J. A. (1997). Educational risks for students experiencing homelessness. *Journal of School Psychology, 35*(1), 27–46.

May, H., & Supovitz, J. A. (2006). Capturing the cumulative effects of school reform: An 11-year study of the impacts of America's choice on student achievement. *Educational Evaluation and Policy Analysis, 28*(3), 231–257.

May, H., & Supovitz, J. A. (2011). The scope of principal efforts to improve instruction. *Educational Administration Quarterly, 47*(2), 332–352.

Mayrowetz, D., Murphy, J., Seashore Louis, K., & Smylie, M. (2009). Conceptualizing distributed leadership as a school reform. In K. Leithwood, B. Mascall, & T. Strauss (Eds.). *Distributed leadership according to the evidence* (pp. 167–195). London, UK: Routledge.

Mayrowetz, D., & Weinstein, C. S. (1999). Sources of leadership for inclusive education: Creating schools for all children. *Educational Administration Quarterly, 35*(3), 423–449.

Mazzarella, J. (1985). The effective high school principal: Sketches for a portrait. *R & D Perspective.* Center for Educational Policy and Management, University of Oregon, Eugene.

McDougall, D., Saunders, W. M., & Goldenberg, C. (2007). Inside the black box of school reform: Explaining the how and why of change at Getting Results schools. *International Journal of Disability, Development and Education, 54*(1), 51–89.

McGee, G. W. (2003, April). *Closing Illinois' achievement gap: Lessons from the 'Golden Spike' high poverty high performing schools.* Paper presented at the Annual Meeting of the American Educational Research Association, Chicago, April, 2003.

McKeever, B. (2003). *Nine lessons of successful school leadership teams: Distilling a decade of innovation.* San Francisco, CA: WestEd.

McKenna, M. C., & Walpole, S. (2010). Planning and evaluating change at scale: Lessons from Reading First. *Educational Researcher, 39*(6), 478–483.

McLaughlin, M. W. (1994). Somebody knows my name. In *Issues in restructuring schools* (Issue Report No. 7). Madison: Center on Organization and Restructuring of Schools, University of Wisconsin-Madison.

McLaughlin, M. W., & Talbert, J. E. (2001). *Professional communities and the work of high school teaching.* Chicago, IL: University of Chicago Press.

McLaughlin, M. W., & Yee, S. M. L. (1988). School as a place to have a career. In A. Lieberman (Ed.), *Building a professional culture in schools* (pp. 23–44). New York, NY: Teachers College Press.

Meehan, M. L., Cowley, K. S., Schumacher, D., Hauser, B., & Croom, N. D. M. (2003). *Classroom environment, instructional resources, and teaching differences in high-performing Kentucky schools with achievement gaps.* Charleston, WV: AEL, Inc.

Meier, D. (2003). So, what does it take to build a democratic school. *Phi Delta Kappan, 85*(1), 15–21.

Memphis Latino Student Success Collaborative. (n.d.). *Memphis Latino Student Success Collaborative Integrated Action Plan.* Unpublished document.

Mendez, L. M. R., Knoff, H. M., & Ferron, J. M. (2002). School demographic variables and out-of-school suspension rates: A quantitative and qualitative analysis of a large, ethnically diverse school district. *Psychology in the Schools, 39*(3), 259–277.

Meyer, J. W., & Rowan, B. (1975). *Notes on the structure of educational organizations: Revised version.* Paper presented at the annual meeting of the American Sociological Association, San Francisco.

Miller, B., Moon, J., & Elko, S. (2000). *Teacher leadership in mathematics and science: Casebook and facilitator's guide.* Portsmouth, NH: Heinemann.

Miller, L. S. (1995). *An American imperative: Accelerating minority educational advancement.* New Haven, CT: Yale University Press.

Miller, R., & Rowan, B. (2006). Effects of organic management on student achievement. *American Educational Research Journal, 43*(2), 219–253.

Mitchell, A. (1997, Fall). Teacher identity: A key to increased collaboration. *Action in Teacher Education, 19*(3), 1–14.

Mitchell, C., & Castle, J. B. (2005). The instructional role of elementary school principals. *Canadian Journal of Education/Revue Canadienne de l'education, (28)*3, 409–433.

Mitchell, C., & Sackney, L. (2006). Building schools, building people: The school principal's role in leading a learning community. *Journal of School Leadership, 16*(5), 627–640.

Mojkowski, C., & Fleming, D. (1988). *School-site management: Concepts and approaches.* Andover, MA: Regional Laboratory for Educational Improvement of the Northeast and Islands.

Moles, O. (1996). New directions in research and policy. In A. Booth & J. Dunn (Eds.), *Family-school links: How do they affect educational outcomes?* (pp. 247–254). Mahwah, NJ: Erlbaum.

Moller, G., & Katzenmeyer, M. (1996). The promise of teacher leadership. In G. Moller & M. Katzenmeyer (Eds.), *Every teacher as a leader: Realizing the potential of teacher leadership* (pp. 1–18). San Francisco, CA: Jossey-Bass.

Moller, J., & Eggen, A. B. (2005). Team leadership in upper secondary education. *School Leadership and Management, 25*(4), 331–347.

Moore, J. (2005a). *Collaborations of schools and social service agencies.* National Center for Homeless Education at SERVE, Greensboro, NC. Retrieved from http://www.serve.org/nche

Moore, J. (2005b). *Unaccompanied and homeless youth review of literature: Review of literature (1995–2005).* National Center for Homeless Education at SERVE, Greensboro, NC. Retrieved from http://www.serve.org/nche

Morrissey, M. S. (2000). *Professional learning communities: An ongoing exploration.* Austin, TX: Southwest Educational Development Laboratory.

Mukuria, G. (2002). Disciplinary Challenges. *Urban Education, 37*(3), 432–452.

Mulford, B., & Silins, H. (2003). Leadership for organisational learning and improved student outcomes—what do we know. *Cambridge Journal of Education, 33*(2), 175–195.

Mullen, C. A., & Hutinger, J. L. (2008). The principal's role in fostering collaborative learning communities through faculty study group development. *Theory into Practice, 47*(4), 276–285.

Munoz, M., Ross, S., & McDonald, A. (2007). Comprehensive school reform in middle schools: The effects of different ways of knowing on student achievement in a large urban district. *Journal for Students Placed at Risk, 12*(2), 167–183.

Murnane, R. J., & Levy, F. (1996). *Teaching the new basic skills: Principles for educating children to thrive in a changing economy.* New York, NY: The Free Press.

Murphy, J. (1988). Methodological, measurement, and conceptual problems in the study of administrator instructional leadership. *Educational Evaluation and Policy Analysis, 10*(2), 117–139. Reprinted in R. J. S. Macpherson & J. Weeks (Eds.), *Pathways to knowledge in educational administration.* Armidale, N.S.W., Australia: Australian Council for Educational Administration.

Murphy, J. (1989). Educational Reform in the 1980s: Explaining some surprising success. *Educational Evaluation and Policy Analysis, 11*(3), 209–223.

Murphy, J. (1990). Principal instructional leadership. In L. S. Lotto & P. W. Thurston (Eds.), *Advances in educational administration: Changing perspectives on the school.* (Volume 1, Part B). Greenwich, CT: JAI Press.

Murphy, J. (1991). *Restructuring schools: Capturing and assessing the phenomena.* New York, NY: Teachers College Press.

Murphy, J. (1992). School effectiveness and school restructuring: Contributions to educational improvement. *School Effectiveness and School Improvement, 3*(2), 90–109.

Murphy, J. (1996). *The privatization of schooling: Problems and possibilities.* Newbury Park, CA: Corwin.

Murphy, J. (1999). New consumerism: The emergence of market-oriented governing structures for schools. In J. Murphy & K. S. Louis (Eds.), *The handbook of research on school administration.* San Francisco, CA: Jossey-Bass.

Murphy, J. (2005). *Connecting teacher leadership and school improvement.* Thousand Oaks, CA: Corwin.

Murphy, J. (2006). The evolving nature of the American high school: A punctuated equilibrium model of institutional change [Invited article]. *Leadership and Policy in Schools, 5*(4), 1–39, 285–324.

Murphy, J. (2008a). The place of leadership in turnaround schools: Insights from organizational recovery in the public and private sectors. *Journal of Educational Administration, 46*(1), 74–98.

Murphy, J. (2008b). Turnaround insights from the organizational sciences: A review of the empirical evidence and the development of a staged model of recovery with potential implications for the PK–12 education sector. *Leadership and Policy in Schools, 17*(4), 331–357.

Murphy, J. (2009, November). Turning around failing schools: Policy insights from the corporate, government and non-profit sectors. *Educational Policy, 23*(6), 796–830.

Murphy, J. (2010a). *The educator's handbook for understanding and closing achievement gaps.* Thousand Oaks, CA: Corwin.

Murphy, J. (2010b). Turning around failing schools: Insights for educational leaders. *Journal of Educational Change, 11*(2), 157–176.

Murphy, J. (2012). *Homeschooling in America.* Thousand Oaks, CA: Corwin.

Murphy, J. (2013a). *The architecture of school improvement: Essential lessons.* Thousand Oaks, CA: Corwin.

Murphy, J. (2013b). The architecture of school improvement. *Journal of Educational Administration, 51*(3), 252–263.

Murphy, J., & Beck, L. G. (1995). *School-based management as school reform: Taking stock.* Newbury Park, CA: Corwin.

Murphy, J., Beck, L., Crawford, M., Hodges, A., & McGaughy, C. (2001). *The productive high school: Creating personalized academic communities.* Thousand Oaks, CA: Corwin.

Murphy, J., & Datnow, A. (2003a). *Leadership lessons from comprehensive school reforms.* Thousand Oaks, CA: Corwin.

Murphy, J., & Datnow, A. (2003b). Leadership lessons from comprehensive school reform designs. In J. Murphy & A. Datnow (Eds.), *Leadership for school reform: Lessons from comprehensive school reform designs.* Thousand Oaks, CA: Corwin.

Murphy, J., Elliott, S. N., Goldring, E., & Porter A. (2007). Leadership for learning: A research-based model and taxonomy of behaviors. *School Leadership & Management, 27*(2), 179–201.

Murphy, J., & Hallinger, P. (1993). Restructuring schooling: Learning from ongoing efforts. In J. Murphy & P. Hallinger (Eds.), *Restructuring schooling: Learning from ongoing efforts.* New Park, CA: Corwin.

Murphy, J., Hallinger, P., & Heck, R. (2013). Leading via teacher evaluation: The case of the missing clothes. *Educational Researcher, 42*(6), 349–354.

Murphy, J., Hallinger, P., Lotto, L. S., & Miller, S. K. (1987). Barriers to implementing the instructional leadership role. *Canadian Administrator, 27*(3), 1–9.

Murphy, J., Hallinger, P., & Mesa, R. P. (1985a). Strategies for coupling schools: The effective schools approach. *NASSP Bulletin, 69*(478), 7–13.

Murphy, J., Hallinger, P., & Mesa, R. P. (1985b). School effectiveness: Checking progress and assumptions and developing a role for state and federal government. *Teachers College Record, 86*(4), 615–641.

Murphy, J., Hallinger, P., Weil, M., & Mitman, A. (1984). Instructional leadership. A conceptual framework. *Planning and Changing, 14*(3), 137–149.

Murphy, J., & Meyers, C. V. (2008). *Turning around failing schools: Leadership lessons from the organizational sciences.* Thousand Oaks, CA: Corwin.

Murphy, J., & Meyers, C. V. (2009). Rebuilding organizational capacity in turnaround schools: Insights from the corporate, government, and nonprofit sectors. *Educational Management, Administration and Leadership, 37*(1), 9–29.

Murphy, J., & Shiffman, C. (2002). *Understanding and assessing charter schools.* New York, NY: Teachers College Press.

Murphy, J., Smylie, M., Mayrowetz, D., & Louis, K. S. (2009, April). The role of the principal in fostering the development of distributed leadership. *School Leadership & Management, 29*(2), 181–214.

Murphy, J., & Tobin, K. (2011). *Homelessness comes to school.* Thousand Oaks, CA: Corwin.

Murphy, J., Weil, M., Hallinger, P., & Mitman, A. (1982). Academic press: Translating high expectations into school policies and classroom practices. *Educational Leadership, 40*(3), 22–26.

Murphy, J., Weil, M., Hallinger, P., & Mitman, A. (1985, Spring). School effectiveness: A conceptual framework. *The Educational Forum, 49*(3), 361–374.

Murphy, J., Weil, M., & McGreal, T. L. (1986). The basic practice model of instruction. *Elementary School Journal, 87*(1), 83–95.

Myers, M. S. (1970). *Every employee a manager: More meaningful work through job enrichment.* New York, NY: McGraw-Hill.

Newlon, J. H. (1934). *Educational administration as social policy.* New York, NY: Scribner.

Newmann, F. M. (1981). Reducing student alienation in high schools: Implications of theory. *Harvard Educational Review, 51*(4), 546–564.

Newmann, F. M. (1992). Conclusion. In F. M. Newmann (Ed.), *Student engagement and achievement in American secondary schools* (pp. 182–217). New York, NY: Teachers College Record.

Newmann, F. M., King, M. B., & Youngs, P. (2000). Professional development that addresses school capacity: Lessons from urban elementary schools. *American Journal of Education, 108*(4), 259–299.

Newmann, F. M., Rutter, R. A., & Smith, M. S. (1989). Organizational factors that affect school sense of efficacy, community, and expectations. *Sociology of Education, 62*(4), 221–238.

Newmann, F. M., Smith, B., Allensworth, E., & Bryk, A. S. (2001). Instructional program coherence: What it is and why it should guide school improvement policy. *Educational Evaluation and Policy Analysis, 23*(4), 297–321.

Newmann, F. M., & Wehlage, G. G. (1995). *Successful school restructuring.* Madison, WI: University of Wisconsin-Madison, Center of Organization and Restructuring of Schools.

Newmann, F. M., Wehlage, G. G., & Lamburn, S. D. (1992). The significance and sources of student engagement. In F. M. Newmann (Ed.), *Student engagement and achievement in American secondary schools* (pp. 11–39). New York, NY: Teachers College Press.

Nichols, J. D., Ludwin, W. G., & Iadicola, P. (1999). A darker shade of gray: A year-end analysis of discipline and suspension data. *Equity & Excellence in Education, 32*(1), 43–54.

Noguera, P. (1996). Responding to the crisis confronting California's black male youth: Providing support without furthering marginalization. *The Journal of Negro Education, 65*(2), 219–236.

North Carolina State Department of Public Instruction. (2000). *Closing the achievement gap: Views from nine schools.* Raleigh: Author.

Nunez, R. da Costa, & Collignon, K. (2000). Supporting family learning: Building a community of learners. In J. H. Stronge & E. Reed-Victor (Eds.), *Educating homeless students: Promising practices* (pp. 115–133). Larchmont, NY: Eye on Education, Inc.

Nystrand, M. (1997). *Operating dialogue: Understanding the dynamics of language and learning in the English classroom.* New York, NY: Teachers College Press.

Oakes, J., & Guiton, G. (1995). Matchmaking: The dynamics of high school tracking decisions. *American Educational Research Journal, 32*(1), 3–33.

O'Conner, C. (1997). Dispositions toward (collective) struggle and educational resilience in the inner city: A case analysis of six African-American high school students. *American Educational Research Journal, 34*(4), 593–629.

Odell, C. W. (1939). *The secondary school.* Champaign, IL: Garland.

Odell, S. J. (1997, Fall). Preparing teachers for teacher leadership. *Action Teacher Education, 19*(3), 120–124.

O'Donnell, R. J., & White, G. P. (2005). Within the accountability era: Principals' instructional leadership behaviors and student achievement. *NASSP Bulletin, 89*(645), 56–71.

Ogawa, R., & Bossert, S. (1995). Leadership as an organizational quality. *Educational Administration Quarterly, 31*(2), 224–243.

Ogden, E. H., & Germinario, V. (1995). *The nation's best schools: Blueprints for excellence.* Lancaster, PA: Technomic.

O'Hair, M. J., & Reitzug, W. C. (1997). Teacher leadership: In what ways? For what purpose? *Action in Teacher Education, 19*(3), 65–76.

Olivier, D., & Hipp, K. K. (2006). Leadership capacity and collective efficacy: Interacting to sustain student learning in a professional learning community. *Journal of School Leadership, 16*(5), 505–519.

Olsen, B., & Kirtman, L. (2002). Teacher as mediator of reform: An examination of teacher practice in 36 California restructuring schools. *The Teachers College Record, 104*(2), 301–324.

Opdenakker, M., Maulana, R., & Brock, P. (2012). Teacher-student interpersonal relationships and academic motivation within one school year: Developmental changes and linkage. *School Effectiveness and School Improvement, 21*(1), 95–199.

Orr, M. T., Berg, B., Shore, R., & Meier, E. (2008). Putting the pieces together: Leadership for change in low-performing urban schools. *Education and Urban Society, 40*(6), 670–693.

Osterman, K. F. (2000). Students' need for belonging in the school community. *Review of Educational Research, 70*(3), 323–367.

Page, R. N. (1991). *Lower track classrooms: A curriculum and cultural perspective.* New York, NY: Teachers College Press.

Palincsar, A., Magnusson, S., Marano, N., Ford, D., & Brown, N. (1998). Designing a community of practice: Principles and practices of the GIsML (Guided Inquiry supporting Multiple Literacies) community. *Teaching and Teacher Education, 14*(1), 5–19.

Patterson, N., Beltyukova, S., Berman, K., & Francis, A. (2007). The making of sophomores: Student, parent, and teacher reactions in the context of systemic urban high school reform. *Urban Education, 42*(2), 124–144.

Payne, J. L. (1995). *Profiting from education: Incentive issues in contracting out.* Washington, DC: Education Policy Institute.

Pellicer, L. O., & Anderson, L. W. (1995). *A handbook for teacher leaders.* Thousand Oaks, CA: Corwin.

Penuel, W., & Davey, T. (1998). *Meta-analysis of McKinney programs in Tennessee.* Paper presented at the Annual Meeting of the American Educational Research Association, San Diego, CA, April 13–17, 1998.

Penuel, W. R., Fishman, B. J., Yamaguchi, R., & Gallagher, L. P. (2007). What makes professional development effective? Strategies that foster curriculum implementation. *American Educational Research Journal, 44*(4), 921–958.

Penuel, W. R., Riel, M., Joshi, A., Pearlman, L., Kim, C. M., & Frank, K. A. (2010). The alignment of the informal and formal organizational supports for reform: Implications for improving teaching in schools. *Educational Administration Quarterly, 46*(1), 57–95.

Penuel, W., Riel, M., Krause, A., & Frank, K. (2009). Analyzing teachers' professional interactions in a school as social capital: A social network approach. *The Teachers College Record, 111*(1), 124–163.

Phillips, J. (2003). Powerful learning: Creating learning communities in urban school reform. *Journal of Curriculum and Supervision, 18*(3), 240–258.

Pitner, N. (1988). The study of administrator effects and effectiveness. In N. Boyan (Ed.), *Handbook of research in educational administration* (pp. 99–122). New York, NY: Longman.

Potter, D., Reynolds, D., & Chapman, C. (2002). School improvement for schools facing challenging circumstances: A review of research and practice. *School Leadership & Management, 22*(3), 243–256.

Pounder, D. G. (1999). Teacher teams: Exploring job characteristics and work-related outcomes of work group enhancement. *Educational Administration Quarterly, 35*(3), 317–348.

Pounder, D. G., Ogawa, R. T., & Adams, E. A. (1995). Leadership as an organization-wide phenomena: Its impact on school performance. *Educational Administration Quarterly, 31*(4), 564–588.

Powell, A. G., Farrar, E., & Cohen, D. K. (1985). *The shopping mall high school: Winners and losers in the educational marketplace.* Boston, MA: Houghton-Mifflin.

Powell, D. R. (1991). How schools support families: Critical policy tensions. *The Elementary School Journal, 91*(3), 307–319.

Prawat, R. S., & Peterson, P. L. (1999). Social constructivist views of learning. In J. Murphy & K. S. Louis (Eds.), *Handbook of research on educational administration* (2nd ed., pp. 203–226). San Francisco, CA: Jossey-Bass.

Prestine, N. A. (1995). Crisscrossing the landscape: Another turn at cognition and educational administration. *Educational Administration Quarterly, 31*(1), 134–142.

Printy, S. M. (2004). The professional impact of communities of practice. *UCEA Review, 46*(1), 20–23.

Printy, S. M. (2008). Leadership for teacher learning: A community of practice perspective. *Educational Administration Quarterly, 44*(2), 187–226.

Purkey, S. D., & Smith, M. S. (1983, March). Effective schools: A review. *Elementary School Journal, 83*(4), 427–452.

Putnam, R. D. (1995). Bowling alone: America's declining social capital. *Journal of Democracy, 6*(1), 65–77.

Quint, J. (2006). *Meeting five critical challenges of high school reform: Lessons from research on three reform models.* New York, NY: Manpower Demonstration Research Corporation.

Quint, S. (1994). *Schooling homeless children: A working model for America's public schools.* New York, NY: Teachers College Press.

Rallis, S. F. (1990). Professional teachers and restructured schools: Leadership challenges. In B. Mitchell & L. L. Cunningham (Eds.), *Educational leadership in changing contexts of families, communities, and schools: Eighty-ninth yearbook of the national society for the study of education* (pp. 184–209). Chicago, IL: National Society for the Study of Education.

Ravitch, D. (1983). *The troubled crusade: American education, 1945–1980.* New York, NY: Basic Books.

Raywid, M. (1995). Professional community and its yield at Metro Academy. In K. S. Louis and S. Kruse (Eds.), *Professionalism and community: Perspectives on reforming urban schools* (pp. 43–75). Thousand Oaks, CA: Corwin.

Reese, W. J. (1995). *The origins of the American high school.* New Haven, CT: Yale University Press.

Reitzug, U. C., & Patterson, J. (1998). I'm not going to lose you! Empowerment through caring in an urban principal's practice with students. *Urban Education, 33*(2), 150–181.

Reyes, P., Wagstaff, L. H., & Fusarelli, L. D. (1999). Delta forces: The changing fabric of American society and education. In J. Murphy & K. S. Louis (Eds.),

Handbook of research on educational administration (2nd ed., pp. 183–201). San Francisco, CA: Jossey-Bass.

Reynolds, G. M. (2002). *Identifying and eliminating the achievement gaps and in-school and out-of-school factors that contribute to the gaps.* Naperville, IL: North Central Regional Educational Laboratory.

Riehl, C., & Sipple, J. (1996). Making the most of time and talent: Secondary school organizational climates, teaching task environments, and teacher commitment. *American Educational Research Journal, 33*(4), 873–901.

Riester, A. F., Pursch, V., & Skria, L. (2002). Principals for social justice: Leaders of school success for children from low-income homes. *Journal of School Leadership, 12*(3), 281–304.

Robinson, V. M. J. (2007). *School leadership and student outcomes: Identifying what works and why.* Sydney, NSW: Australian Council for Educational Leaders.

Robinson, V. M. J. (2008). Forging the links between distributed leadership and educational outcomes. *Journal of Educational Administration, 46*(2), 241–256.

Robinson, V. M. J., Lloyd, C. A., & Rowe, K. J. (2008). The impact of leadership on student outcomes: An analysis of the differential effects of leadership types. *Educational Administration Quarterly, 44*(5), 635–674.

Rodgers, M., Sowden, A., Petticrew, M., Arai, L., Roberts, H., Britten, N., & Popay, J. (2009). Testing methodological guidance on the conduct of narrative synthesis in systematic reviews: Effectiveness of interventions to promote smoke alarm ownership and function. *Evaluation, 15*(1), 047–071.

Rodríguez, L. (2008). Teachers know you can do more: Understanding how school cultures of success affect urban high school students. *Educational Policy, 22*(5), 758–780.

Roney, K., Coleman, H., & Schlichting, K. A. (2007). Linking the organizational health of middle grades schools to student achievement. *NASSP Bulletin, 91*(4), 289–321.

Roscigno, V. J. (1998). Race and the reproduction of educational disadvantage. *Social Forces, 76*(3), 1033–1061.

Rosenholtz, S. J. (1989). *Teachers' workplace: The social organization of schools.* White Plains, NY: Longman.

Ross, S., Sterbinsky, A., & McDonald, A. (2003). *School variables as determinants of the success of comprehensive school reform: A quantitative study of 69 inner-city schools.* Paper presented to American Educational Research Association, Chicago, IL.

Rossmiller, R. A. (1992). The secondary school principal and teachers' quality of work life. *Educational Management Administration & Leadership, 20*(3), 132–146.

Roth, J. L., & Brooks-Gunn, J. (2003). Youth development programs: Risk, prevention and policy. *Journal of Adolescent Health, 32*(3), 170–182.

Roth, J. L., Brooks-Gunn, J., Murray, L., & Foster, W. (1998). Promoting healthy adolescents: Synthesis of youth development program evaluations. *Journal of Research on Adolescence, 8*(4), 423–459.

Rothman, H. R., & Cosden, M. (1995). The relationship between self-perception of a learning disability and achievement, self-concept and social support. *Learning Disability Quarterly, 18*(3), 203–212.

Rothstein, R. (2004). *Class and schools: Using social, economic, and educational reform to close the black-white achievement gap.* Washington, DC: Economic Policy Institute.

Rouse, H., & Fantuzzo, J. (2009). Multiple risks and educational well-being: A population-based investigation of threats to early school success. *Early Childhood Research Quarterly, 24*(1), 1–14.

Rowan, B. (1995). Research on learning and teaching in K–12 schools: Implications for the field of educational administration. *Educational Administration Quarterly, 31*(1), 115–133.

Rowan, B., & Miller, R. J. (2007). Organizational strategies for promoting instructional change: Implementation dynamics in schools working with comprehensive school reform providers. *American Educational Research Journal, 44*(2), 252–297.

Rowley, J. (1988, May/June). The teacher as leader and teacher educator. *Journal of Teacher Education, 39*(3), 13–16.

Rumberger, R. (2011). *Dropping out: Why students drop out of high school and what can be done about it.* Cambridge, MA: Harvard University Press.

Rumberger, R., & Palardy, G. (2005). Does segregation still matter? The impact of student composition on academic achievement in high school. *Teachers College Record, 107*(9), 1999–2045.

Russell, J. S., Mazzarella, J. A., White, T., & Maurer, S. (1985). *Linking the behaviors and activities of secondary school principals to school effectiveness: A focus on effective and ineffective behaviors.* Eugene: University of Oregon, Center for Educational Policy and Behavior.

Rutherford, W. L. (1985). School principals as effective leaders. *Phi Delta Kappan, 6*(1), 31–34.

Rutter, M., Maughan, B., Mortimore, P., & Ouston, J. (1979). *Fifteen thousand hours: Secondary schools and their effects on children.* Cambridge, MA: Harvard University Press.

Sackney, L. E., & Dibski, D. J. (1992). *School-based management: A critical perspective.* Paper presented at the Seventh Regional Conference of the Commonwealth Council for Educational Administration, Hong Kong.

Sadker, M., & Sadker, D. (1994). *Failing at fairness: How America's schools cheat girls.* New York, NY: Scribner.

Sanders, M. G. (2001). The role of "community" in comprehensive school, family, and community partnership programs. *The Elementary School Journal*, 19–34.

Sanders, M. G., & Harvey, A. (2002). Beyond the school walls: A case study of principal leadership for school-community collaboration. *Teachers College Record, 104*(7), 1345–1368.

Sarason, S. B. (1994). *Parental involvement and the political principle: Why the existing governance structure of schools should be abolished.* San Francisco, CA: Jossey-Bass.

Sather, S. E. (1999). Leading, lauding, and learning: Leadership in secondary schools serving diverse populations. *Journal of Negro Education*, 511–528.

Saunders, W. M., Goldenberg, C. N., & Gallimore, R. (2009). Increasing achievement by focusing grade-level teams on improving classroom learning: A prospective, quasi-experimental study of Title I schools. *American Educational Research Journal, 46*(4), 1006–1033.

Scanlan, M., & Lopez, F. (2012). Vamos! How school leaders promote equity and excellence for bilingual students. *Educational Administration Quarterly, 48*(4), 583–625.

Scheerens, J. (1997). Conceptual models and theory-embedded principles on effective schooling. *School Effectiveness and School Improvement, 8*(3), 269–310.

Scheurich, J. J. (1998). Highly successful and loving, public elementary schools populated mainly by low-SES children of color. *Urban Education, 33*(4), 451–491.

Schlechty, P. C. (1990). *Schools for the 21st century: Leadership imperatives for educational reform.* San Francisco, CA: Jossey-Bass.

Scribner, J. P., Cockrell, K. S., Cockrell, D. H., & Valentine, J. W. (1999). Creating professional communities in schools through organizational learning: An evaluation of a school improvement process. *Educational Administration Quarterly, 35*(1), 130–160.

Sebastian, J., & Allensworth, E. (2012). The influence of principal leadership on classroom instruction and student learning: A study of mediated pathways to learning. *Educational Administration Quarterly, 48*(4), 626–663.

Sedlak, M. W., Wheeler, C. W., Pullin, D. C., & Cusick, P. A. (1986). *Selling students short: Classroom bargains and academic reform in the American high school.* New York, NY: Teachers College Press.

Sergiovanni, T. J. (1990). *Value-added leadership: How to get extraordinary performance in schools.* San Diego, CA: Harcourt, Brace, & Jovanovich.

Sergiovanni, T. J. (1991a). The dark side of professionalism in educational administration. *Phi Delta Kappan, 72*(7), 521–526.

Sergiovanni, T. J. (1991b). *The principalship: A reflective practice perspective* (2nd ed.). Boston, MA: Allyn & Bacon.

Sergiovanni, T. J. (1992). Why we should seek substitutes for leadership. *Leadership, 49*(5), 41–45.

Sergiovanni, T. J. (1994). Organizations or communities? Changing the metaphor changes the theory. *Educational Administration Quarterly, 30*(2), 214–226.

Shannon, S. G., & Bylsma, P. (2002). *Addressing the achievement gap: A challenge for Washington state educators.* Olympia, WA: Washington Office of the State Superintendent of Public Instruction.

Shear, L., Means, B., Mitchell, K., House, A., Gorges, T., Joshi, A., . . . & Shlonik, J. (2008). Contrasting paths to small-school reform: Results of a 5-year evaluation of the Bill & Melinda Gates Foundation's National High Schools Initiative. *Teachers College Record, 110*(9), 1986–2039.

Sheldon, S. B. (2002). Parents' social networks and beliefs as predictors of parent involvement. *The Elementary School Journal,* 301–316.

Sherrill, J. A. (1999). Preparing teachers for leadership roles in the 21st century. *Theory into practice, 38*(1), 56–61.

Shouse, R. (1996). Academic press and sense of community: Conflict, congruence, and implications for student achievement. *Social Psychology of Education, (1)*1, 47–68.

Silins, H., & Mulford, B. (2004). Schools as learning organisations: Effects on teacher leadership and student outcomes. *School Effectiveness and School Improvement, 3*(4), 443–466.

Silins, H., & Mulford, B. (2010). Re-conceptualising school principalship that improves student outcomes. *Journal of Educational Leadership, Policy and Practice, 25*(2), 74–93.

Silins, H. C., Mulford, W. R., & Zarins, S. (2002). Organizational learning and school change. *Educational Administration Quarterly, 38*(5), 613–642.

Silva, D. Y., Gimbert, B., & Nolan, J. (2000, August). Sliding the doors: Locking and unlocking possibilities for teacher leadership. *Teachers College Record, 102*(4), 779–804.

Sindelar, P., Shearer, D., Yendol-Hoppey, D., & Liebert, T. (2006). The sustainability of inclusive school reform. *Exceptional Children, 72*(3), 317–331.

Singham, M. (2003, April). The achievement gap: Myths and reality. *Phi Delta Kappan, 84*(8), 586–591.

Sisken, L. S. (1994). *Realms of knowledge: Academic departments in secondary schools.* Washington, DC: Falmer Press.

Siu, W. (2008). Complexity theory and school reform. *NASSP Bulletin, 92*(2), 154–164.

Sizer, T. R. (1964). *Secondary schools at the turn of the century.* New Haven, CT: Yale University Press.

Sizer, T. R. (1984). *Horace's compromise: The dilemma of the American high school.* Boston, MA: Houghton Mifflin.

Smerdon, B. A., & Borman, K. M. (2009). Secondary school reform. In B. A. Smerdon & K. M. Borman (Eds.), *Saving America's high schools* (pp. 1–17). Washington, DC: The Urban Institute Press.

Smerdon, B. A., Borman, K. M., & Hannaway, J. (2009). Conclusions: Implications for future reform efforts, research, and policy. In B. A. Smerdon & K. M. Borman (Eds.), *Saving America's high schools* (pp. 201–215). Washington, DC: The Urban Institute Press.

Smylie, M. A. (1992). Teacher participation in school decision making: Assessing willingness to participate. *Educational Evaluation and Policy Analysis, 14*(1), 53–67.

Smylie, M. A. (1996). Research on teacher leadership: Assessing the state of the art. In B. J. Biddle, T. L. Good, & I. F. Goodson (Eds.), *International handbook of teachers and teaching* (pp. 521–592). Boston, MA: Kluwer Academic.

Smylie, M. (2010). *Continuous school improvement.* Thousand Oaks, CA: Corwin.

Smylie, M. A., & Brownlee-Conyers, J. (1992). Teacher leaders and their principals: Exploring the development of new working relationships. *Educational Administration Quarterly, 28*(2), 150–184.

Smylie, M. Λ., Conley, S., & Marks, H. M. (2002). Exploring new approaches to teacher leadership for school improvement. In J. Murphy (Ed.), *The educational leadership challenge: Redefining leadership for the 21st century* (pp. 162–188). Chicago, IL: University of Chicago Press.

Smylie, M. A., & Denny, J. W. (1989, March). *Teacher leadership: Tensions and ambiguities in organizational perspective.* Paper presented at the annual meeting of the American Educational Research Association, San Francisco, CA.

Smylie, M. A., & Hart, A. W. (1999). School leadership for teacher learning: A human and social capital development perspective. In J. Murphy & K. S. Louis, *Handbook of research on educational administration* (2nd ed., pp. 421–441). San Francisco, CA: Jossey-Bass.

Smylie, M. A., Mayrowetz, D., Murphy, J., & Louis, K. S. (2007, July). Trust and the development of distributed leadership. *Journal of School Leadership, 17*(4), 469–503.

Snell, J., & Swanson, J. (2000, April). *The essential knowledge and teacher leaders: A search for a conceptual framework.* Paper presented at the annual meeting of the American Educational Research Association, New Orleans, LA.

Somech, A., & Bogler, R. (2002). Antecedents and consequences of teacher organizational and professional commitment. *Educational Administration Quarterly, 38*(4), 555–577.

Southworth, G. (2002). Instructional leadership in schools: Reflections and empirical evidence. *School Leadership & Management, 22*(1), 73–91.

Spears, H. (1941). *Secondary education in American life.* New York, NY: American Book.

Spillane, J. (2005). Distributed leadership. *The Educational Forum, 69*(2), 43–150.

Spillane, J. P., Camburn, E., Pareja, A. (2009). School principals at work: A distributed perspective. In K. Leithwood, B. Mascall, & T. Strauss (Eds.), *Distributed leadership according to the evidence* (pp. 87–110). London, UK: Routledge.

Spillane, J. P., Diamond, J. B., Walker, L. J., Halverson, R., & Jita, L. (2001). Urban school leadership for elementary science instruction: Identifying and activating resources in an undervalued school subject. *Journal of Research in Science Teaching, 38*(8), 918–940.

Spillane, J. P., Hallett, T., & Diamond, J. B. (2003). Forms of capital and the construction of leadership: Instructional leadership in urban elementary schools. *Sociology of Education,* 76 (1), 1–17.

Spillane, J. P., Halverson, R., & Diamond, J. B. (2001). Investigating school leadership practice: A distributed perspective. *Educational Researcher, 30*(3), 23–28.

Spillane, J. P., & Louis, K. S. (2002). School improvement processes and practices: Professional learning for building instructional capacity. In J. Murphy (Ed.), *The educational leadership challenge: Redefining leadership for the 21st century: Yearbook of the National Society for the Study of Education* (pp. 83–104). Chicago, IL: University of Chicago Press.

Spradlin, T. E., Kirk, R., Walcott, C., Kloosterman, P., Zaman, K., McNabb, S., & Zapf, J. (2005). *Is the achievement gap in Indiana narrowing? Special report.* Bloomington, IN: Center for Evaluation and Education Policy.

Sprick, B., & Rich, M. (2010). *A proposal to strengthen family and community engagement within the elementary and secondary education act: An implementation guide.* Chicago, IL: Appleseed.

Spring, J. (1990). *The American school 1642–1990: Varieties of historical interpretation of the foundations and developments of American education* (2nd ed.). New York, NY: Longman.

Steele, C. M. (1992). Race and the schooling of Black Americans. *Atlantic Monthly, 269*(4), 68–78.

Steele, C. M. (1997). A threat in the air: How stereotypes shape the intellectual identities and performances of women and African Americans. *American Psychologist, 52*(6), 613–629.

Steele, C. M., & Aronson, J. (1995). Stereotype threat and the intellectual test performance of African Americans. *Journal of Personality and Social Psychology, 69*(5), 797–811.

Stein, M. K., & Coburn, C. E. (2008). Architectures for learning: A comparative analysis of two urban school districts. *American Journal of Education, 114*(4), 583–626.

Stewart, E. B. (2008). School structural characteristics, student effort, peer associations, and parental involvement: The influence of school- and individual-level factors on academic achievement. *Education and Urban Society, 40*(2), 179–204.

Stiefel, L., Schwartz, A. E., & Ellen, I. G. (2006). Disentangling the racial test score gap: Probing the evidence in a large urban school district. *Journal of Policy Analysis and Management, 26*(1), 7–30.

Stigler, J. W., & Hiebert, J. (1999). *The teaching gap: Best ideas from the world's teachers for improving education in the classroom.* New York, NY: The Free Press.

Stoll, L., Bolam, R., McMahon, A., Wallace, M., & Thomas, S. (2006). Professional learning communities: A review of the literature. *Journal of Educational Change, 7*(4), 221–258.

Stone, M., Horejs, J., & Lomas, A. (1997). Commonalities and differences in teacher leadership at the elementary, middle, and high school level. *Action in Teacher Education, 19*(3), 49–64.

St. Pierre, T. L., Mark, M. M., Kaltreider, D. L., & Aikin, K. J. (1997). Involving parents of high-risk youth in drug preventions: A three year longitudinal study in Boys & Girls Clubs. *Journal of Early Adolescence, 17*(1), 21–50.

Strahan, D. (2003). Promoting a collaborative professional culture in three elementary schools that have beaten the odds. *The Elementary School Journal, 104*(2), 127–146.

Stringfield, S., & Reynolds, D. (2012). *Creating and sustaining secondary schools success at scale—Sandfields, Cwmtawe, and the Neath-port Talbot local education authority's high reliability schools reform.* Paper presented at the National Conference on Scaling Up Effective Schools, Nashville, TN.

Stronge, J., & Hudson, K. (1999). Educating homeless children and youth with dignity and care. *Journal for a Just and Caring Education, 5*(1), 7–18.

Sui-Chu, E. H., & Willms, J. D. (1996). Effects of parental involvement on eighth-grade achievement. *Sociology of Education, 69*(2), 126–141.

Suleiman, M., & Moore, R. (1997). *Teachers' roles revisited: Beyond classroom management.* Paper presented at the ATE summer workshop, Tarpon Springs, FL.

Supovitz, J. (2002). Developing communities of instructional practice. *The Teachers College Record, 104*(8), 1591–1626.

Supovitz, J. (2008). Instructional influence in American high schools. In M. M. Mangin & S. R. Stoelinga (Eds.), *Effective teacher leadership: Using research to inform and reform* (pp. 144–162). New York, NY: Teachers College Press.

Supovitz, J. A., & Christman, J. B. (2003). *Developing communities of instructional practice: Lessons from Cincinnati and Philadelphia.* Philadelphia, PA: Consortium for Policy Research in Education, University of Pennsylvania.

Supovitz, J. A., & Klein, V. (2003). *Mapping a course for improved student learning: How innovative schools systematically use student performance data to guide improvement.* Philadelphia, PA: Consortium for Policy Research in Education.

Supovitz, J. A., & Poglinco, S. M. (2001). *Instructional leadership in a standards-based reform.* Philadelphia, PA: Consortium for Policy Research in Education.

Supovitz, J. A., & Turner, H. M. (2000). The effects of professional development on science teaching practices and classroom culture. *Journal of research in science teaching, 37*(9), 963–980.

Supovitz, J., Sirinides, P., & May, H. (2010). How principals and peers influence teaching and learning. *Educational Administration Quarterly, 46*(1), 31–56.

Sweeney, J. (1982). Research synthesis on effective school leadership. *Educational Leadership, 39*(5), 346–352.

Sweetland, S. R., & Hoy, W. K. (2000). School characteristics and educational outcomes: Toward an organizational model of student achievement in middle schools. *Educational Administration Quarterly, 36*(5), 703–729.

Sykes, G., & Elmore, R. F. (1989). Making schools more manageable. In J. Hannaway & R. L. Crowson (Eds.), *The politics of reforming school administration* (pp. 77–94). New York, NY: Falmer Press.

Teddlie, C., & Stringfield, S. (1985). *Six different kinds of effective and ineffective schools.* Paper presented at the annual meeting of the American Educational Research Association, Chicago, IL.

Teitel, L. (1996). Finding common ground: Teacher leaders and principals. In G. Moller & M. Katzenmeyer (Eds.), *Every teacher as a leader: Realizing the potential of teacher leadership* (pp. 139–154). San Francisco, CA: Jossey-Bass.

Theoharis, G. (2007). Social justice educational leaders and resistance: Toward a theory of social justice leadership. *Educational Administration Quarterly, 43*(2), 221–258.

Thompson, C. L. (2002). *Research-based review of reports on closing achievement gaps: Report to the education cabinet and the joint legislative oversight committee.* Chapel Hill, NC: The North Carolina Education Research Council.

Thompson, C. L., & O'Quinn, S. D., III. (2001). *Eliminating the black-white achievement gap: A summary of research.* Chapel Hill, NC: North Carolina Education Research Council.

Tichy, N. M., & Cardwell, N. (2004). *The cycle of leadership: How great leaders teach their companies to win.* New York, NY: Harper Business.

Tierney, W., Gupton, J., & Hallett, R. (2008). *Transitions to adulthood for homeless adolescents: Education and public policy.* Center for Higher Education Policy Analysis (CHEPA).

Timperley, H. (2005). Distributed leadership: Developing theory from practice. *Journal of Curriculum Studies, 37*(4), 395–420.

Timperley, H. (2009). Distributed leadership to improve outcomes for students. In K. Leithwood, B. Mascall, & T. Strauss (Eds.), *Distributed leadership according to the evidence* (pp.197–222). London, UK: Routledge.

Troen, V., & Boles, K. (1994). Two teachers examine the power of teacher leadership. In D. R. Walling (Ed.). *Teachers as leaders: Perspectives on the professional development of teachers* (pp. 275–286). Bloomington, IN: Phi Delta Kappa.

Tschannen-Moran, M., & Barr, M. (2004). Fostering student learning: The relationship of collective teacher efficacy and student achievement. *Leadership and Policy in Schools, 3*(3), 189–209.

Tushman, M. L., & Romanelli, E. (1985). Organizational evolution: A metamorphosis model of convergence and reorientation. In L. L. Cummings & B. M. Straw (Eds.), *Research in organizational behavior* (pp. 171–222). Greenwich, CT: JAI Press.

Tyack, D. B. (1974). *The one best system: A history of America urban education.* Cambridge, MA: Harvard University Press.

Tyack, D. B. (1993). School governance in the United States: Historical puzzles and anomalies. In J. Hannaway & M. Carnoy (Eds.), *Decentralization and school improvement* (pp. 1–32). San Francisco, CA: Jossey-Bass.

Uline, C. L., & Berkowitz, J. M. (2000). Transforming school culture through teaching teams. *Journal of School Leadership, 10*(1), 416–444.

Urbanski, A. & Nickolaou, M. B. (1997, June). Reflections on teacher leadership. *Educational Policy, 11*(2), 243–254.

Useem, E. L., Christman, J. B., Gold, E., & Simon, E. (1997). Reforming alone: Barriers to organizational learning in urban school change initiatives. *Journal of Education for Students Placed at Risk (JESPAR), 2*(1), 55–78.

U.S. Commission on Civil Rights (2004). *Closing the achievement gap: The impact of standards-based education reform on student performance* [Draft report for commissioners' review]. Washington, DC: Author.

Valentine, J. W., & Prater, M. (2011). Instructional, transformational, and managerial leadership and student achievement: High school principals make a difference. *NASSP Bulletin, 95*(1), 5–30.

Venezky, R., & Winfield, L. (1979). *Schools that succeed beyond expectations in teaching reading* (Technical Report No. 1). Newark, NJ: University of Delaware.

Vescio, V., Ross, D., & Adams, A. (2008). A review of research on the impact of professional learning communities on teaching practice and student learning. *Teaching and Teacher Education, 24*(1), 80–91.

Visscher, A. J., & Witziers, B. (2004). Subject departments as professional communities? *British Educational Research Journal, 30*(6), 785–800.

Voelkl, K. E. (1997). Identification with school. *American Journal of Education, 105*(3), 294–318.

Vostanis, P., Grattan, E., Cumelia, S., & Winchester, C. (1997). Psychosocial functioning of homeless children. *Journal of the American Academy of Child and Adolescent Psychiatry, 36*(7), 881–889.

Wahlstrom, K. L., & Louis, K. S. (2008). How teachers experience principal leadership: The roles of professional community, trust, efficacy, and shared responsibility. *Educational Administration Quarterly, 44*(4), 458–495.

Walker, J. (2009). Reorganizing leaders' time: Does it create better schools for students? *NASSP Bulletin, 93*(4), 213–226.

Walker, J., & Slear, S. (2011). The impact of principal leadership behaviors on the efficacy of new and experienced middle school teachers. *NASSP Bulletin, 95*(1), 46–64.

Wasley, P. A. (1991). *Teachers who lead: The rhetoric of reform and realities of practice.* New York, NY: Teachers College Press.

Waters, T., Marzano, R. J., & McNulty, B. (2003). *Balanced leadership: What 30 years of research tells us about the effect of leadership on student achievement.* Aurora, CO: Mid-continent Research for Education and Learning.

Waxman, H. C., Padron, Y. N., & Garcia, A. (2007). Educational issues and effective practices for Hispanic students. In S. J. Paik & H. J. Walberg (Eds.), *Narrowing the achievement gap: Strategies for educating Latino, Black, and Asian students* (pp. 131–151). New York: Springer Science+Business Media.

Wayman, J., & Stringfield, S. (2006). Technology-supported involvement of entire faculties in examination of student data for instructional improvement. *American Journal of Education, 112*(4), 549–571.

Webb, R. (2005). Leading teaching and learning in the primary school. *Educational Management Administration & Leadership, 33*(1), 69–91.

Weick, K. E. (1976). Educational organizations as loosely coupled systems. *Administrative Science Quarterly, 21*(2), 1–19.

Weil, M., & Murphy, J. (1982). Instructional processes. In H. E. Mitzel (Ed.), *The encyclopedia of educational research* (5th ed., Vol. 2).

Weis, L. (1990). *Working class without work: High school students in a de-industrializing economy.* New York, NY: Routledge.

Wellisch, J. B., MacQueen, A. H., Carriere, R. A., & Duck, G. A. (1978). School management and organization in successful schools. *Sociology of Education, 51*(3), 211–226.

Wells, M., Widmer, M. A., & McCoy, J. K. (2004). Grubs and grasshoppers: Challenge-based recreation and the collective efficacy of families with at-risk youth. *Family Relations, 53*(3), 326–333.

Wenger, E. (1998). *Communities of practice: Learning, meaning, and identity.* Cambridge, MA: Cambridge University Press.

Wenger, E. (2000). Communities of practice and social learning systems. *Organization, 7*(2), 225–246.

Wenger, E., & Snyder, W. (2000). Communities of practice: The organizational frontier. *Harvard Business Review, 78*(1), 139–146.

Wepner, S. B., Ferrara, J., Rainville, K. N., Gómez, D. W., Lang, D. E., & Bigaouette, L. (2012). *Changing suburbs, changing students: Helping school leaders face the challenges.* Thousand Oaks, CA: Corwin.

Whitaker, K. S. (1997, Summer). Developing teacher leadership and the management team concept: A case study. *Teacher Education, 33*(1), 1–16.

Wigginton, E. (1992). A vision of teacher leadership. In C. Livingston (Ed.), *Teachers as leaders: Evolving roles* (pp. 167–173). Washington, DC: National Education Association.

Williams, L. (2003). *Fragmented: Improving education for mobile students.* Washington, DC: Poverty & Race Research Action Council.

Wilson, B., & Corbett, H. (1999). *No excuses: The eighth grade year in six Philadelphia middle schools.* Philadelphia, PA: Philadelphia Education Fund.

Wilson, B. L., & Corcoran, T. B. (1988). *Successful secondary schools: Visions of excellence in American public education.* New York, NY: Falmer.

Wilson, M. (1993). The search for teacher leaders. *Educational Leadership, 50*(6), 24–27.

Wilson, S. M., & Berne, J. (1999). Teacher learning and the acquisition of professional knowledge: An examination of research on contemporary professional development. In A. Iran-Nejad and P. D. Pearson (Eds.), *Review of Research in Education* (pp. 173–209). Washington, DC: American Educational Research Association.

Wimpelberg, R. K. (1986, April). *Bureaucratic and cultural images in the management of more and less effective schools.* Paper presented at the annual meeting of the American Educational Research Association, San Francisco.

Witziers, B., Bosker, R. J., & Krüger, M. L. (2003). Educational leadership and student achievement: The elusive search for an association. *Educational Administration Quarterly, 39*(3), 398–425.

Wohlstetter, P., Datnow, A., & Park, V. (2008). Creating a system for data-driven decision-making: Applying the principal-agent framework. *School Effectiveness and School Improvement, 19*(3), 239–259.

Woloszyk, C. (1996). *Models for at-risk youth.* Final Report. Kalamazoo, MI: Upjohn Institute for Employment Research.

Woods, P. A., Bennett, N., Harvey, J. A., & Wise, C. (2004). Variabilities and dualities in distributed leadership. *Educational Management Administration & Leadership, 32*(4), 439–457.

Woronoff, R., Estrada, R., & Sommer, S. (2006). *Out of the Margins: A report on regional listening forums highlighting the experiences of lesbian, gay, bisexual, transgender, and questioning youth in care.* Child Welfare League of America.

Wraga, W. G. (1994). *Democracy's high school: The comprehensive high school and educational reform in the United States.* Lanham, MD: University Press of America.

Wynne, E. (1980). *Looking at schools: Good, bad, and indifferent.* Lexington, MA: D. C. Heath.

Yarger, S. J., & Lee, O. (1994). The development and sustenance of instructional leadership. In D. R. Walling (Ed.), *Teachers as leaders: Perspectives on the professional development of teachers* (pp. 223–237). Bloomington, IN: Phi Delta Kappa.

York-Barr, J., & Duke, K. (2004). What do we know about teacher leadership? Findings from two decades of scholarship. *Review of Educational Research, 74*(3), 255–316.

Young, V. (2006). Teachers' use of data: Loose coupling, agenda setting, and team norms. *American Journal of Education, 112*(4), 521–548.

Youngs, P. (2007). How elementary principals' beliefs and actions influence new teachers' experiences. *Educational Administration Quarterly, 43*(1), 101–137.

Youngs, P., & King, M. B. (2002). Principal leadership for professional development to build school capacity. *Educational Administration Quarterly, 38*(5), 643–670.

Yu, H., Leithwood, K., & Jantzi, D. (2002). The effects of transformational leadership on teachers' commitment to change in Hong Kong. *Journal of Educational Administration, 40*(4), 368–389.

Yukl, G. (2010). *Leadership in organizations.* Upper Saddle River, NJ: Prentice Hall.

Zaccaro, S. J., Kemp, C., & Bader, P. (2004). Leader traits and attributes. In J. Antonakis, A. T. Cianciolo, & R. J. Sternberg (Eds.), *The nature of leadership* (pp. 101–124). Thousand Oaks, CA: Sage.

Zimpher, N. L. (1988, January/February). A design for the professional development of teacher leaders. *Journal of Teacher Education, 39*(1), 53–60.

Index